Growth Through Easy Fun Fabulous Hairstyles!

A Beginners' Ultimate Guide

Photographed
Illustrated
&
Written
By
Nadine Manning

1st Edition

Over 100 Hairstyle Ideas!

WARNING:

DISCLAIMER:

This book is for educational and entertainment purposes. The author is not responsible for any damage or lack of results allegedly caused to an individual directly or indirectly as a result of the information presented in this book. The author is not a licensed cosmetologist. The information that is presented in this book is a combination of being self-taught, personal experience, and research.

ISBN #
978-0-9914722-5-3
Get on the **VIP list** at:
www.LearnHairAndDo.com

Created by: Nadine Manning

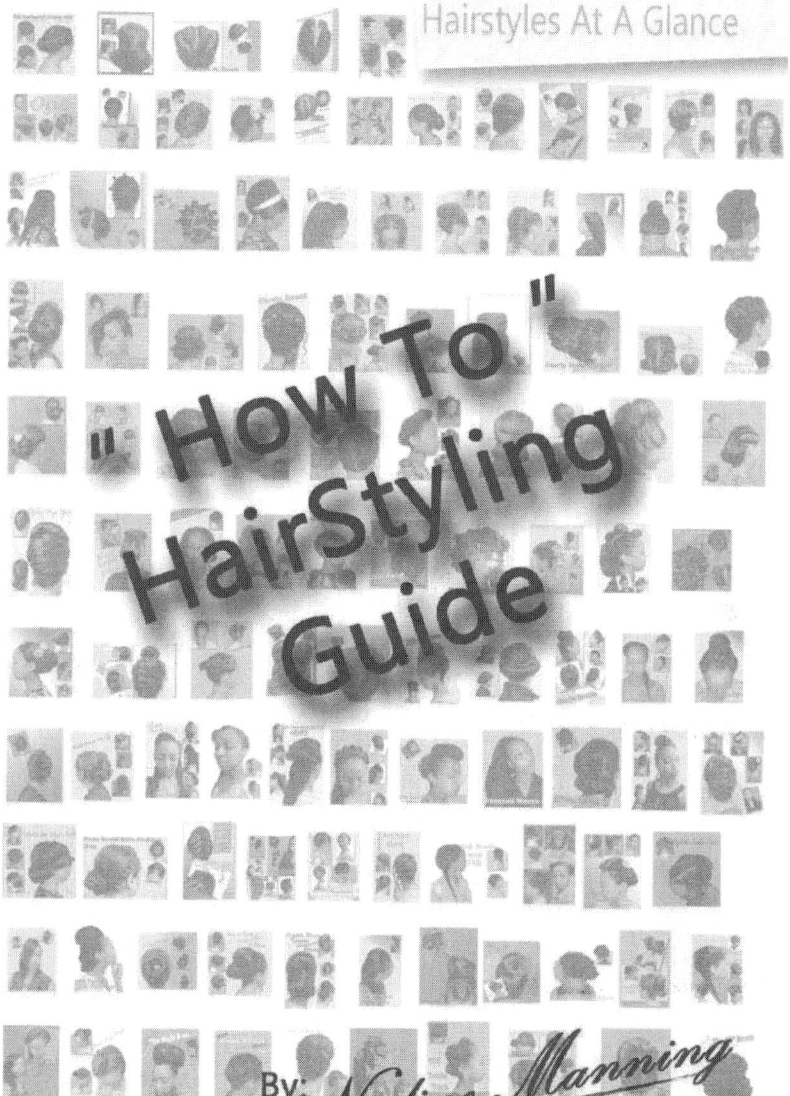

" How To " HairStyling Guide

By: *Nadine Manning*

Table Of Contents

Introduction

I want to take the time to thank you for purchasing my book. I created this book to provide a simple starter guide and overview of what is required to grow black hair to longer lengths. As far as ***protective and no heat hairstyling*** goes *(which this book is mainly about)*, I noticed that there weren't a lot of styling ideas available to choose from, only the basic BUN, BRAIDS, and TWISTS. Even though those styles serve their purpose it can become a little boring after a while to have the same couple of hairstyles in rotation over and over. So I decided to play around with different ways to style black hair in ways that are conducive to growth, simple to create yet stylish. By time I knew it I'd accumulated a whole catalog of over 100 protective and no heat hairstyles!

The hairstyles that are demonstrated in this book are mostly done on my relaxed hair. **HOWEVER**, don't be discouraged if you have natural hair, because most **styles can easily be translated to other hair textures** as well. Just know that because of various hair textures, hairstyles might look slightly different.

Side note: Just a word about relaxed hair verses natural hair. Which is better? There has been a lot of debate over this subject. It has been said that those who choose to relax their hair must hate their natural hair because of the chemicals that they use to straighten it. And also because of this relaxed hair can't grow long. It is believed that only those with natural hair can grow their hair long. Well, I say "relaxed" or "natural" doesn't matter. It depends on the person caring for each types of hair. A person who may have chemically relaxed hair might be able to grow their hair longer verses someone who has natural hair and neglects to care for it and vice versa. It all depends on the knowledge they have and how they use that knowledge to care for their hair in whatever state they choose to wear their hair in. The way you choose to wear your hair (relaxed or natural) is a personal choice and no one should feel bad about it. I know for **me, my relaxed hair is easier to handle. I like my hair straight and I'm able to take care of it so that it can grow long. I must say though, I love both natural & relaxed hair, they are both beautiful. The versatility of our textured hair is awesome! So whatever state your hair is in right now enjoy it girl…it's your hair.*

How the book is divided up

This book is divided up into two main parts. **Part one** and **Part two**. Part one of this book is all about hairstyling ideas. You'll find things like, **protective and no heat hairstyle ideas**. These styles are an important part of the success of the growth of black hair. I've included a banquet of many different styles for almost any occasion. Don't be afraid to tweak any style to your liking and taste.

**even though protective and no heat hairstyles are important in your hair care regimen, it is important to note that it is not the only component to growing black hair long. In section two I'll discuss other important factors that are essential and conducive to the growing of black hair.*

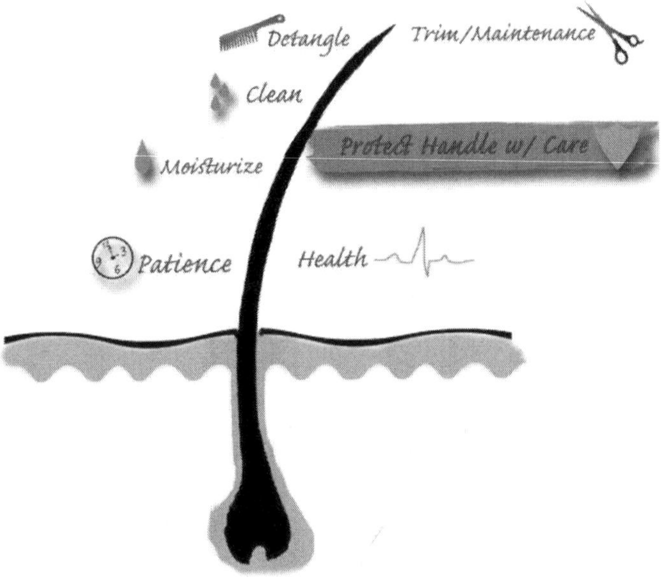

The "**Tips before styling**" section has basic styling information you should know before you start any styling. I've included things such as: how to create cornrows, two strand twists with hair extensions, pin curling hair, and how to properly take gel out of your hair to eliminate damage, etc. I even explain to you how to properly use a comb and brush to eliminate unnecessary breakage of your hair!

"Hairstyles that flatter your face shape" section is a fun section and I know you are going to love it. Basically, I break down the different face shapes and give you ideas of how to wear your hair to flatter your specific face shape.

Protective and no heat hairstyles section is a compilation of many different hairstyles that are easy to create. (Even though I said no heat, the only time you use heat, is if you choose to roller set your hair and go under a hooded dryer after a wash. Sometimes you can even leave the rollers in your hair to simply air dry. After that you might use a flat iron to straighten the roots of relaxed hair.) But this is the only time you would be applying heat to your hair after washing it. As far as the actual styling of the hair goes NO HEAT is required.

You will notice that some of the hairstyles require adding braiding hair for twists and braids. I also made an effort to do hairstyles that have low manipulation when doing these styles.

That being said, which ever hairstyle that you so choose to incorporate into your hair care regimen, mainly the adding of the extension hair to your real hair, only do so as little as possible and carefully when applying it. Also do not wear the hairstyles with the extension hair for long periods of time because this will only defeat the goal in mind, which is to retain length and thus have longer hair.

Part two of this book is the **hair care section.** In this section I go a little more into depth and explain what hair is, and how black hair is different from other types and how to properly take care of it.

In part two, I share a little bit about my hair story as well. Also if you are relaxed, I give some tips on how to properly do touch ups. After that section you'll find the **"hair assessment and goals"** section. This section is important when you are just starting out on a healthy hair journey, because it documents your starting point, pin point any problems you currently have right now and give tips how to correct the problems so you can reach your goal. Then I go into what I think are the fundamentals of achieving a healthier head of hair, such as your mindset, how to properly detangle your hair and so on.

Part One

Hair Styling Ideas Section

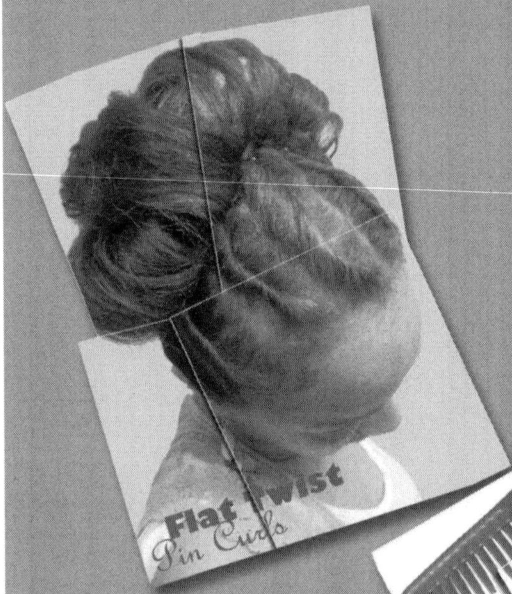

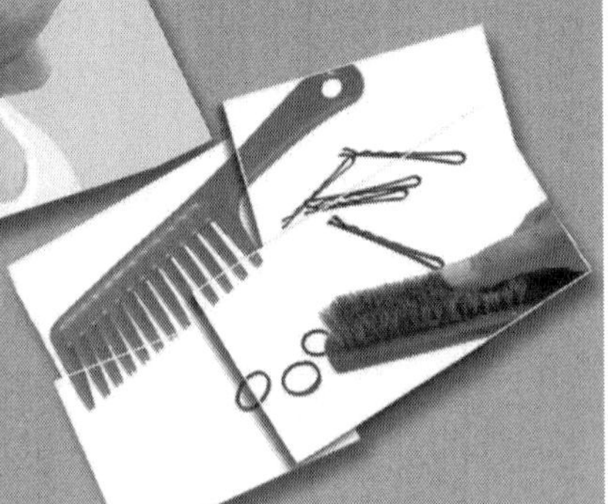

Tips Before Styling

Tips before styling section includes a few useful suggestions I think you should know before you begin to style your hair. Before any hairstyle, be sure to add moisture to the hair. This will help keep the hair pliable and prevent unnecessary breakage. When applying any kind of extension hair to your real hair please be cautious and mindful of the tension. Extension hair should always be applied gently and not too tight.

Using a comb correctly

As simple as it may seem, using a comb incorrectly or correctly can mean the difference between length retention and no length retention of the hair. Both the type of comb and the manner in which you part the hair are very important.
Let's talk about the types of combs you should be using in a healthy hair care regimen. There are two must have types, the **large teeth** comb and a **medium teeth rat tail** comb. The large teeth comb is an important tool to have because when it comes to detangling the hair, using a smaller teeth comb will not effectively do the job of safely detangling. In fact, it will defeat the whole purpose of the growing process. When detangling the hair from knots, the goal is to go through the process with minimal breakage at the end of the session.

Using a large teeth comb to detangle the hair. Start by first going through the hair in sections using your **fingers** (*the best detangling tool*). Do so starting from the ends of your hair and gently work your way up to the roots all the while separating any knots you come across.

Now take your large teeth comb and go through the hair in sections again, gently comb through the hair starting from the very ends of the hair and work your way up to the root. After you have completed each section simply take a butterfly clip and section off each detangled section. If you have thick, longer, or wet hair this will prevent the already detangled section of hair to stay in a detangled state and also out of your way while working on another section of hair.

Using a medium teeth comb. A medium teeth comb is great for parting the hair. Because the teeth are smaller than that of the large teeth comb, it creates a sleeker part. However, when parting your hair don't take it for granted and think that you are only parting your hair. Take heed and pay attention to how you maneuver the comb throughout the hair. If you have medium length hair or longer, sometimes what happen is you part the hair and inadvertently drag the comb roughly against the hair which causes premature breakage of the hair. Instead, after you make a part slowly lift the comb up off the head and then continue parting the rest of the hair.

Pin curling hair

Pin curling the hair is an excellent way to get curls without using heat. There are two different ways you can go about pin curling your hair.

1). Raised pin curl or
2). Flat pin curl

Raised pin curls resemble the shape of a roller that you use to do a rollerset. Therefore, when creating a raised pin curl do so by pretending to roll the hair onto an imaginary roller by mimicking the same motion you would use to roll the hair on the roller.

1. Start by taking the desired amount of hair you would like to pin curl and comb through it gently to smooth it out. Add a dab of oil moisturizer to it.
2. Locate the end of the hair and begin to roll the end under forming a loop. Then continue to roll the hair up to the root all the while keeping the loop intact.
3. Use a hair pin to secure the raised pin curl you just created just like you would a roller for a rollerset. (against the scalp in between the loop opening)

If you want to do a pin curl and sleep overnight on it a raised pin curl is not such a good idea, try a **flat pin curl** instead. Follow the same instructions for the raised pin curl. Before securing the pin curl with hair pins, take your thumb and index finger and place it on both sides of the raised pin curl. While the pin curl is still between your fingers, start to close the gap between your thumb and index fingers until they are touching each other. Next, take the raised pin curl you just flattened between your fingers and lay it against the head. Secure with a hair pin. Use a silk or satin scarf to tie your head.

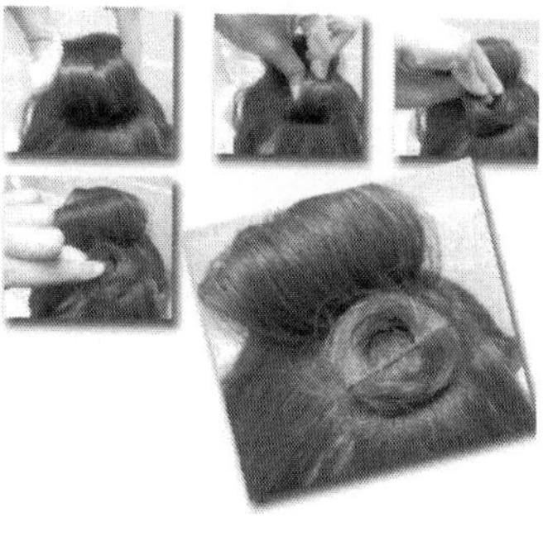

Position of Rollers Placed on the Head

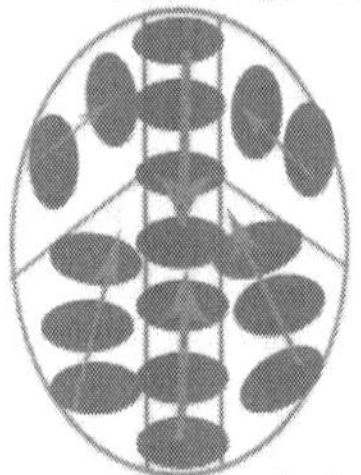

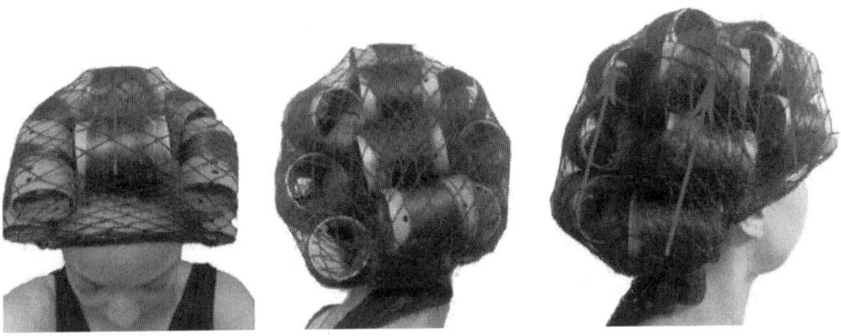

After you've washed your hair you have the choice of air drying or using heat to dry. If you choose to use heat, indirect heat is the way to go. One of the best ways to use indirect heat to dry your hair is by doing a roller set and then go under a hooded dryer. With this method you eliminate hair flying all over the place. Also you would be able to avoid any hard brushing and scraping of the hair strands every time you pass the brush through the hair while using the hand held blow dryer, which will inevitably break off the hair prematurely.

Steps to do a roller set.

Supplies:
-Rollers (choose size according to length of your hair)
-large hair Pins
-large teeth comb & medium teeth comb
-Water bottle with water
-Butterfly clips
-Triangle hair net

Instructions:

1. First, gently and thoroughly detangle the whole head of hair.
2. Place the roller right on the hair line right in the middle of the front of the head horizontally *(this will serve as a measurement for your part)*
3. Next, take the comb and make two parallel parts going straight back to the nape of the neck. (*See diagram*) section off this middle portion of hair with a butterfly clip for now.
4. Proceed to the side of the head. Take the roller and again place it against the head next to the hair line in the front of the head. (*make sure that the roller is facing horizontally against the head*)
5. Part the hair vertically accordingly to the size or width of the roller. *(See diagram)* section off both sections of hair on both sides of the part with a butterfly clip.
6. Proceed to the other side of the head and do the same thing to that side.
7. At this point you should have 5 sections of hair. Undo the butterfly clip from the middle section of hair; this is where you are going to begin the roll set.
8. To determine the size of the section of hair you will be parting off to place on the roller, simply take the roller and place the part with the hole on the head to determine the width of the section of hair. When you have done so, simply proceed with parting.
9. **Placing the hair on the roller**. Take the first section of hair and spray it with water, take the medium teeth comb and comb through the hair to smooth it out to the ends of the hair. (*bring the section of*

hair forward towards the front of the head and make sure that it is nice and smooth, especially the ends).

10. Place the roller on top of the hair and begin to roll the hair towards the root, all the while holding the hair with some tension to keep the hair straight while rolling. When you get to the roots secure the roller on the head with a hair pin.
11. Follow steps 8-10 for the remaining rollersets in this section of hair. Except, when you reach to the forth rollerset or the middle of the head, hold the hair 90 degrees off the head instead of towards the front of the head and rollerset the remaining hair going upward (*see diagram and photo*).
12. **Roller setting the sides of the head**. Proceed to the side of the head and undo the butterfly clip from the back section. Use the roller to determine the size of the section of hair you will be parting off. Do so by placing the circle side on the head, then go ahead and make your part.
13. Saturate the hair with water from the water bottle as you see the hair drying out. Start rolling the rollers in this section upward and secure with hair pins.
14. Remove the butterfly clip from the next section and repeat steps 12 & 13
15. Proceed to the next side of the head and repeat steps 12-14

*REMEMBER TO STATURATE THE HAIR WITH WATER FROM THE WATER BOTTLE AS YOU SEE THE HAIR DRYING OUT.

Using flexi rods

Flexi rods are great for creating curls without using direct heat to the hair. They come in different sizes. Just choose the size that is appropriate for the length of your hair and also for the size of curl you would like to achieve.

Before you start to roll the hair on the flexi rod, be sure to apply some type of setting lotion or mousse to the hair so that the hair can set in place properly.

Hold the section of hair you would like to roll on the flexi rod and place the tip or the end of the hair on the flexi rod about ½ an inch away from the end. Roll the rod to secure the ends of the hair on it then proceed rolling the rod so the hair starts to spiral on it. When the hair reaches about ½ an inch away from the other end of the rod, roll it so that the hair stops spiraling on it but wrapping around itself until it cannot wrap any more. To secure the flexi rod in place, simply bend and coil both ends of the flexi rod.

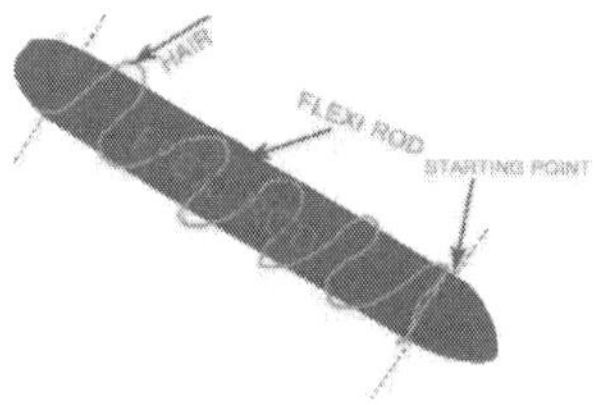

Removing gel or any other products used to hold the hair in place.

Things like gel or hair spray are great products to use when you want to sculpt your hair. What about when it is time to undo the sculpted masterpiece you created? How will you dismantle it? Some might take a brush or a comb and start to rake through the hair. That is an absolute no-no. If you like the hair that is on your head and you want to grow it longer don't do that! That will only cause massive breakage.

Here's a safer approach to taking the product out of your hair. Simply **wash it out,** but take heed of the manner in which you wash the product out of your hair. Don't just go in the shower, wet your hair with water, apply some shampoo and then start scrubbing your hair every which way on your head. This will cause your hair to form unnecessary knots and lose hair in the detangling process.

Just take your time and go through the process slowly and gently.

1. Go in the shower and turn the water on the warm temperature.
2. Relax and let the water run through the hair, completely saturating the hair with water. (*This process will safely loosen the product in the hair*)
3. Let the water continue to run down the hair. NEVER AT ANY POINT TAKE THE HAIR AND PLACE IT ON TOP OF YOUR HEAD AND BEGIN TO SCRUB IT. Just let the water continue to run down the hair.
4. Take some detangling moisturizing shampoo, place some in your hands and then apply it to your hair, starting from the roots working your way down the hair length until you reach the ends of your hair.
5. Wash your hair by running your hands down the length of the hair in sections.
6. To wash the roots and the scalp, just grasp a section of hair with one hand and with the other hand spread your fingers out and just reach in between the hair and now begin to wash your scalp. *(If you have shoulder length hair or longer this is great because this process will reduce the amount of tangles you might create verses if you bundled your hair on your head and washed it that way.)*
7. Rinse the conditioner out of your hair by letting the water run through the hair and at the same time stroking your hair in a downward motion to help and assist the shampoo out of the hair.
8. After the shampoo is out of the hair, wring the excess water out of your hair and apply some conditioner. Apply the conditioner the same way you did the shampoo. Leave the conditioner in the hair for about ten minutes, then rinse.

(Tip: *you can add some coconut oil in the conditioner for extra conditioning*)

9. Rinse the conditioner out of the hair when the ten minutes are up.

Wrapping your hair to reduce breakage

Wrapping and tying your hair at night before you go to bed is important. It provides protection from the twisting and turning you might be doing while you sleep. If you go to bed without neatly tucking away your hair and leave it out freely while you sleep, the friction that is caused between your head and the pillow will over time break your hair off.

There are two different ways you can wrap your hair. **Traditional wrap** and the **criss cross wrap.** Let's explore both ways.

Traditional Wrapping

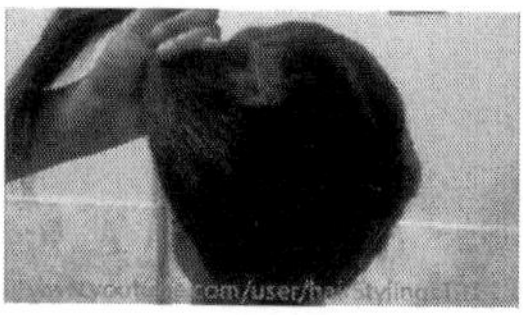

Traditional wrapping is done by combing the entire head of hair around the surface of the head into one seamless circle. This method is great for straight hair or relaxed hair that does not have a lot of new growth. With straighter roots the hair can easily be maneuvered around the head without too much manipulation such as combing and brushing.

Supplies you'll need:

- Large hair pins
- Soft brush
- Large teeth comb
- Moisturizer (*to add moisture to hair*)
- Natural oil (*such as coconut oil, to seal in the moisture*)
- Silk or satin scarf

Here's how to do a traditional wrap:

1. First gently comb through and detangle the hair starting from ends to root.
2. **Moisturize the hair** by placing a pea or dime size amount of moisturizer in the palm of your hand *(amount depends on the length of your hair. Less if your hair is shorter and more if your hair is longer*)
3. Lightly rub your palms together and then apply the product to the hair starting from the ends then work your way up the hair strand to the root of the hair in a downward smoothing motion.

4. Take the oil and place a pea sized amount in the palm of your hand (*be mindful of the amount you dispense to apply. Appling too much oil will weigh down the hair and cause it to look limp.*) This process of applying the moisture and then the oil is call MOISTURIZING & SEALING.
5. **Start the wrapping process** by placing the large tooth comb on top of the head in the center and start combing the hair out from the center so that it starts to fan out from the center.
6. Next make a part from the center of the head towards the front.
7. Place the teeth of the comb right in line with the part and begin to comb the front section of hair to the **right,** smooth the hair with the soft brush if needed.
8. Place your hand on the smoothed portion of hair to temporarily hold the hair in place. Then take the large hair pin and slide one in the front and one on top where the center is. Add more hair pins to this already smoothed portion if needed.
9. Continue to comb and smooth the hair around the contour of the head in small neat steps. As you do so slide the large hair pins on the top and on the bottom to secure the wrap in place. (**Tip**: *when you place the hair pin on top, place it in the center.*)
10. When you reach back to where you started you will have hair left over from the wrap. To make the wrap one seamless wrap, simply undo the hair pins next to it and include the left over hair in that section, smooth it out and replace the hair pins back. Tie your hair with a silk or satin scarf.

Criss Cross Wrapping

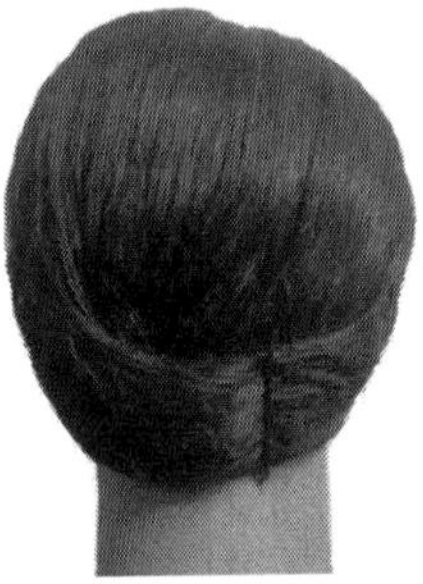

Criss cross wrapping is great if you are transitioning from relaxed to natural hair and are dealing with two different textures, or if you are post relaxed and have a lot of new growth or even if you are natural. This is *my* preferred method of wrapping my hair. Because of the amount of manipulation that is done during this process, such as the amount of combing and brushing, breakage is greatly reduced thus keeping more of the hair intact.

Supplies you'll need:

- Large hair pins
- Duck bill clips (*for temporarily holding the hair in place*)
- Soft brush
- Large tooth comb
- Moisturizer (*to add moisture to hair*)
- Natural oil (*such as coconut oil, to seal in the moisture*)
- Silk or satin scarf

Here's how to do a criss cross wrap:

1. Comb through the hair gently to get rid of any knots and tangles.
2. Comb the entire head of hair back.
3. Moisturize and seal the hair.
4. Split the hair diagonally into two at the nape of the neck.
5. Criss cross your hands in the back of your head and grasp both sections of hair you just split into two.
6. While still grasping the two sections of hair, move your hands apart and place the hair that is in your hands on the sides of your head parallel to your hair line on the side. (*Let go of one side for now and let's focus on pinning down and securing one side at a time*).
7. Hold the side you choose to work with first with some tension to keep it straight and lay it down on the side of the head (*be sure to smooth it out before doing so*). Now proceed to start placing the hair pins to secure the hair in place.
8. Go to the other side of the head and do the same to that side.
9. Tie your head with a satin or silk scarf.

TIP: ***If you don't want to leave the hair pins in your hair while you sleep, try placing the duck bill clips in your hair the same way you would the hair pins. Except when you are done tying your hair remove the duckbill clips by sliding them out from underneath the scarf.***

No snag hair accessories

No Snag accessories and hair tools are extremely important when it comes to your hair. What are they? They are hair accessories that do not get caught up in your hair and pull it when you try to remove it from your hair. They are better quality in the way that they are constructed. Take for instance, a **comb**. One that is well made will not have any jagged edges in between the teeth of the comb that will catch the hair strands and snag on it while it passes through the hair and, as a result, break off the hair strand prematurely. The comb must have smooth surface all over, especially in between the teeth of the comb.

Hair bands should be seamless as well. Choose ones that do not have the metal piece that holds the hair band together.

Hair pins should have smooth intact ball tips. If they are not intact your hair can be snagged by the jagged tips and pull on the hair in such a way where it is kind of painful- not to mention the possibility of breaking off the hair before it's time to naturally shed from the scalp. Just be sure to carefully examine any kind of hair accessories, and tool before purchasing and using it.

Clip on Hair Pieces

Clip on hair pieces are an excellent, quick and easy way to add volume and length to short and medium length hair. Some of the hairstyles that are demonstrated in this book are longer styles. However, if you want to achieve the same look just simply add hair pieces to the appropriate areas and proceed with the hairstyle as directed.

You can either buy or make your own. If you would like to make your own clip on hair piece its super simple. Here's how:

Things you'll need:

- Weft hair (*make sure the color and texture matches your own hair*)
- Small wig clips
- Hair weaving needle (*curved or straight*)
- Hair weaving thread (*close to the color of your own hair*)
- Pair of scissors

Instructions:

1) Take the weft or weaving hair out of the package, unravel a small portion of the weaving hair, and then hold it against the head right at the location where you would like to add more volume or length. Measure the appropriate width then use the scissors to cut off just the amount that you need.
2) Depending on how many pieces of clip on hair pieces you would like to make, just continue to measure and cut until you have the amount of pieces you want.
3) Now, take the weaving needle and thread it with the weaving thread. (*12 inches of thread will do for now, then cut the thread. Even out the ends of the tread and knot the very ends.*)
4) Ok, take the wig clip and place it against the seam of the weaving hair (*the comb of the wig clip should be facing up and the teeth facing down, see picture*).
5) Take the threaded needle and begin to sew the wig clips on the weft one at a time. The wig clip already comes with holes in them so just simply pass the thread through them.
6) To make sure that the wig clip is secure on the weft hair, simply make a knot at the end. Do so by first cutting the thread close to the wig clip (about an inch will do). Then knot it a few times and cut the excess thread above the knot.
7) **To clip the hair pieces in your hair** make a part in the desired area you would like a fuller or longer look. Clip the top section of hair out of the way with a butterfly clip.
8) Take a small teeth comb and back comb the roots of the section of hair you'll be placing the hair piece in.(*The back combing will create texture and more anchor for the clip to stay*)
9) Now take the hair piece and place the part with the seam and clips along the part you've parted earlier. Push the clips in the back combed section and push the clips against the head to snap them shut.

2 Ways To Do Bantu Knot

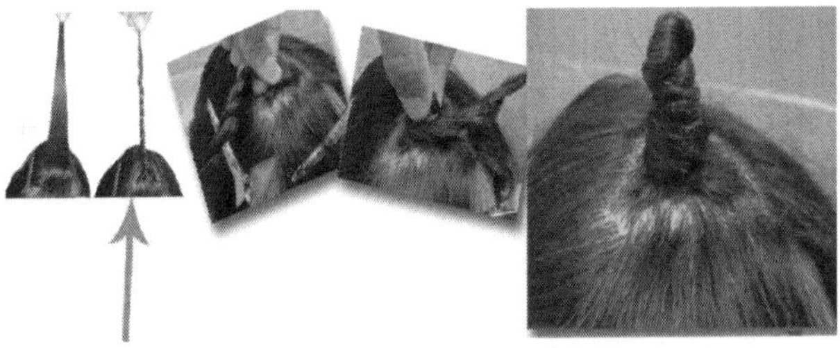

How To Bantu Knot

1. Hold the hair about 1 inch from the root and begin to roll it between your fingers. When the hair begins to coil on itself start to wrap the hair around the base of the Bantu knot. As you wrap the hair around the base roll the hair between your fingers and then wrap the hair around the base again. Continue to do this for the remaining length of the hair.
2. TIP: As you wrap the hair around the base gently assist the hair that is already wrapped on the top up a little by sliding it up.
3. Be sure that the ends are wrapped neatly around the base. Secure the hair by placing a small cloth hair band around the base of the Bantu knot.

TIP: When Bantu knotting the hair remember to bring the hair around the base of the hair each time to wrap it around .This will help to form a neat curl pattern. And also part the hair in half moon shapes that are positioned in a brick layered pattern.

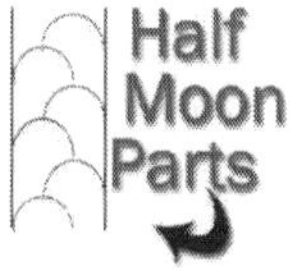

Creating Cornrows

The best way I think you as a beginner would grasp how to learn the cornrowing process is by first practicing the proper finger positions on a single braid or plait. Then when you are comfortable with doing that proceed to do the actual cornrow.

Supplies you'll need:

- Comb
- Butterfly clips *(for sectioning off the hair)*

How to do cornrows:

Practicing for the cornrow on the right *(regular raised cornrow).*

1. Grab a small section of hair.
2. Split it into three equal parts.
3. *To begin the braid you need proper finger positioning.* **With the right hand**. Hold the RIGHT piece of hair close to the root between your middle finger and ring finger.
4. With your index finger and thumb hold the MIDDLE piece of hair.

5. **With the left hand**, hold the LEFT piece of hair between the middle and ring finger.
6. *Practicing finger movement.* While still maintaining the same finger positions, start by using the pointer finger on the left hand side and slide it behind the middle hair and in front of the right hair.
7. Hook the hair with the pointer finger.
8. And bring it over to the left side.
9. And hold it in place with the pointer finger and thumb. Drop all the hair that you're holding with your right hand and immediately assume your fingers back into position again by holding the middle piece of hair with your middle and ring finger.
10. The same thing you've done from steps 4- 9 is the same exact thing you'll be doing on this side. *The braiding process is like a back and forth rhythm.* Take the pointer finger on the right hand and slide it behind the middle hair and in front of the left hair.
11. Hook it with the pointer finger.
12. And bring it to the right side.
13. Hold the hair between your pointer finger and thumb. Drop all the hair that you're holding with your left hand and immediately assume your fingers back in position again by holding the middle piece of hair with your middle and ring finger.
14. CONTINUE with this process, back and forth.
15. HOLD the hair up straight for this braiding practicing process.
16. And braid the hair to the end.
17. **ACTUAL CORNROW**. To begin, assume your finger positions from steps 3-5 and begin to braid the hair in the same rhythm you practiced. STOP! And pay attention. Instead of standing the hair up straight while braiding like you would in the practice session, you'll be braiding the hair flat on the head for the actual cornrow. To allow the hair to stick, whenever you use the pointer finger to hook the hair, pick up a small piece of hair under it at the side and merge those two together as one and hold the hair in place with your pointer and thumb simultaneously as you hook and collect some of the hair at the side that's under the hooked hair. *Whew! I hope you understood that. Just read it over and try to visualize it. This is going to take some practice before you get the hang of it.*

<u>Ok let's recap for a moment</u>. To begin the cornrow, pick up 3 small pieces of hair from the front of the part. Assume your finger positions. (*Hold the hair close to the finger tips and with some tension*) use the pointer finger that is not holding any hair, and begin to hook the hair from the opposite side and pick up some hair underneath it *(Important: The pointer finger and the thumb should be traveling to the other side at the same time to hook and hold the hair in place*)

Let go of the hair that you're holding with your other hand and hold it back with your middle and ring finger. Hook the hair on the other side in the same manner in which you did the other.

Tip: When doing the actual cornrow, you will be holding the hair more towards the tips of your fingers with some tension. Also, as you cornrow the hair the fingers should stay as close to the previous hair you just cornrowed and the hair should always be held with a little tension, so that as the cornrow is being formed the hair is not loose (Be careful not pull the hair too tight).

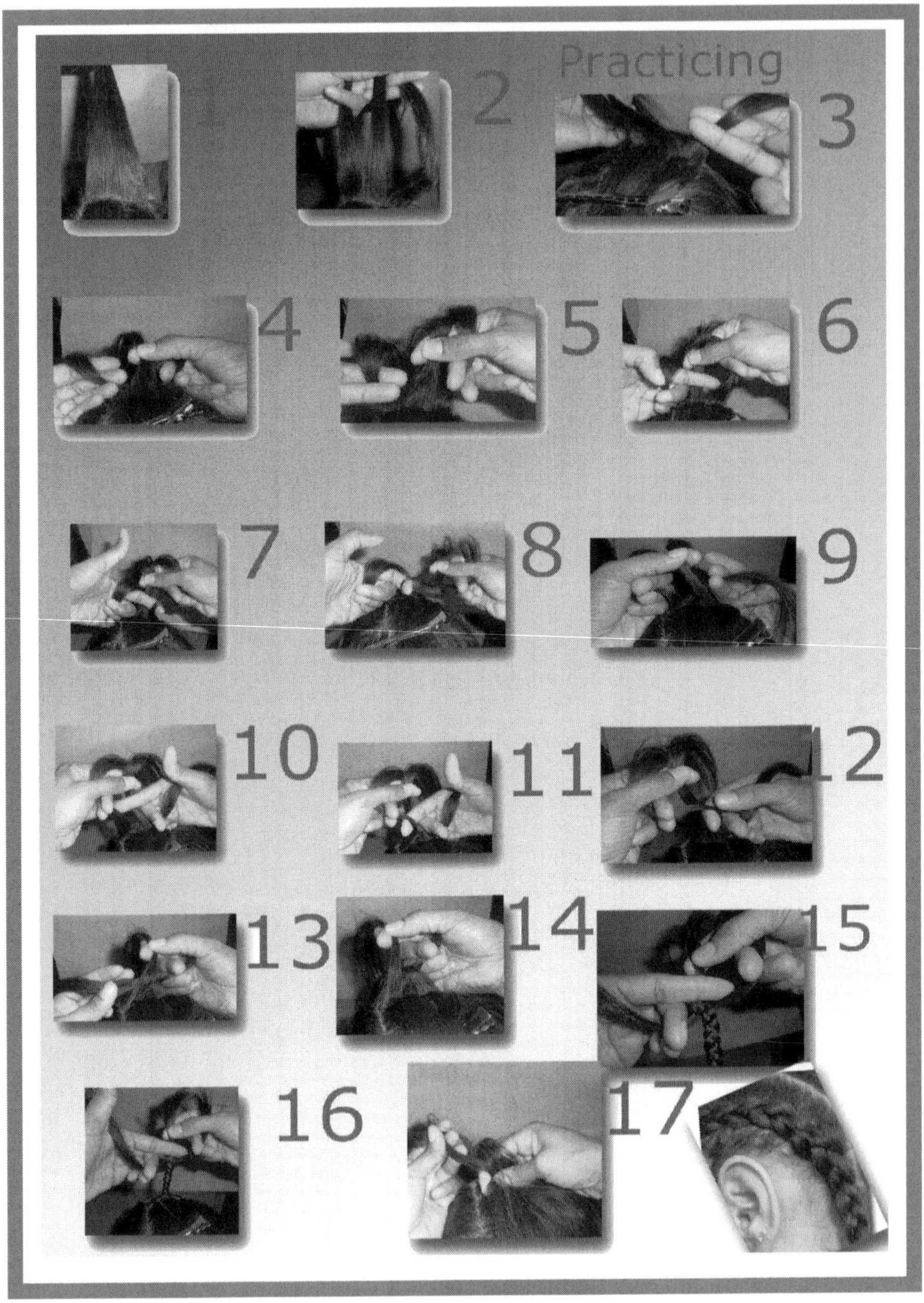
Practicing
2
3
4
5
6
7
8
9
10
11
12
13
14
15
16
17

Senegalese Twists *(example of how to attach braiding hair to your own hair to create Senegalese twists)*

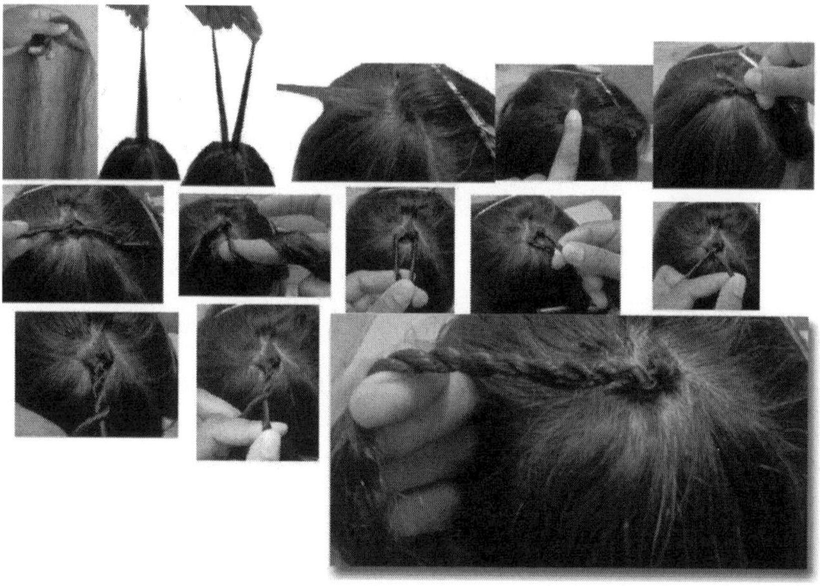

Items you'll need:

- Braiding hair
- Butterfly clips
- Moisturizer
- Mousse
- Hot water
- 2 Towels
- Mug with handle

Instructions for Senegalese twists:

1. First detangle hair completely from ends to roots. Do so in sections. Moisturize the hair from root to end.
2. Next part the hair in the front of the head from ear to ear across the head. Section off the back portion of hair with a butterfly clip for later. Now go to the front of the head and make a part starting from the front of the head where the hair line is in the middle. Now, you should have two equal parts of hair at the top part of the head. Section off one section with a butterfly clip.
3. Now you should have a section of hair in the back and two sections in the front.
4. Section off a piece of hair at the front side of the head. This should be shaped like a half moon. Section off the rest of the hair with a butterfly clip so it doesn't interfere with the hair you are going to use to create the Senegalese twist with.
5. **Doing the Senegalese twist**. Take a small section of hair and split it into 2 equal parts. Take a piece of braiding hair (*about the size of the section of hair you just split into 2*) and place the middle of the braiding hair against the scalp right between the hair you split into 2.
6. Pick up both the right section of hair along with the right portion of the braiding hair and begin to roll both of them together between your fingers from the root, (*please see the last photo in the first row*). **Use one hand to roll the Hair and the other to hold.** As you roll the hair between your fingers once, immediately take the other hand to hold the roll hair so that is does not unravel or become undone. With the other hand grasp the same piece of hair again and make another roll between your fingers on top of the last roll- continue to repeat this process until you have about 5 to 6 rolls done. Now wrap the hair around your middle finger (*see second picture in second row*) to hold it in place and to keep it from unraveling while you go to the next side and twist the hair.
7. While holding the hair with your middle finger, repeat the same process of rolling the hair on the other side.
8. After you have finished rolling, remove the middle finger from the hair. While still holding the hair on both sides **cross over the right side of hair to the left *(over the other piece of hair)* and now the originally left piece is now on the right side.** *(At this point both pieces of hair should be forming a criss cross shape).*
9. Adjust your grasp on both pieces of hair so that you are maintaining the "**X**" shape.
10. Now simultaneously roll each pieces of hair between your fingers to the **right once** and then cross them over each other to the **left**.
11. Continue this process of rolling and crossing over until you reach the end of the hair.
12. Make another half-moon part and REPEAT steps 5 – 11 to twist the hair.

13. **SEALING THE ENDS**
14. When the whole head of hair is completely done in Senegalese twists, place a large towel over your shoulders and begin to dip the ends of the twists in the hot water in small sections at a time (*about 1 minute for each section*)
15. Put the hot water down carefully and immediately take the towel and wrap it around the wet hot hair to soak up the water. This will also prevent the hot water from burning YOU.
16. Lastly apply a generous amount of mousse to the hair.

Since the braiding hair is synthetic the hot water helps to bind the fibers together.

Tip: To make the ends of the Senegalese twist have a tapered look, take the bundle of braiding hair and feather or make both ends of the bundle of hair more uneven by pulling on both sides a little at time simultaneously.

Video: "How to do Senegalese twist"
www.youtube.com/hairstylings101

CLICK ON: Senegalese twist

Flat Twist

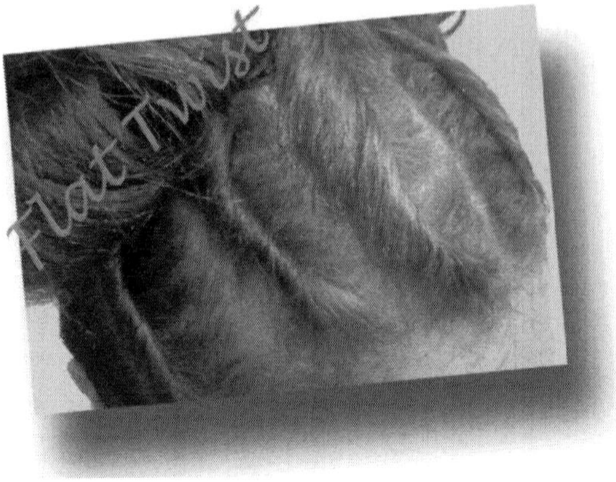

Supplies for doing flat twists:

- Comb
- Butterfly clip
- Hair pins or small hair bands
- Gel
- Silk or satin scarf

How to do flat twists:

1. First comb through the hair gently to detangle it.
2. Take the comb and determine the width or size you would like the flat twist to be. For instance if you would like the flat twist to be about 1 inch wide, start the part one inch away from side of the head in the front and start to part the hair going back. How long the flat twist should be is up to you. For instance, do you want it ¼, ½ or all the back to the nape of the neck?
3. Part the first section and then use the butterfly clip to section off the rest of the hair.
4. Comb through the section of hair you are going to flat twist and then take a small amount of gel and apply it along the root.
5. With your thumb and index finger grasp the front of the hair within the part right at the root and begin to roll the hair into a twist in between your fingers.
6. Take your other hand and place your index finger on the end of the flat twist, hold it for a moment. Let go off the flat twist with your other hand and immediately put it back re-grasping the hair at the root again.

7. REPEAT steps 5 &6 until you get to the end, then secure the flat twist with a hair band or hair pin which ever works best for you.
8. Undo the butterfly clip and make another part to make another flat twist. REPEAT steps 4 -8.
9. When you've completed all the flat twists, tie your hair with a silk or satin scarf to allow the flat twist to dry and set.

How To Attach Extension Braid

1. Divide the section of hair you would like to add the extension hair to into 3 equal parts.
2. Follow the steps of how to prepare the braiding hair and assume proper finger positions.
3. Place the braiding hair with its already 3 divided sections on top of your own hair matching the 3 sections of hair. **Pair** and **merge** each 3 sections of hair and re-assume your finger positions and begin to braid the hair as if it's your own. Remember to keep your fingers close to the hair you already braided. The hair that you're holding between your fingers should be positioned close to the tips of the fingers. And you should be holding the hair with a little tension while braiding. This will to create a neat look.

Pictures of some tools you'll be using in this book

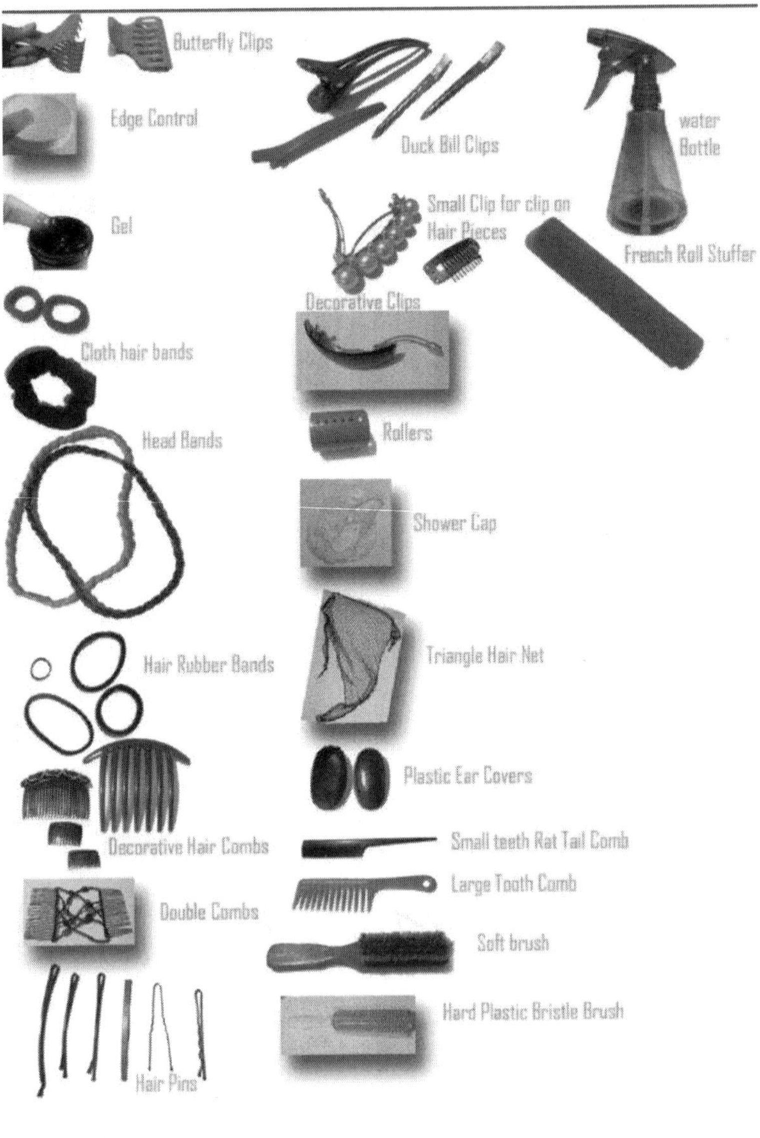

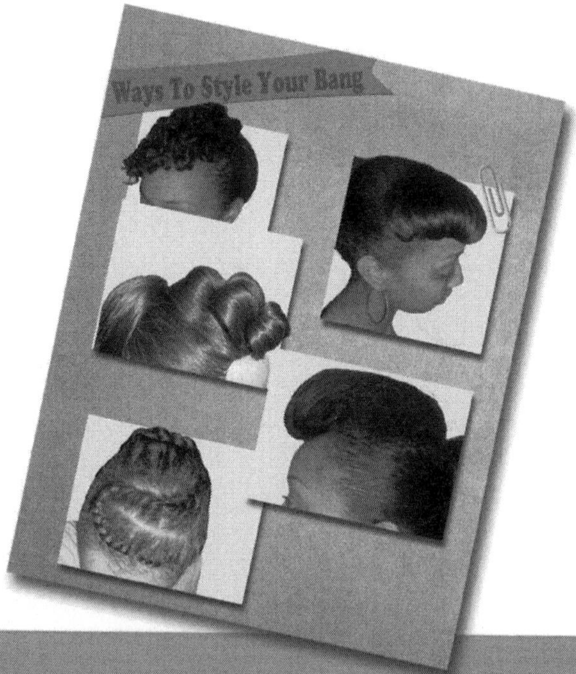
Ways To Style Your Bang

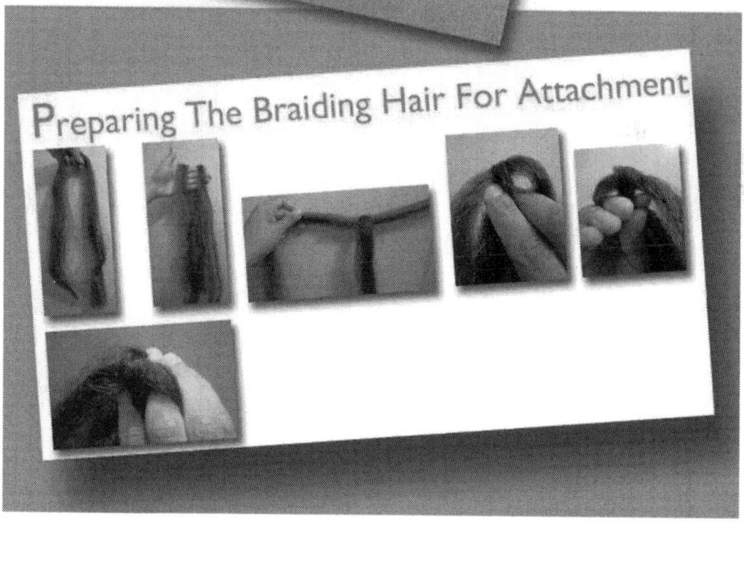
Preparing The Braiding Hair For Attachment

How To Make A Perfect Bun

Bun Maker

Have you ever wanted to know how to create a perfect bun but every time you attempt to do so it turns out to be a little lopsided, hair sticking out, not full enough or just some other issue going on? Well I'm going to share with you a great tool to use the next time you decide to style your hair into bun. There's something call a bun maker it looks like a donut and it comes in different colors and sizes according to the length and color of your hair. *See the picture above.*

To use a bun maker, simply gather all your hair into one and place a hair band around the hair to secure the ponytail in place.

Next, take the ponytail and put it through the hole of the bun maker, slide the bun maker all the way down to the base of the ponytail.

Fan the ponytail out so that the hair is evenly covering the bun maker, now begin to tuck the hair under the bun maker to hide the excess hair, do so all the way around until all the hair is completely tucked under. Use hair pins to further secure the bun in place. And wahlah! You just created a perfect bun!

Would you like to make your very own bun maker? Let me show you how.

Supplies you'll need:

- An old sock
- A pair of scissors

Instructions how to make a bun maker:

1. First take the sock and locate the part for the toes.
2. Next take the scissors and begin to cut the tip off.
3. Now fold the edge over the sock and begin to roll the sock into a donut shape. Congratulations you've just make your very own sock bun! (*see picture below for the picture instructions*)

Hairstyles that flatter your face shape

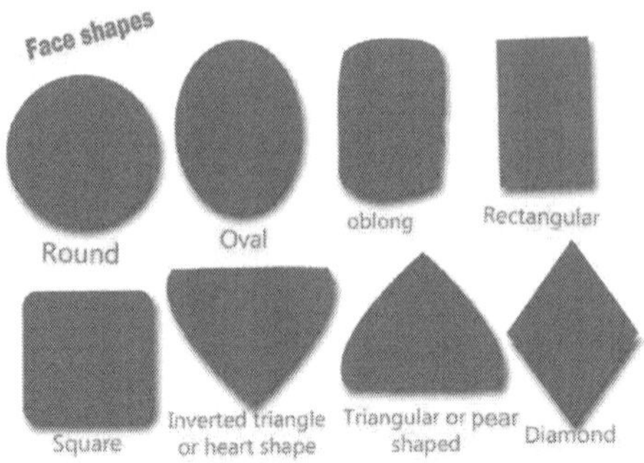

I include this section because I thought you would find it a little fun to discover what your face shape is and what hairstyles flatters the shape of your face the most. This is also a great guide for picking out wig styles for your protective styling.

Oval: The length of the face is about 1 ½ times wider than the width. And the forehead is a little wider than the chin.
STYLES: The contour of an oval face shape is said to be the most desirable shape to have. This is because this shape can pretty much carry off any hairstyle type. Because of this all other face shapes when comes to hairstyles are styled to give the illusion of an oval shape.

Round: The face length is shorter than that of an oval shape. Therefore the length and the width are about the same.
STYLES: You want the face to appear longer. Choose hairstyles that have height on top of the head and a sleeker look at the sides.

Oblong: I would say this shape is a mix between oval and rectangular shape.
STYLES: Choose a style that is short (about chin length) and has volume on the sides of the head. The hair on the top should be closer to the head.

Rectangular: The widths of the top and bottom portion of the face are about the same, and the length is longer than the width.
STYLES: Keep the style shorter at about chin length. Hair should be covering the forehead area and also the hair on the bottom should be close to the face.

Square: The width on top and bottom of the face are about the same. The bottom of the face has a squared off shape, the length of the face is about the same as the width.
STYLES: Soften up the face by framing it with soft layers not blunt cuts.

Triangular or pear shape: Are narrower on the top portion of the face and wider on the bottom.
STYLES: You want camouflage the narrowness of the top portion of the head. You can hide it with a soft bang or add volume to the sides at the top of the head.

Inverted triangle or heart shape: Wider on top of the face and narrower on the bottom.
STYLES: Balance out this shape by keeping the style close on top of the head. As the style progress down the length of the face it should have more volume, more at the bottom.

Diamond: The forehead and chin areas are narrower than the width of the cheekbone area.
STYLES: Hairstyle should be fuller on the top and sleeker at cheekbone area and fuller at the bottom. *hair at the cheekbone area should be comb towards the face not away.

Protective And No Heat Hairstyle Ideas !

The Horizontal French Roll
Double rolls

The Horizontal French Roll

Wow, this hairstyle is so simple and elegant at the same time. This style is perfect for relaxed, naturals or those that are transitioning from relaxed to natural.

Items you'll need:

- ✓ Comb
- ✓ Soft brush
- ✓ Edge control or gel
- ✓ Hair pins
- ✓ Something to stuff the roll with or braiding hair
- ✓ Hair ties or hair bands

How to create the style:

1. Start to prepare the braiding hair by braiding it, do so according to the length and thickness of your own hair. For example, I pinch off 1/3 of the braiding hair and create a long braid from it. Now my hair is currently at about bra strap length, so that amount is perfectly fine for me. If your hair is about shoulder length, you might want pinch off less braiding hair to create the braid.

   After you have created a braid from the hair, start to fold the braided hair onto itself so that it is about 4 inches long. At this point it should look like a small log.

   Use the rubber bands to wrap around the folded braid to secure it in place.

2. Comb and detangle your hair carefully, make sure the whole head of hair is combed back.
3. Now place the log of hair you created earlier **horizontally** on the back of your head, less than half way up from the nape of your neck.
4. Start to use the hair pins to pin the log in place.
5. After that, use your own hair to fold over the braided hair, so that it completely covers the braided hair; don't forget to fold over the sides as well.
6. Now use the hair pins to pin and secure your hair
7. Use the edge control or gel and put it on the edges and nape of your hair. Use the soft brush to brush down any fly aways.

YOU'RE DONE!

Naturally Long, Thick, Full Hair

If you already have natural long, thick, full hair you can absolutely create this same style.

Just follow the steps below. Exclude adding the braid or stuffing to your hair.

1. Comb your whole head of hair back. Brush the edges with a soft brush.
2. Gather all your hair into a low ponytail and run your hands down to the ends of your hair, take a small hair band and place it at the end.
3. Now start to roll the hair from the ends all the way up, just like you are about to create a pin curl. Make sure that it is snug.
4. Use the hair pins to start securing the hair in place. Check and make sure the roll itself is not too slack or loose. Adjust the sides of the roll as well.
5. Now take some edge control or gel and use the brush to smooth out the perimeter of hair.

The Double Roll

To create the double roll you see on the bottom left corner, you basically will use the same technique to create the roll. The only difference is the hair will be sectioned off into two instead of one. Here's how.

1. First, part the hair into two halves going horizontally
2. Next section off the bottom half.
3. Proceed to the top half of hair and take off a section of hair from any one side you want.
4. Now, add that small section of hair with the bottom section. At this point you should have two sections of hair still, however now the section on top is slanted to the side and the one on the bottom starts from the top and curve to the bottom end (take a look back at the picture to have a clear picture of what I'm saying).
5. At this point you'll be creating the rolls. First, take the top section loosen it gently and comb through it, also use a soft brush to smooth out the edges
6. Hold the hair 90 degrees off the head and use the comb to gently back comb the roots *(this will create some body, volume and height for the top)*.
7. Now begin to fold the hair under itself hiding all the ends (make sure not to tuck too tight but just snug enough). Now begin to pin the hair into place.
8. Proceed to the bottom section. Place the braided log hair a little below the part horizontally and fold your own hair over to cover it completely. Be sure to tuck in all the ends, now proceed to pin and secure the roll.
9. Add some edge control or gel to smooth the edges.

Pretty Bow
Hair Style

Pretty Hair Bow Hairstyle

This style is indeed very pretty. I can see a little girl wearing this style as well as a grown person.

Items you'll need:

- ✓ Comb
- ✓ Soft brush
- ✓ Hair pins
- ✓ Hair band
- ✓ Edge control

Here's how to create the style:

1. Gently comb through hair getting rid of any tangles.
2. Use the comb to make a part horizontally across the head (start about 1 ½ inch up from the nape of the neck). Section that bottom piece off with a hair band.
3. Proceed to the top section; gather all the hair from the top into a low pony tail, and secure it with a hair band.
4. Now pick up the pony tail and take out a small piece of hair from the bottom of the pony tail. Use a hair pin to pin down the hair so that it is now out of the way.
5. Take the remaining hair in your hand and proceed to splitting it into two equal pieces. Pin down one piece so that piece can be out of the way as well.
6. *Let's recap for a second. At this point you should now have hair parted into 2 sections bottom and top. Bottom section is smaller than the top. The bottom is section off and the top section is in a ponytail and that ponytail is split into 2 with a small piece of hair from the bottom pinned away.*
7. Ok. Now take one section of hair within the pony tail and proceed to create a raised pin curl with it (do so facing your ears and also when pin curling the hair, do so going under)
8. Now use a hair pin to slide within the hole of the pin curl and secure it into place.
9. REPEAT steps 7 & 8 when working with the other section of hair within the pony tail.
10. Remember the small piece of hair you section off in step # 4? Well now take the hair pin out to set free that piece (look at the picture). Notice the middle between the two raised pin curl hair? Well now you are going to create that look by taking the small piece of hair and bring it up over the middle section (covering the seam or middle) secure with a pin. Bring the rest of the hair back down and secure with a hair pin. Continue to go back and forth just like that until there's no more hair to work with.
11. Final step. Look at the picture again. Notice under the bow there's a section that is rolled and tuck under? Ok well now take off the hair band

off that section that you place on it in (step # 2). Gently comb through the hair.

12. Place a small hair band at the very end of the hair (to help keep the hair together if you have longer hair). Begin to roll the hair under itself until you're unable to do so. Now use the pin to secure that hair into place. Do so underneath the roll.
13. That's it. You are done!

Side Twist
With Puffy Top

Side Twists with Puffy Top

Items you'll need:

- ✓ Braiding hair *(for fullness optional)*
- ✓ Hair pins
- ✓ Comb
- ✓ Soft brush
- ✓ Butterfly clip *(to keep hair out of the way)*

Here's how to create this style:

1. First use the comb and gently comb through and detangle hair.
2. Now use the comb to make a "U" shape part at the top front of your head (this should be about 4 ½ inches wide. And about 3 ½ to 4 inches long)
3. Now hold the hair up 90 degrees from the head, proceed to gently back comb the roots of the hair (this will create volume for the puffy top). DO NOT BACK COMB TOWARDS THE FRONT. ONLY IN THE BACK WITHIN THAT SECTION OF HAIR.
4. At this point fold the hair in the back, hiding all the ends of the hair. Use some hair pins and secure the fold into place. And tah dah! You have just created a puffy top.
5. Let's move on to the back section now. Gently comb through the hair and carefully detangle it. With your hands, NOT the comb. Divide the section into two equal parts. And section off one side with a butterfly clip.
6. Take the braiding hair from the package and pinch off a piece (the size you choose will depend on the thickness you are trying to achieve for the twist).
7. **Attaching the braiding hair to your own hair.** After you've decided the amount you want, go ahead and hold the long piece of hair in the **middle** so that both ends are hanging loose. Starting from the side of the head towards the front, pick up two small pieces of hair and begin to attach the braiding hair to yours. *Creating a Senegalese twist see "tips you should know before styling" section in the front of this book to learn how to do the attachment process.*
8. After attaching the twist, criss cross and twist the hair down about two times. Now lay the twist down flat to the scalp still holding the 2 sections of the twist with your fingers.
9. Begin to do a 2 strand flat twist with the braiding hair and your hair together. When you can no longer do a 2 strand flat twist, just continue to twist the hair to the very end. If you find that the twist is unraveling, just use a small hair band to secure the end.
10. Proceed to the next side and follow steps 7-9

11. After you've completed the twist on both sides, take the tail of one twist and lift it up and bring it horizontally to the other side, secure with a hair pin. Take the remaining of that hair and lay it across going the other way horizontally, pin to secure. Keep going back and forth until there is no more hair to pin.
12. Proceed to the next side. And do the very same thing with that hair. Look back at step 11.
13. That's it!
14. **Do you have natural or, relaxed, long hair?** Just follow the steps above. Just exclude the braiding hair.

Romantic Side Swept Curls

Romantic side Swept Curls

Wow! This style is simple but just so beautiful to look at. This style is great for any special occasion. Great on relaxed hair or transitioning hair types. Ideal for short, medium or long hair.

Items you'll need:

- ✓ Hair mousse
- ✓ Hair pins
- ✓ Comb
- ✓ Soft brush
- ✓ Flexi rods
- ✓ Time

Here's how to create the style:

1. Comb through hair gently and carefully to get rid of any tangles. Always start from the bottom an work your way up to avoid premature breakage of hair
2. Decide what side of the head you want the side swoop to be. Go ahead and brush or comb hair over to that side.
3. Now take the mousse and squirt about a palm full into your hands and apply it to the length of your hair
4. Section off a small piece of hair. Take the flexi rod and hold it at one end then hold it up right. Now take the small section of hair and place the end of the hair on the flexi rod next to where you are holding it. Begin to rotate the flexi rod so that the hair begins to wrap around it. Continue to do so, so that the hair is covering a good amount of the rod.
5. Now bend and curve each ends of the rod so that it stays in place
6. Repeat steps 4 &5 to the rest of the hair.
7. Allow a couple of hours to dry (the hair shouldn't take that long to dry given that the mousse was applied to dry not wet hair). *if you are allowing the hair to dry overnight remember to cover with a silk or satin scarf*
8. **When hair is completely set and dry** start taking the rods out. Undo the curved ends of the rods and proceed to unravel the hair from the flexi rod slowly and gently.
9. After all the rods are out, take your fingers to slowly and gently fluff out the curls.
10. Starting from the front side of the head, take a section of the now curly hair and loosely roll it up to the side of your head. Now take a couple of hair pins and secure the rolled up curls into place.
11. Continue this process until you reach the back of the head
12. Proceed to the other side of the head without the curls and pull some of the hair towards the back of the head (not too tight) just enough for it to look neat.

13. Fold over that section of hair upwards into a curl and place it against the head in the back and pin to secure.
14. Take a look back at the picture to see if your finish hair style looks like the one you see.
15. You are done!

Wrap Braid

The Wrap Braid

This style is so unique. And I must say, I really love it!
This hairstyle is great for medium to long length hair. If you are natural, I would recommend stretching the hair a little by using large rollers after washing your hair. After the hair is dried place the hair in a criss cross wrap overnight and tie with a silk or satin scarf then proceed with the hairstyle.

Items you'll need:

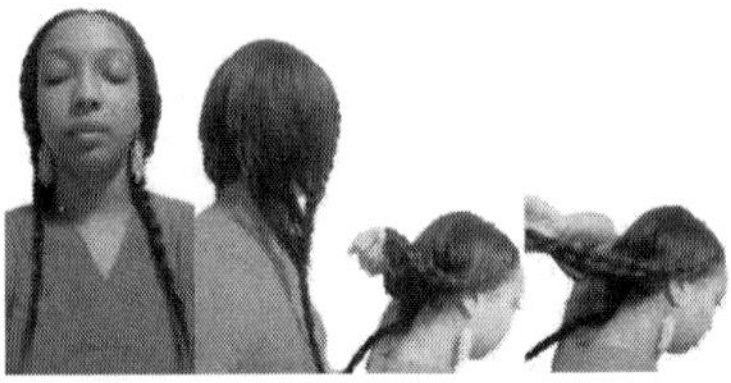

- ✓ Comb
- ✓ Soft brush
- ✓ Hair pins
- ✓ Small hair bands
- ✓ Butterfly clip
- ✓ Clip in hair pieces for length (*color and texture as your own hair*)

Here's how to create this style:

1. First, use the comb to gently comb through the hair and get rid of any tangles. Next, place the clip on hair pieces on your hair.
2. Make a middle part in the front of the head about 1 inch long. Then divide the hair in the back into two with your hands (a comb is not necessary) and section off one of the section of hair with a butterfly clip.
3. Grab three strands of hair close to where the middle part is in front of the head and start to loosely cornrow the hair *stay close to the hair line when creating the cornrow* when you reach the temples of your head stop creating the cornrow onto the head. Do this by holding the cornrow off the head and straight down pointing to the floor and slightly pulling on it.
4. Complete the cornrow off the head by grabbing pieces of hair from the loose hair behind it. Do so until you reach the very end of the hair. Now use a hair band to secure the end of the cornrow.
5. Proceed to the next side of the head and remove the butterfly clip. Follow steps 3 & 4.
6. After both sides are braided lift the braid like you see in picture and lay it horizontally across the back of the head creating a pouch like style below the braid.
7. If any hair is crossing over the hair line on the other side, simply fold it under the braid to hide it. Place hair pins along the braid to secure it in place.
8. Proceed to the next side and do the same thing.
9. Now, adjust the pouch underneath the braid too so that it is nice and neat.

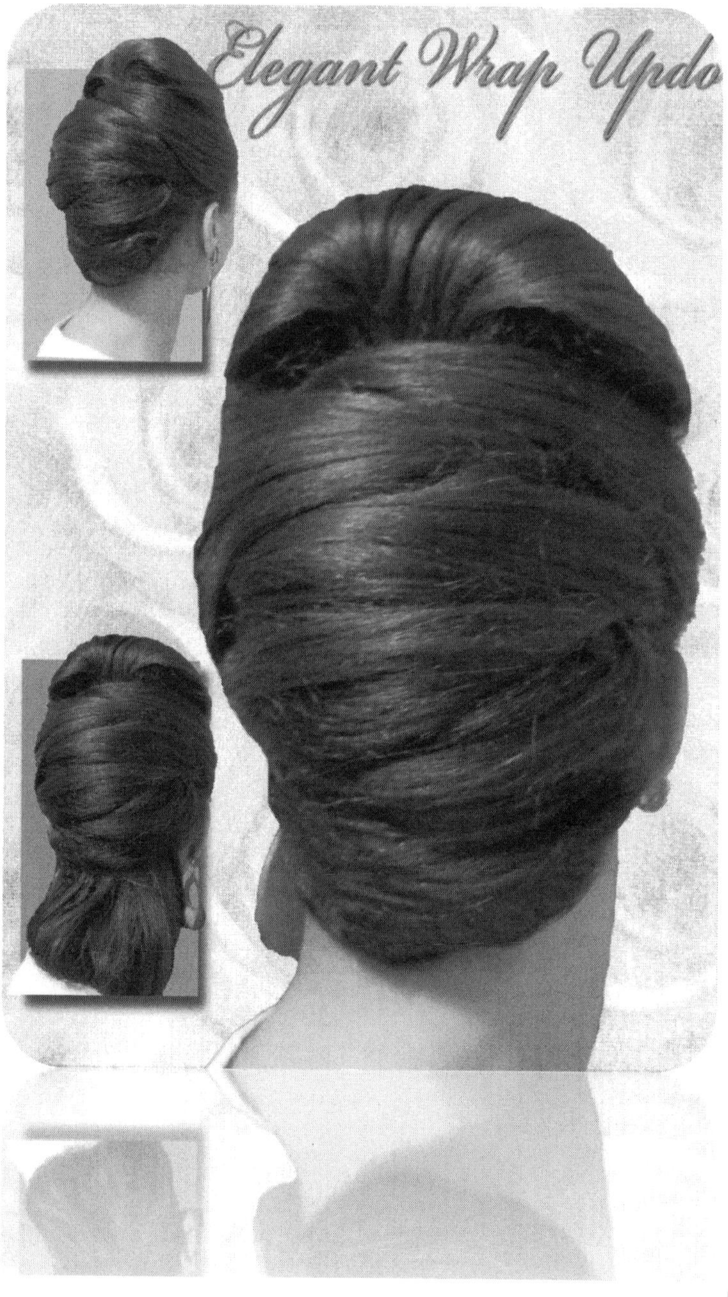
Elegant Wrap Updo

Elegant Wrap Updo

This elegant updo can be done on medium to long hair

Items you'll need:

- ✓ Soft brush
- ✓ Comb
- ✓ Lots of hair pins

Here's how to create this style:

1. First comb through the hair gently and carefully getting rid of any tangles
2. Make a "U" part shape at the front center of the head. About 4 inches wide and 2 inches back. Then gently back comb the roots of the hair in the back to create volume in the front.
3. Next fold the section of hair down and secure it with a couple of hair pins.
4. Take a piece of hair from the front side of the head and smooth it out with a soft brush. Now bring it across the back of the head horizontally and lay it down flat, now it is covering the hair pins you just placed at the top. When you reach the other side (the point where you made the "U" shape part, slightly bend the remaining hair downwards), take a hair pin and secure the hair at that point.
5. Proceed to the other side and do the same thing, make sure when you are going across, stay close to the bottom end of the previous strip you just laid
6. Continue to do this process until you reach the bottom of the head.
7. Remember to take the strips of hair from the sides of the head when criss crossing them.

Simple Updo
With a Hint
of Braids

Simple Updo with a Hint of Braids

Items you'll need:

- ✓ Comb
- ✓ Soft brush
- ✓ Hair pins
- ✓ Edge control or gel
- ✓ Butterfly clip

Here's how to create this style:

1. First comb through the hair gently to get rid of any tangles. Do so starting from the bottom and work your way up carefully and slowly to avoid breakage.
2. Use the comb to make a side part at the front left side of your head (about 1 inch to1 ½) going back. STOP, do not lift the comb yet. **You can choose any side you want to make the part, left or right **
3. Now turn the comb facing your right ear, and continue making the part going all the way back to the back of your head, reaching the nape of your neck. Remember to stay parallel to the perimeter of the edge of your hair line when creating the part
4. Now create an underhand French braid with this section of hair. Braid all the way to the end. *See picture.*
5. Use your ears as guides and make a part going horizontally across the head. From ear to ear, In the middle of the head.
6. Section off the bottom portion of the hair below the part with a butterfly clip
7. Take the top portion of hair gently comb through it, use a soft brush to smooth edges (add some gel if you like).
8. Now hold the hair about 90 degrees off the head and back comb the roots gently. This will create some volume.
9. Now gather the hair about 5 inches from the root, and place it down where see the part. Place it so that it is on the part. Take a couple of hair pins and secure the hair into place.
10. Proceed to the bottom section. Take out the butterfly clip and gently comb through the hair. Be careful not snag the portion of hair that's on the top. From the bottom left side of the nape of your neck, grab a small portion of hair and braid it. Set that braid aside for a moment.
11. Now gather all the loose hair you see and begin to create a raised pin curl facing upward. Now pin down the pin curl you just created (when doing this, be sure to cover any loose hair that may be sticking out from the portion of hair from the top). *Stop a moment and adjust any hair you see out of place.*
12. Now take the braids you created earlier and wrap it around the middle section one at a time (just between the 2 bumps you see in the picture). Whenever you wrap the braids through the middle, pass it under the

bottom bump and come back around through the 2 middle bumps. Do so until there is no more braided hair left. Now use hair pins to pin and secure the braids down in place.

Tip: When you braid the two braids and find that they are not long enough. Simply add a small amount of braiding hair to compensate for the length

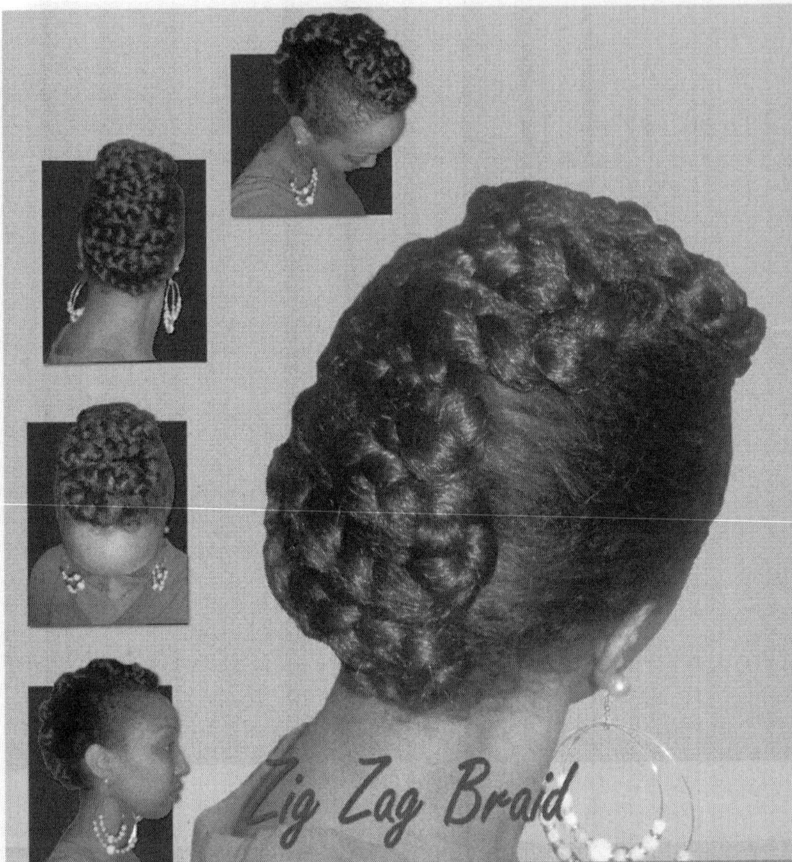
Zig Zag Braid

Zigzag Braid

This hair style is great for short to medium length hair. However, if you already have long hair, about bra strap length, you can achieve a similar look. Just go straight to the end of these instructions.

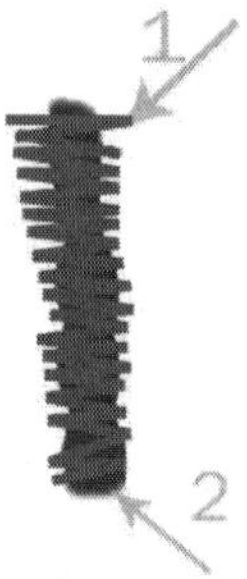

Items you'll need:

- ✓ Braiding hair
- ✓ Comb
- ✓ Soft brush
- ✓ Lots of hair pins

Here's how to create the style:

First prepare the braiding hair by dividing it into 3 pieces, fold and braid each one. Set aside until later.

1. Comb through and carefully detangle hair.
2. Comb hair up into the center of the head into a Mohawk fashion.
3. Next, create an inverted braid starting from the very front of the head coming all the back to the nape of the neck. Then tuck in the remaining hair from the braid into itself at the nape and pin to secure.
4. Now take one of the pre braided hair and place it horizontally across the underhanded braided you created with your own hair in the front of the head. Only part of the pre braided hair should be placed over your braid, about 2 inches of it starting from one of the end.
5. Place a couple of hair pins to secure that 2 inch length (small portion) braid onto to your head.
6. Now start to zigzag the pre braided hair back and forth on top and along the already underhanded braid going all the way down to the nape of the neck. Remember to pin as you go to secure the braids.
7. As you make your down just be mindful of any gaps in between any zigzag. There should be NONE.

That's it!

The drawing is a demonstration of what the pre braided hair and your braided hair should look like. The black log underneath the zigzag represents your braided hair. And the brown zigzag part represents pre braided hair going back and forth all the way down to the nape of the neck.

Have long hair already? Try this.

Items you'll need:

- ✓ No snag hair bands
- ✓ Lots of hair pins
- ✓ Comb
- ✓ Soft brush
- ✓ Edge control or gel

Creating the hair style:

1. Make about five to six small pony tails starting from the front of the head going all the way back to the nape of the neck.
2. Make sure that they are all lined up straight in a row in a Mohawk fashion.
3. Next split each one into two equal parts and proceed to braid each one completely. Add a small hair band to the end of each braid to stop them from unraveling.
4. Go back to the front of the head and pick up the first braid in the first ponytail and place the braid down on the head in the front vertically in a straight line. Now scrunch it together so that it resembles a zigzag and place hair pins to secure it down into place.
5. Next take the other braided hair and do the same thing, however now you'll be placing the hair going the opposite direction facing the nape. Remember to place hair pins to secure into place. Continue this process until you've completed all the braids.

TOP

The Braided Bang

Items you'll need:

- ✓ Comb
- ✓ Soft brush
- ✓ Braiding hair (optional)
- ✓ Hair pins
- ✓ Hair band

Here's how to create the style:

1. First, comb through hair gently to get rid of any tangles.
2. Next, create the bang area by starting to part the hair towards the front part of the head. Do this by using the ears as markers, start from back of the ears and start to part the hair horizontally going across the head. Stop when you reach the back of the next ear on the other side of the head.
3. Section off the back portion of the hair with a hair band. Now comb the front portion of hair forward so that is covering your face and parts of the sides.
4. Staring from the side of the head (you can choose any side) next to where the part is but starting about eye brow level, simply start to braid the hair across the face staying in a straight line
5. When you reach to the other side of the head next to where the part is and there is no more hair to braid across, simply create a single braid going down to the end. Now you have 2 options, depending on the length of your hair you can **1)** tuck the hair under the braid you just created and pin it to secure it in place or **2)** or bring the braid up alongside the part going upward and pin to secure. If there's any remaining braided hair left sticking out just simply add it to the bun in the next step.
6. Ok, proceed to the back and undo the hair band and comb the hair up into a high ponytail close to the front of the bang. Make sure to use the soft brush to brush around the perimeter of the hair to smooth it out. Gather the hair and secure it with the hair band.
7. At this point you have two options. 1) First, you can use your own hair to make into a bun or 2) use the braiding hair to make a bigger braid.
8. **USING YOUR OWN HAIR TO MAKE A BUN:** Simply divide your pony tail into 3 sections and proceed to braid to the end then wrap each one around the base of the ponytail one at time and secure with a hair pin.
9. **USING THE BRAIDNG HAIR TO CREATE A BIGGER BRAID:**
10. Use the whole pack of braiding hair and divide it into 3 sections. Start from the base of the ponytail and begin to braid the braiding hair into your real hair until you reach the end, then secure with a hair band.
11. Now begin to wrap the hair around unto itself until there is no more to wrap. Remember to secure the hair with hair pins as you go. Put some edge control or gel on the edges and use a soft brush to smooth out the edges.

From This
To This !
Dress it Up !
Backwards Ponytail

The Backwards Ponytail

Items you'll need:

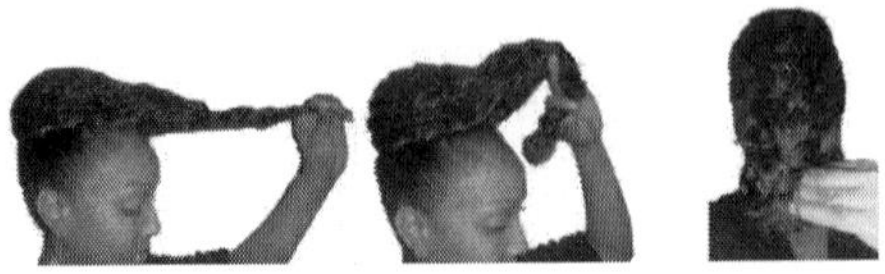

- ✓ Hair band
- ✓ Hair pins
- ✓ Comb
- ✓ Soft brush
- ✓ Edge control or gel
- ✓ A flower clip for style (optional)
- ✓ Draw string clip on ponytail (curly or straight) about 10 or 12 inches long

Here's how to create the style:

1. Comb through hair gently to get rid of any tangles.
2. Place some gel or edge control around the perimeter of hair and use a soft brush to brush and smooth out the edges.
3. Gather all the hair into a high pony tail and secure it with a hair band.
4. Braid the ponytail all the way to the end and wrap it around the base as snug as you can but not too tight and secure with a hair pin.
5. Now place the ponytail over the braided bun (make sure that the drawstring in the pony tail is facing your face). Set the clips that are in the ponytail in your hair and secure. Now draw the drawstring to tighten into place.
6. Gather the ponytail hair in front of your face right at your forehead and braid from that point to the end. Secure the end with a small hair band.
7. Tuck the braided portion under the hair itself hiding the braid. (At this point, you can slant the hair to the side a little or just leave it in the middle. Up to you). Now secure hair with a couple of hair pins.
8. Proceed to the sides and place hair pins alongside the hair just to secure the hair into place as well.
9. OPTIONAL: Take the flower clip and place it at one side of hair just to dress it up a little.

Raised Pin Curl
Updo

Raised Pin Curl Updo

Items you'll need:

- ✓ Comb
- ✓ Soft brush
- ✓ Hair pins
- ✓ Edge control or gel
- ✓ Small double comb w/ decorative elastic in middle
- ✓ Butterfly clips (for sectioning)

Here's how to create the style:

1. First comb through hair gently to get rid of any tangles.
2. YOU'LL BE DIVIDING THE HAIR INTO 3 SEPARATE SECTIONS. 1st –start from the back of the head and begin to part the hair horizontally across (about 1 ½ to 2 inches up from the nape of neck). Use the butterfly clip to section off the top section of hair for now.
3. Now take the bottom portion of hair and make one twist at the base (as if you are going to do a French roll) and stop. Next, use the double comb and place it over the twist just like you see in the picture.
4. Ok. Proceed to the top section of hair and undo the butterfly clip. At this point, make a "U" shape part in the front bang area centered in the middle. (*This should be about 4 inches wide and 4 inches going back).* Again use the butterfly clip to section off this portion of hair for later.
5. Now you should be left with a portion of loose hair in the middle. Gather it together and smooth the sides and twist it once at the roots and secure it with a couple of hair pins. (*Or use a small hair band to secure the hair at the roots).*
6. Now let's recap for a moment: remember the hair is separated into 3 sections. One at the bottom, middle and top.
7. Take the loose hair that is sticking out from the bottom and middle sections (DO NOT UNDO THEM) and simply merge them together. Comb it so that it is neat and begin to create a raised pin curl with it facing the front of your head. Use hair pins to secure it into place.
8. Undo the butterfly clip from the top and begin to make a 1 inch part going horizontally across within the part, create another pin curl going forward and secure with hair pins. Continue to do this until there is no more hair left.

Stacked Pin Curls
Banana Clip Split
Pin Curls

Stacked Pin Curls

Items you'll need:

- ✓ Banana clip
- ✓ Small hair pins
- ✓ Edge control or gel
- ✓ Comb
- ✓ Soft brush
- ✓ Butterfly clip
- ✓ Hair band

Here's how to create the style:

1. First, comb through the hair gently starting from the ends of the hair working your way up the roots.
2. Next, make a "U" shape part at the front center of the head and place a butterfly clip to section off the hair for later.
3. Proceed to the back of the of head and place some edge control or gel around the perimeter of hair
4. Next, smooth the edges by brushing it with a soft brush, then gather up all the hair into a ponytail in the center of the head and place the hair band to secure it.
5. Now use the banana clip and place it around the ponytail vertically (the banana clip should be laying long ways along the length of the head) then clip the banana clip into place.
6. Remove the hair band from the ponytail and adjust the hair within the banana clip by extending the roots of the hair to each end of the banana clip filling it out.
7. Take a 1/3 of the hair within the banana clip starting from the top and create a raised pin curl. Do so by rolling the hair under itself starting from the end and work your way up to the head then secure it into place with a hair pin. Continue doing this until there is no more hair.
8. Proceed to the front and remove the butterfly clip from the bang area. Now pinch off a tiny amount of hair off of it and create a pin curl, slant it a little to the side and lay it flat, pin it into place.
9. Pin curl the remaining hair (going under), slanting it a little to the same side. Lay it flat onto its side then pin it into place.

Banana Clip Split Pin Curls

Items you'll need:

- ✓ Banana clip
- ✓ Small hair pins
- ✓ Edge control or gel
- ✓ Comb
- ✓ Soft brush
- ✓ Hair band

Here's how to create the style:

1. Comb through hair gently and get rid of any tangles.
2. Make a part at the side (any side) about 1 inch long
3. Put some gel at the perimeter of hair and use the soft brush to brush and smooth the edges.
4. Use the brush or comb to swoop the front side of the hair to the side just like you see in the smaller picture.
5. Gather all the hair together into a ponytail (make sure that it is nice and neat). Place the hair band around the hair to secure the ponytail for now.
6. Now take the banana clip and place it around the ponytail horizontally going across the head, clip and secure it into place.
7. Remove the hair band from the ponytail and adjust the roots of the hair filling the entire banana clip from end to end.
8. Now, comb through the hair so that it is neat and proceed to split the hair into two sections in the middle horizontally.
9. Pin curl the top portion going up then place it down on the head next to the edge of the banana clip, then fan the pin curl out a little so that it is covering most of the top part of the banana clip. Pin to secure in place.
10. Proceed to the bottom part and do the very same thing that you just did on the top however the pin curl will be facing down.
11. **Optional: Need more length? Simply add a couple pieces of clip-in wefts horizontally on the head right where you'll be placing the banana clip. Do so before step # 5.*

Banana Clip
Twist
Two Strand
Flat Twist

Banana Clip Twist

This hair style is great for maintaining the length of long hair.

Items you'll need:

- ✓ Banana clip
- ✓ Hair pins
- ✓ Comb
- ✓ Soft brush
- ✓ Gel
- ✓ Hair band
- ✓ Butterfly clip

Here's how to create the style:

1. Comb through hair gently to get rid of any tangles.
2. Lightly add some gel around the perimeter of hair.
3. Use the brush to brush and smooth out the hair.
4. Gather all the hair together and place a hair band around it.
5. Now take the banana clip and place it horizontally around the base of the ponytail and clip it into place. Remove the hair from the ponytail and adjust the roots of the hair that are in the banana clip. (Make sure that the hair is filling the banana clip from end to end).
6. Starting from the top part of the banana clip, pick up two small portion of hair and begin to do two strand flat twist to the hair going downward all the way to the end of the banana clip. STOP.
7. Split the hair into 2 equal parts. Use the butterfly clip to hold ½ of the hair for a moment.
8. Create a 2 strand twist with the other half and bring it up alongside the banana clip. Use some small hair pins to secure the twist into place.
9. Remove the banana clip and repeat step # 8 for the other side.

Two Strand Flat Twists

Repeat steps 1-5 for **"Banana Clip Twist"**. Now begin to create a flat twist staring from the top of banana clip to the very ends of the hair. Use a small hair band the same color of your hair and place it at the end of the hair to prevent it from unraveling.

2 Side braids & Beautiful Back Pin Up
or
2 Side Twists With Pin Up Back

2 Side Braids With Beautiful Back Pin Up

Items you'll need:

- ✓ Comb
- ✓ Hair pins
- ✓ Small hair bands

Here's how to create the style:

1. Comb through hair gently (from ends to roots).
2. Part the hair in the front of the head down the middle about 1 ½ to 2 inches.
3. Starting from the part but close to the hair line, start to braid the hair (FOLLOWING THE HAIR LINE). STOP when you pass about 2 inches from your ears.
4. Go to other side and repeat step #3.
5. Now take each braid and finish braiding each one separately to the end and secure with a small hair band. At this point there's still supposed to be loose hair in the middle, so go ahead and make about 2 separate braids and secure those with a small hair band.
6. Now take each braid and make swirly patterns in the back and pin each one down with some hair pins to secure.

2 Side Twist With Pin Up Back

For this hairstyle simply follow the steps above for *"2 side braids with beautiful back pin up"* instead of braids at the side create flat twist. Then add the decorative clip on flowers at the back.

Beehive updo

Beehive Updo

This hairstyle is good for relaxed, transitioning and natural hair types that are medium or long in length.

Items you'll need:

- ✓ White head band
- ✓ Comb
- ✓ Soft brush
- ✓ Hair pins
- ✓ Gel
- ✓ Butterfly clip *(for sectioning off hair)*
- ✓ Braiding hair to stuff the hair with (*the same color as your own hair*)

Here's how to create the style:

1. First, comb through the hair gently to detangle it.
2. Next, make a part from ear to ear horizontally across the head (*both front and back should be equally divided*). Section off the front section of hair for now.
3. **Creating the roll in the back**. Proceed to the back and begin to comb the back section of hair to the right side of the head. Then take some of the braiding hair from the package (*the amount depends on how big you like the French roll to be in the back*). Hold the braiding hair into a log shape, enough so that your own hair can adequately cover the log. Place the log vertically on the back of the head.
4. Begin to use the hair pins to pin the log/braiding hair on the head to secure it, and then start covering the log/braiding hair with your own hair. (*As you bring the hair over, tuck the excess hair under the log/braiding hair and use the hair pins to secure the hair in place*).
5. **Creating the beehive in the front**. Remove the butterfly clip from the front section of hair and make a side part going back on the front left side (*the part should be about 1 inch in length*). Turn the comb to the right side of the head facing the right ear and continue to part the hair to the ear. Use the butterfly clip to section off the front section of hair for now.
6. Take another portion of braiding hair *(amount of braiding hair depends on the length of your actual hair and the ability to cover the braiding hair completely*). Comb through the loose hair in the front and place braiding hair underneath the hair horizontally and shape the braiding hair into a nice oval shape. Use the hair pins to secure the braiding hair on the head. Begin to cover the braiding hair with your own hair neatly. As you cover over the braiding hair with your own hair be sure to tuck the remaining loose hair under. Use pins to secure the hair in place.
7. **Creating a seamless look**. Remove the butterfly clip from the front section of hair and apply a small amount of gel on the edges of the hair. Use the soft brush and start smoothing out the edges. Brush and swoop the front piece of hair to the right and slightly upward. Take the

remaining hair from this section at the side and bring it to the back and cover the small gap between the top and back section of hair. Tuck the remaining hair under the French roll and use the hair pins to secure the hair in place.

8. Lastly, take the white head band and place it on the front of the head.

Elegant
French Roll/
Pin Curl
Updo

Elegant French Roll With Pin Curl Updo

Items you'll need:

- ✓ Comb
- ✓ Soft brush
- ✓ Hair pins
- ✓ Butterfly clip (for sectioning off the hair)

Here's how to create the style:

1. Comb through hair gently.
2. Make a 4 by 4 inch "U" shape part in the front of the head. Take the butterfly clip and section off the hair for now.
3. Brush the sides of the head so that it is smooth.
4. Proceed to the bottom and back of the head and create a very small French roll about 2 inches up from the nape of neck. Secure with hair pins.
5. Now take a small piece of hair right above the French roll and create a raised pin curl going under on the left side then pin to secure.
6. Take another small piece of hair from above the raised pin curl you just created and create another one. This time you are going to place this one to the right side. Pin to secure.
7. Continue to do this pattern until you reach the last piece of hair. Instead of placing this pin curl to the side, place it on top.
8. Now undo the butterfly clip in the front. Gently comb through the hair. Hold the hair up about 90 degrees from the head and proceed to back comb the roots gently (this will add volume to this section).
9. Fold the hair onto itself inward starting from the ends working your way towards the roots. Use hair pins to pin down the hair to the scalp.

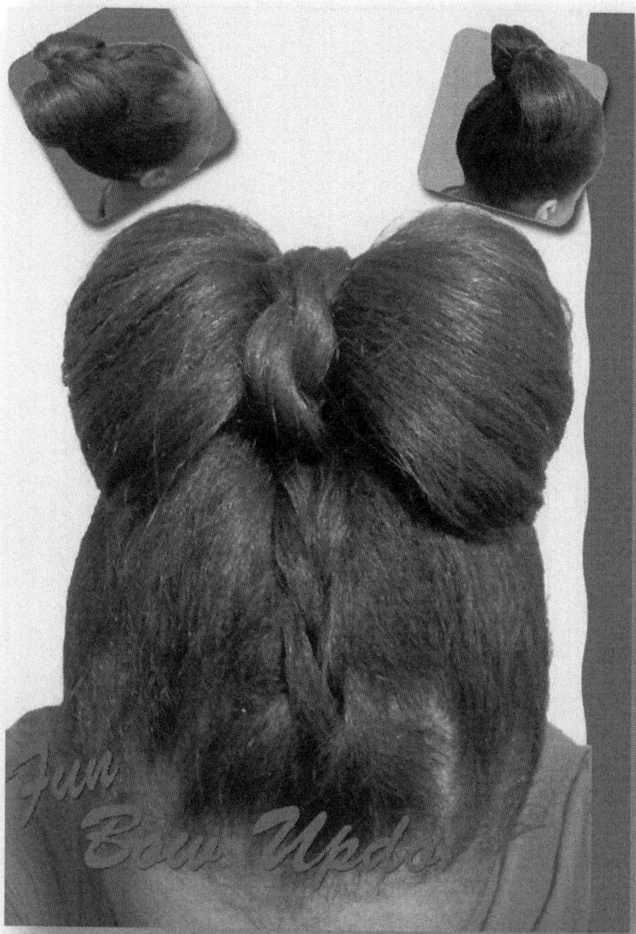
Fun
Bow Updo

Fun Bow Updo
Items you'll need:

- ✓ Comb
- ✓ Soft brush
- ✓ Hair pins
- ✓ Gel
- ✓ 2 butterfly clips
- ✓ Hair band

Here's how to create the style:

1. Make a part a "U" shape part at the front center of the head 2 inches across and 4 inches back.
2. Section off the back portion of hair with a butterfly clip.
3. Go back to the front of the head and create a cornrow going back within the "U" part shape section of hair.
4. Remove the butterfly clip from the back portion of hair and place some gel around the perimeter of the hair.
5. Use the soft brush to brush the hair up into a high ponytail right where the braid is and add the braid to it as well. Place a hair band to secure the ponytail into place.
6. Hold the ponytail and pinch off a small amount of hair from the bottom of the ponytail and section off that hair with a butterfly clip until later.
7. Now, split the remaining hair into 2 equal parts and section off the other portion of hair with the other butterfly clip for later.
8. Next, comb through the loose hair to smooth it out and proceed to create a raised pin curl going under, facing your left ear. Now lay the pin curl on its side (the side that is facing your face) and use the hair pins to pin and secure the hair into place.
9. Proceed to the next side, remove the butterfly clip from the other portion of hair and repeat the same steps as step #8.
10. Now remove the butterfly clip from the back from the smallest section of hair that you section off earlier. Proceed to create a 2 strand twist with it.
11. After you have completed the twist, bring it over to the front between the two pin curls secure with a hair pin.
12. Then bring it back again to the back and secure with a hair pin.
13. Keep doing this process until there is no more hair left.

fun
Braided Updo

Fun Braided Updo

Items you'll need:

- ✓ Comb
- ✓ Soft brush
- ✓ Braiding hair (optional) *same color as your own hair
- ✓ Hair pins
- ✓ 2 hair bands
- ✓ Edge control, gel, or moisturizing hair lotion
- ✓ Butterfly clip

Here's how to create the style:

1. First, comb through hair gently to get rid of any tangles.
2. Take the comb and proceed to make a part starting from the front going all the way to the back (at the nape of the neck). This should be 2 equal parts, section off one portion of hair with the butterfly clip and leave for later.
3. Add some edge control, gel or moisturizing hair lotion to the perimeter of the other portion of hair and use the soft brush to smooth out the hair.
4. Gather the hair up into a high pony tail; use one of the hair bands to secure the hair into place.
5. Now take the braiding hair from the pack and split it into 2 sections (set one aside). *You can add a different color to the braiding hair for highlights if you want.*
6. Start attaching the braiding hair to the pony tail at the base and braid the pony tail into the braiding hair all the way to the end.
7. Remove the other butterfly clip and add some gel, edge control or moisturizing hair lotion to the perimeter of the hair, take the soft brush to smooth out the edges.
8. Gather the hair up into a pony tail and secure it with a hair band. Take the other portion of braiding hair, place it at the base of the pony tail and proceed to braid the pony tail into the braiding hair. Braid to the very end.
9. Now you should have two long braided ponytails!
10. Take one and wrap it around the base of the other braided ponytail. Bring it back and wrap it around itself at the base too. Continue doing this until there is no more hair wrap. (Remember pin and secure the hair as you go along).
11. Take the other braided ponytail and repeat step #10.

**If you already have long hair you don't have to use the braiding hair, unless you want to add some highlight to your hair. If so, choose the color that you want as your highlights and pinch off a small amount of braiding hair. When it comes time to braid the ponytail attach the highlighted braiding hair to the center of the ponytail. Braid it in about two times and STOP. Now proceed to braid your hair as usual. Do the same to the other side.*

Side View
Pin Curl Bang
With Big Bun

Pin Curl Bang With Big Bun

Items you'll need:

- ✓ Comb
- ✓ Soft brush
- ✓ Hair pins
- ✓ Edge control, moisturizing hair lotion or gel
- ✓ Braiding hair (optional) * match your own hair color to the braiding hair*
- ✓ Butterfly clip (for sectioning off the hair)
- ✓ Hair bands

Here's how to create the style:

1. First comb through hair and detangle it gently.
2. Make a "U" shape part about 2 inches wide and 3 inches going back (this should be at the center front of the head) section off the hair until later on.
3. Now proceed to the back of the head. Add some moisturizing hair lotion, gel, or edge control to the perimeter of the hair. Use the soft brush to brush and smooth hair.
4. Gather the hair together in the back and secure it with a hair band.
5. Create a 2 strand twist or a braid with the hair and then wrap it around itself (Snug) and secure with hair pins.
6. Take about ½ the braiding hair from the pack and add a little bit of another color to the hair if you like.
7. Now take the braiding hair and place a hair pin in the center of the hair. Place the hair pin along with the braiding hair in the middle top of the bun you created earlier. Start wrapping the hair around the bun covering all of it. Remember to pin as you go.
8. Remove the butterfly clip from the front and comb through the hair and start creating a raised pin curl going under and facing your face. Now secure with hair pins.
9. If you would like more volume to the pin curl bang you can simply back comb the roots of the hair gently.

Flat Twist Updo
Closer Look At The Top

Flat Twists Updo

This beautiful flat twist updo can be done with or without braiding hair depending on the length of your hair. In the instruction below I'll be explaining how to create it with braiding hair. If you happen to have long hair already skip adding extensions in and proceed with the hairstyle.

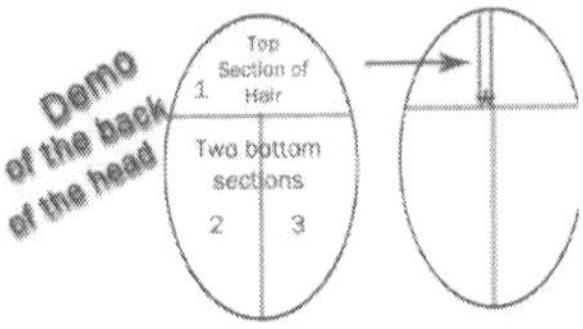

Items you'll need:

- ✓ Gel
- ✓ Comb
- ✓ Lot of small hair pins
- ✓ Braiding hair (optional) about 2 packs
- ✓ Have a few butterfly clips or hair bands for sectioning off hair

Here's how to create the style:

1. First comb through the hair gently to get rid of any knots.
2. Next, make a *part* from ear to ear horizontally going across the head (this *front section should be about 4 inches wide from front to back*). Take the butterfly clip and section off the back portion of hair.
3. **Creating the flat twists in the front of the head**. Start from the middle of the front section of hair and make 2 parallel parts going back. (*The width between the 2 parallel parts should be about 1 inch wide*). Use the butterfly clips to clip and section off the section of hair on both sides.
4. Apply some gel at the root of the hair. Take a small portion of braiding hair (*about the same size as the section of hair you just parted*). Blunt cut the end off, and place it alongside the root of the hair to be flat twist. Starting from the front of the head where the hair line is, begin to **flat twist** the hair. Do this by grabbing both the braiding hair and your own hair simultaneously at the root and twist both hair. While twisting the hair just make sure that your own hair covers the braiding hair. *See "Tips before styling" section for further instruction how to flat twist hair.*
5. When there's no more hair left to be flat twist, roll and **coil** the rest of the hair. Do this by rolling the hair tightly between your fingers in one spot until the hair begins to coil itself. When this happens, move your fingers a little down the length of the hair and REPEAT the process again. When the length of the hair is completely coiled, place it down against the head and use the hair pin to secure the hair.
6. Remove the butterfly clip from the side of the head make another parallel part next to the section of hair you just flat twist. This and all subsequent parts should be the same size. REPEAT steps # 4 & 5 for this section of

hair and the rest of the front portion of hair. **Note: when placing the coils down on the head to secure them, do so towards the center of the head and begin to build a mountain like shape out of them* see photo.*

7. **Styling the back of the head**. Remove the butterfly clip from the back section of hair and proceed to divide the hair in 2 equal parts by parting the hair vertically. Use the butterfly clip to section off the right side for now.
8. Make a horizontal part at the top of this section of hair (the *same size as the previous parts in the front*) follow step # 4 & 5 for flat twisting this section and the rest of the hair in the back. Start the flat twist from the hair line on the side. **Note: before coiling the hair, roll the hair between your fingers without allowing it to coil.* Place it among the mountain of hair in the front that is already coiled and pin at the front and place a hair pin to secure the hair next to the already coiled hair.
9. Take the remaining hair and roll it between your fingers until it coils and then use the small hair pin to secure the hair.
10. Continue to part off small sections of hair, flat twist and secure with hair pins for this section of hair and the next section as well.
11. Tip: as you flat twist, roll and coil the hair, you can use the gel on the hair to create extra hold.

Please refer back to the photo to ensure your hairstyle resembles it.

Big Curly
Ponytail With
Puffy Bang

Big Curly Ponytail with Puffy Bang

Items you'll need:

- ✓ Hair pins
- ✓ Comb
- ✓ Soft brush
- ✓ Hair band
- ✓ Curly clip on ponytail (about 10 or 12 inches long)
- ✓ Butterfly clip
- ✓ Hair pins

Here's how to create the style:

1. Comb hair gently and get rid of any tangles.
2. Make a "U" shape part at the front center of the head about 3 inches wide and 3 inches back.
3. Use the butterfly clip to section off the hair for later.
4. Go to the back and gather up the hair into a high ponytail and place the hair band around the base. Then twist or braid the ponytail and wrap it around the base of the hair. Use hair pins to secure into place.
5. Now place the curly clip-on ponytail over the bun you just created. (Make sure that the drawstring is position downward). Draw it tight into place, but not too tight.
6. Use a comb to comb through the hair to fluff it out a little. *TIP: To make the hair come around the sides and stay like you see in the picture, try to use some small hair pins to secure the hair onto the side of the head.*
7. Now go back to the front and undo the butterfly clip. Comb out the hair a little, use the comb to back comb the roots a little (this will create some volume).
8. Proceed to tucking the hair under itself away from the face. Now use hair pins to secure the hair into place.

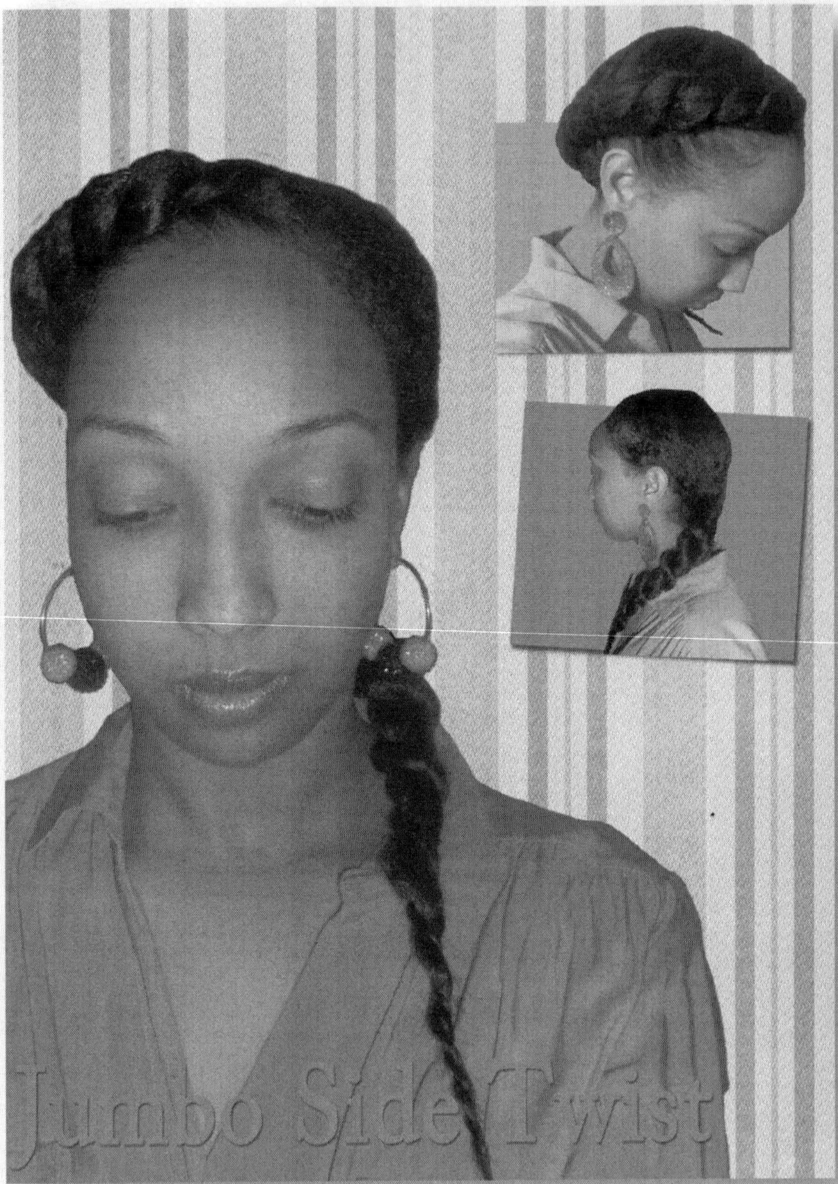
Jumbo Side Twist

Jumbo Side Twist

This hair style is so cute yet so simple. This side twist style is great for those with medium to long hair. For long hair you don't have to add any hair for length, just proceed to doing a two strand flat twist. For medium length hair you would have to use some hair to achieve the length. In this instruction I'll be explaining how to create this style using braiding hair for short to medium hair.

Items you'll need:

- ✓ Comb
- ✓ Soft brush
- ✓ Braiding hair
- ✓ Small hair band

Here's how to create the twist:

1. First comb and gently detangle the hair.
2. Take the comb and comb the entire head of hair to one side of the head also use the soft brush to brush and smooth out the hair line.
3. Now, take the braiding hair out of the pack and divide it into two sections of hair and put back the other one.
4. Take the hair that is in your hand and make the ends of the hair uneven by splitting the hair apart and then putting it back together again but except kind of jagged. This will create the uneven look. REPEAT this step about several times.
5. Now, bend the braiding hair in half.
6. Pick up two pieces of hair from the front of the hair right where the hair line is (use the right eye as a marker) and proceed to start attaching the braiding hair to the two strand of hair you picked up creating a Senegalese twist base. *See how to create Senegalese in "Tips before styling" section.*
7. Twist the hair about 2 times after attaching it, then lay down the twist against the head alongside the hair line. Begin to do a two strand flat twist with the braiding hair and your hair together working your way around the side of the head to the back and stop right at the neck.
8. When you reach to the back side of the head (at the ear) STOP and gather any loose hair from the other side of the head and combine it with braiding hair. Begin to do a two strand twist to the end and place a hair band at the end.

HIGH PUFFY BANG
WITH FRENCH ROLL

High Puffy Bang with French Roll

Items you'll need:

- ✓ Medium size rollers
- ✓ Hair pins
- ✓ Comb
- ✓ Gel
- ✓ Brush
- ✓ Hair mousse or setting lotion
- ✓ Butterfly clip
- ✓ Some time

Here's how to create the style:

1. Make a "U" shape part at the front center of the head (about 2 ½ inches wide and 3 inches back) and section off until later.
2. Proceed to the back. Comb through the hair and brush to smooth the edges then gather up all the hair together.
3. CREATING THE FRENCH ROLL: Starting from the back, at the nape of the neck (in the middle) start rolling the hair just like a huge flat twist. When you reach to the top, any excess hair that you have just simply tuck it under the hair that you already rolled. Use the hair pins to pin alongside the rolled up hair and secure into place.
4. Undo the butterfly clip at the top.
5. Take some hair mousse and add some to the dry hair and comb through hair to smooth out. Place the rollers one at a time rolling them going back. Secure them in place with hair pins. (Wait for the hair to dry. This will depends on the length and thickness of your hair).
6. After hair is completely dried, remove the rollers fluff out the curls a bit and pin to secure.
7. Place some gel on the sides of the hair and use the brush to smooth it out.

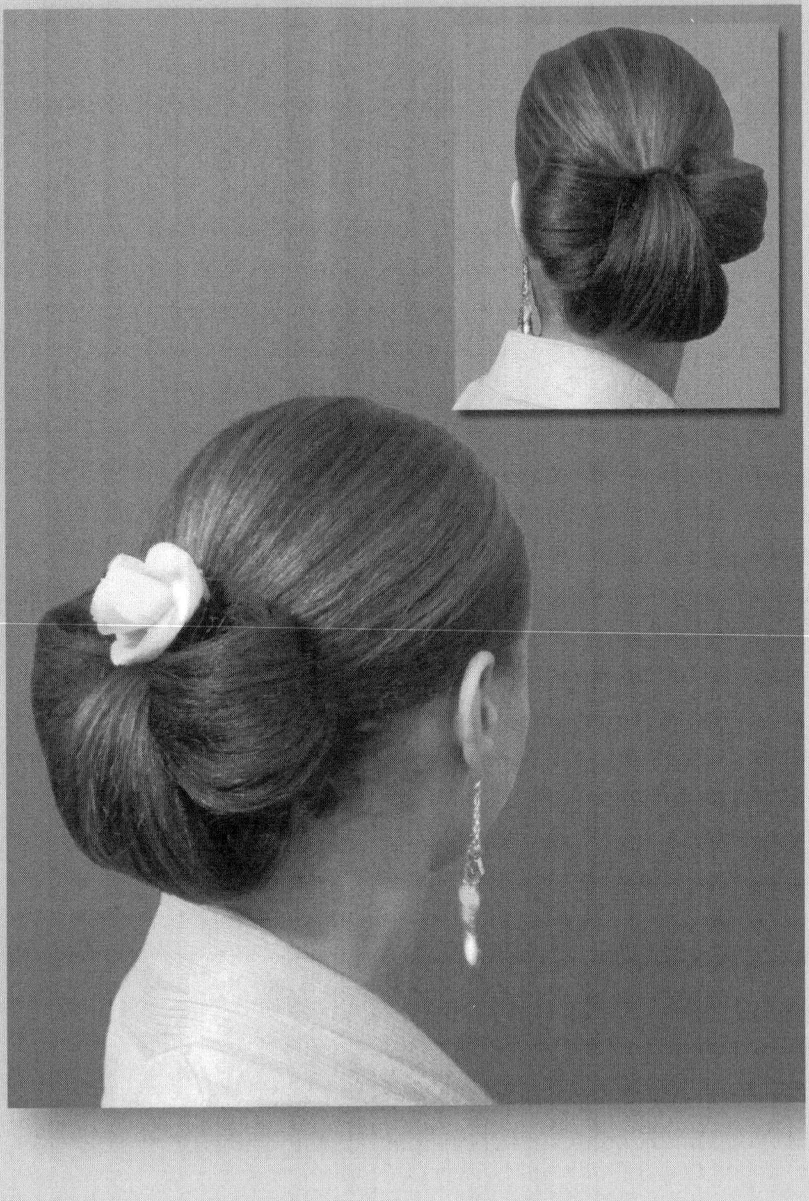

Beautiful Pin Curl Updo

Item's you'll need:

- ✓ Soft brush
- ✓ Comb
- ✓ Hair pins
- ✓ Drawstring clip-on ponytail (*Straight*. Be sure to match the color and texture to your own hair)
- ✓ Hair band
- ✓ Decorative clip

Here's how to create the style:

1. First comb through hair and detangle it.
2. Use the soft brush to brush up the edges.
3. Gather the hair into a low ponytail and place a hair band around it to secure it in place. Create a two strand twist or braid with the ponytail and wrap it around the base of the hair and secure with a hair pin.
4. Place the drawstring clip-on ponytail on top of bun you just created and adjust the combs into place, draw the drawstring tight but not too tight.
5. Take a section of hair from the side of the ponytail and proceed to create a raised pin curl and roll it under itself (*should be facing the ear*) now use the hair pins to secure the hair in place.
6. Repeat the same step to the other side. Now take the bottom section and do a pin curl going under the hair, secure with hair pins. Place the decorative clip on top as you see in the picture.

*If you already have long hair, simple gather all your hair up into a low ponytail and follow steps 5 & 6 for creating the pin curls.

Rope Braid With Braided Bun

Rope Braid With Braided Bun

Items you'll need:

- ✓ Braiding hair
- ✓ Hair band
- ✓ Hair pins
- ✓ Comb
- ✓ Soft brush

Here's how to create the style:

1. Comb through hair and get rid of any tangles.
2. Part hair in the middle at the front about 1 ½ inch going back.
3. Gather all the hair into a low ponytail and place a hair band around it to secure, proceed to braid the hair to the end, and then roll it on the base of the ponytail. Use the hair pins to secure it into place.
4. Take the braiding hair out of pack and pinch off 2 separate pieces of hair, depending on the thickness you would like the braid to be.
5. Take one portion of hair and wrap it around the head just to get an idea of how long it should be and where to cut it. Measure and cut the hair accordingly.
6. Now braid the braiding hair completely. Take one end of the hair and place it at the bottom of the bun, take a couple of hair pins and secure it into place.
7. Wrap the braid around the head going around the front of the head going around the other side of head to the back and pin the other end under the bun. Use a couple of hair pins to secure into place.
   (Put a couple of hair pins in the front to anchor down the braid)
8. Braid the other piece of braiding hair completely to the end.
9. Take the end of the hair and place in the center of the bun, Use a hair pin to secure into place. Now begin to wrap the hair around the bun (each time you wrap use a hair pin to secure the braid in to place). When you are done wrapping the braiding hair, check to make sure that none of your hair is showing.

Relaxed
Curled Up Tail Braid

Relaxed Curled Up Tail Braid

Items you'll need:

- ✓ Comb
- ✓ Soft brush
- ✓ Butterfly clip, hair pins
- ✓ Decorative small clips (optional)

Here's how to create the style:

1. Comb through the hair complete and gently.
2. Go to the front of the head where the middle is, place the comb right there and proceed to make a straight part all the way down, continue to the back of the head until you reach the nape of the neck.
3. Now you should have two equal parts of hair. Section off one portion with a butterfly clip.
4. CREATING THE BRAID: Starting from the front of this portion of hair, pick up three strands of hair from the center and begin to braid the hair back (don't braid too tight, need it to be a little loose).
5. When working your way back while braiding, stay in the middle of the part. When you reach about the middle, slant the braid over towards the middle of the head and continue to braid the hair to the nape of the neck.
6. When you reach the nape of the neck, hold the braid for a second with one hand. Use your other hand to pull/tug on the loops of the braid on both sides for the whole length of the braid to create a wider fluffier braid.
7. Now go back down to the nape of the neck and continue to braid the hair down to the end loosely. Secure the end with a small hair band that is the same color of your hair.
8. Create a spiral shape with the remaining braid at the bottom side of the head. Secure in place with some small hair pins. *(See picture above).*
9. Proceed to the other side of the head and undo the butterfly clip. Follow steps 4-8.
10. After both sides are completed you can leave the hair as is or you can add two small decorative clips in the middle of the spirals on both sides of the head (*see picture*).

If you have short to medium length hair, use some braiding hair to give you the length.

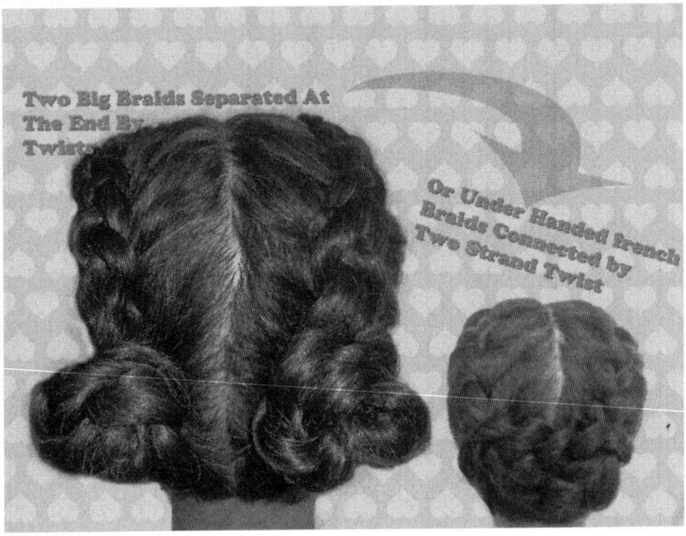
Two Big Braids Separated At
The End By
Twists
Or Under Handed french
Braids Connected by
Two Strand Twist

Two Big Braids Separated At The Ends By Twists

Items you'll need:

- ✓ Comb
- ✓ Two hair bands
- ✓ A few hair pins
- ✓ Butterfly clip

Here's how to create the style:

1. Comb through the hair to get rid of any tangles.
2. Go to the front of the head where the hair line is, locate the middle. Make a straight part from this point going all the back the nape of the neck. You should have two equal parts at this point. Use the butterfly clip to section off one section of the hair.
3. Comb the loose section of hair out, start braiding the hair from the front of the hair within the middle of the part all the way down to the nape of the neck.
4. Place a hair band around the hair to secure into place.
5. Make two separate two strand twists with the remaining hair and wrap them around the base going opposite directions. Secure the twist with hair pins.
6. Undo the butterfly clip on the other side and REPEAT steps 3-5

Under Handed French Braids Connected By Two Strand Twists.

Items you'll need:

- ✓ Comb
- ✓ Hair bands
- ✓ Hair pins
- ✓ Butterfly clip

Here's how to create the style:

1. Comb through hair gently.
2. Begin to part the hair from the front where the hair line is in the middle.
3. Continue parting the hair in a straight line until you reach the bottom where the nape of the neck is.
4. Now you should have two equal parts of hair.
5. Take one section of hair and section it off with the butterfly clip.

6. Now begin to create a under hand braid with the hair (make sure to stay in the middle within the apart). See picture.
7. Continue braiding the hair until you reach at the bottom. Hold the braid for a moment, pick up a hair band and place it around the hair close to the head to secure the hair in place.
8. Undo the butterfly clip on the other side of the head and REPEAT steps 6 & 7.
9. Create two twists on both sides with the loose hair separately, and secure the ends with small hair bands.
10. Take the completed twist from one side and bring it over to the other side of the head wrapping it over the base of the other cornrow where you placed the hair band. Secure the end with small hair pins at the end.
11. Do the same thing to other side of the head.

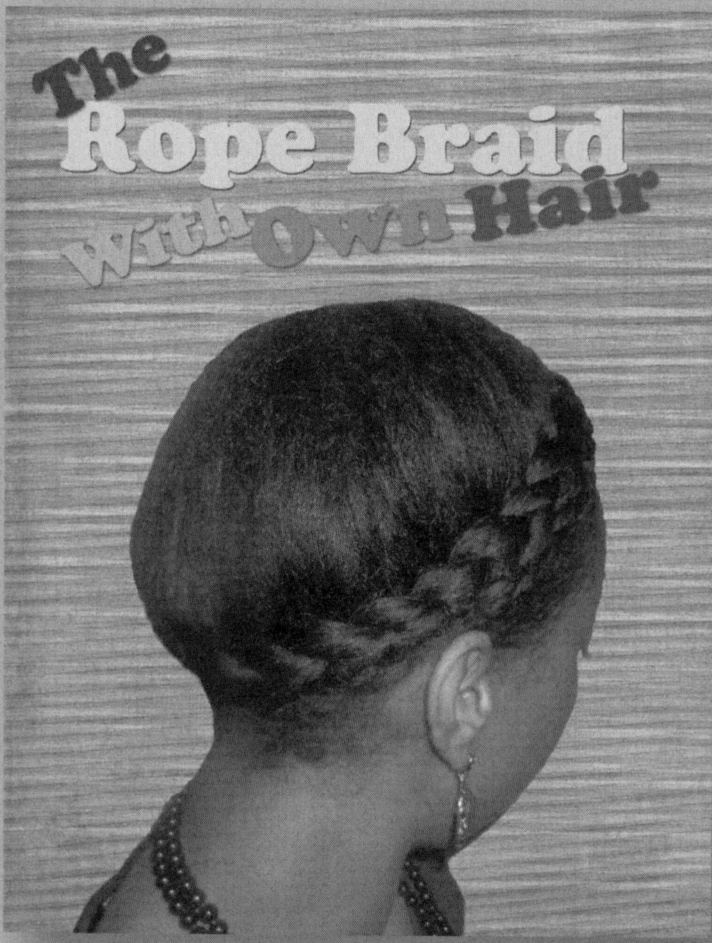
The
Rope Braid
With Own Hair

The Rope Braid With Own Hair

Items you'll need:

- ✓ Comb
- ✓ Soft brush
- ✓ Hair pin

Here's how to create the style:

1. Comb through hair from ends to root gently.
2. Place your pointer finger at the top middle of your head.
3. Place the comb next the finger and begin to comb the hair away from the finger. Keep on doing this and work your way around the finger until you have completed the entire head.
4. Now your whole head should be fanned out.
5. Start from any ear- pick three strands of hair and proceed to start braiding the hair working your way towards the front of the head back to the other ear. Continue the braid until you meet the front of the braid on the other side of the head.
6. Finish braiding off the tail of the braid to the end. Tuck the remaining hair alongside the braid (on the top). Use the hair pins to secure the hair into place. Check the top of the head to see if there's any loose hair sticking up and use the soft brush to smooth it out.

Bantu
Knots

Bantu Knots

Items you'll need:

- ✓ Small black hair bands
- ✓ Comb
- ✓ Moisturizer
- ✓ A couple of butterfly clips

Here's how to create the style:

1. First detangle hair completely from ends to roots. Do so in sections.
2. Next, part the hair in the front of the head from ear to ear across the head. Section off the back portion of hair with a butterfly clip for later. Now go to the front of the head and make a part starting from the front of the head where the hair line is in the middle. Now you should have two equal parts of hair at the top part of the head. Section off one section with a butterfly clip.
3. Now you should have a section of hair in the back and two sections in the front.
4. Section off a piece of hair at the front side of the head. This should shape like a half moon shape. Section off the rest of the hair with a butterfly clip to so that it doesn't interfere with hair you are going to use to create the Bantu knot with.
5. CREATING THE BANTU KNOT: First, grab the hair at the roots close to the head and begin to twist the hair by rolling the hair between your fingers (use the fingers on the other hand to assist you in this process). When you reach about 2 inches from the head *continue to roll the hair at this point without adding more length to the twist, the twist should start feeling kind of stiff at this point.*
6. Now push the twist towards the head, it should start to coil around itself. (make sure that the coil is sitting against the head)
7. Twist the hair some more with your fingers and then wrap it around the base of the Bantu knot.
8. Continue to do this until there is no more hair. Make sure that the end of the twist is also wrapped around the Bantu knot. Place a small hair band to secure the hair.
9. Make another half-moon shape next to the first one and create another Bantu knot.
10. Keep on creating half-moon shapes next to and on top of each other throughout the whole head for your Bantu knots.

Ponytail Weave

Ponytail Hair Weave

Items you'll need:

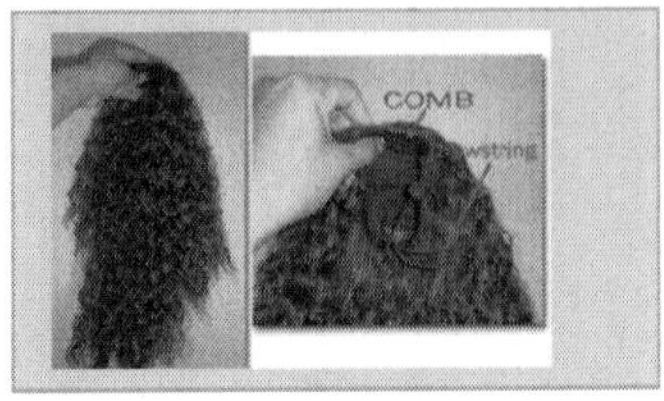

- ✓ Comb
- ✓ Soft brush
- ✓ Gel or edge control
- ✓ Hair pins
- ✓ Drawstring clip on ponytail (curly or straight)

Here's how to create the style:

1. First comb through hair gently from ends to root.
2. Add some gel or edge control around the perimeter of hair and then use the soft brush to brush and smooth out the hair line, the back and the rest of the hair.
3. Gather all the hair up into a ponytail.
4. Make a braid or twist with ponytail
5. Then wrap the braid or twist around itself at the base and secure with hair pins. You just make a bun.
6. Take the drawstring ponytail and place it over the bun you just create (the drawstring should be hanging down in the back.) Adjust the combs that are in the ponytail weave into your hair and then draw the drawstring tight in place (not too tight).
7. Use the soft brush again to smooth out the edges.

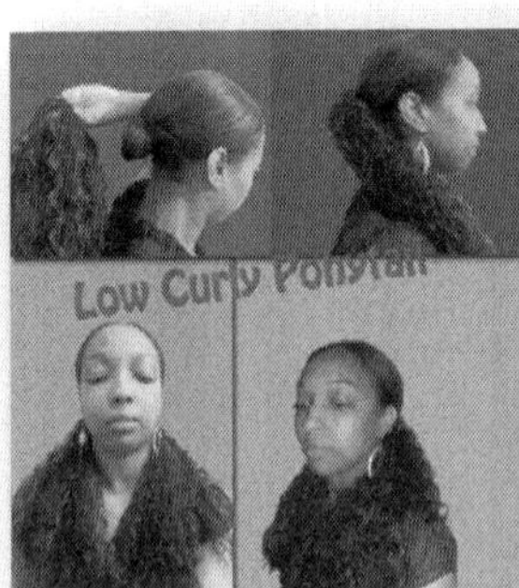

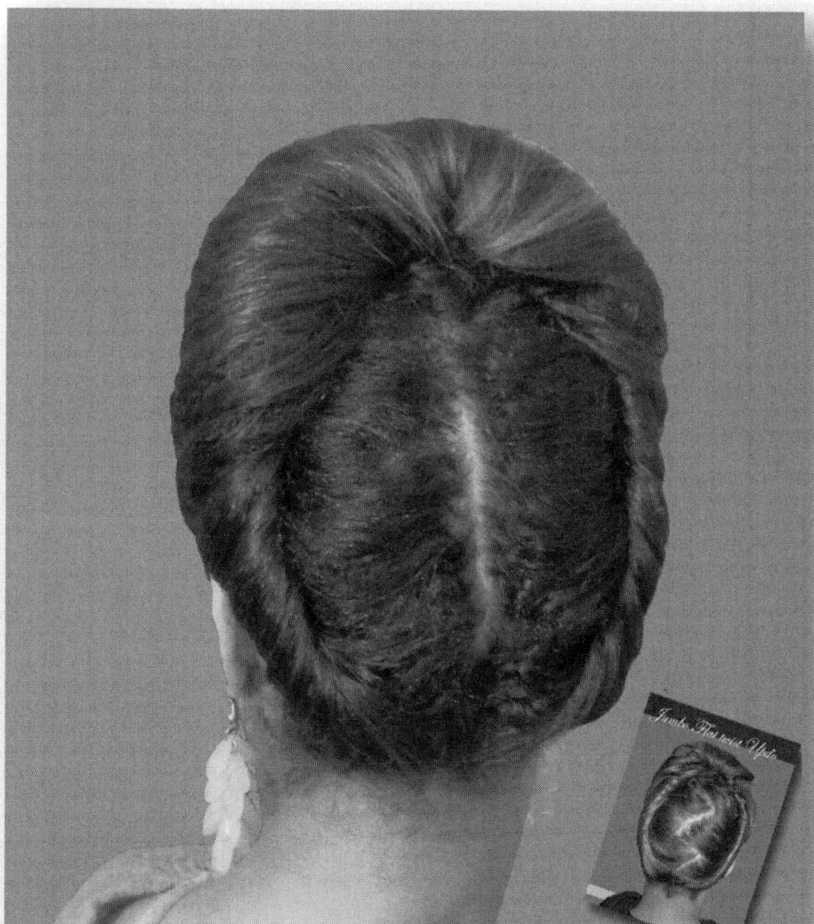

Jumbo Flat Twist Updo

Items you'll need:

- ✓ Comb
- ✓ Hair pins
- ✓ Two butterfly clips (for sectioning off hair)

Here's how to create the style:

1. Gently comb through hair to detangle from end to root in sections.
2. Make a straight part going across the head in the front, from ear to ear. And section off this portion of hair with the butterfly clip.
3. Divide the back part the hair equally into two equal parts (horizontally) do so in a zigzag motion or straight. Just like you see in the picture.
4. Section off one portion of hair with the other butterfly clip.
5. Begin from the back of the head at the nape of neck and start doing a flat twist facing the part. Twist going upward (be sure to stay in the center within the part).
6. When you reach the part at the top STOP and secure the twist with the appropriate size hair pins and also alongside the flat twist as well.
7. Undo the butterfly clip on the opposite side of the flat twist you just made and REPEAT steps # 5 & 6.
8. Undo the butterfly clip at the top front of the hair. Gently comb through the hair. Now hold the hair about 90 degrees from the head and proceed to gently back comb the roots of the hair (this will add a little volume).
9. Now collect the loose hair from the twists and add them to the front portion of hair.
10. Start tucking the hair under its self in the back. Pin the hair to secure it in place.
11. Take a look at it and make any adjustments to it if necessary.

Fake Bob

Fake Bob

Items you'll need:

- ✓ Hair pins
- ✓ A few flexi rods (the size will depends on the length of your hair)
- ✓ Comb
- ✓ Hair mousse

Here's how to create the twist:

1. Comb out hair gently ends to root.
2. Choose a side at the front of the head and make a side part about 2 inches back. Now comb the hair down to the sides and back.
3. Start from one side of the head and section off a small portion of hair, add some mousse to the bottom part of the hair.
4. Take the flexi rod and place it at the end of the hair and begin to roll it up inward, stop at the ear or hair line. Secure the ends of the flexi rod by bending both sides in and curving them.
5. Continue to go all the way around the head by following steps 3 & 4. Allow hair to completely dry. This will depend upon the thickness and length of your individual head of hair.
6. REMOVING THE FLEXI RODS: after the hair is completely dry. Undo the flexi rods by undoing the curve and undoing the bend.
7. Use a big tooth comb to gently and slowly comb through the hair (never force the comb through if you encounter any tangle along the way).
8. Now section by section roll the hair under and up and use hair pins to secure the hair into place.
9. After you have completed all the hair make sure to look in the mirror and adjust any gaps that might be on the sides or back of the hair.

ack View
Jumbo Braids

Jumbo braids

Items you'll need:

- ✓ 2 packs Braiding hair
- ✓ Comb
- ✓ Hair pins
- ✓ Butterfly clip
- ✓ Hair bands

Here's how to create the style:

1. First comb through hair gently.
2. Divide the hair into two equal parts by parting the hair from ear to ear (horizontally) in the middle of the head.
3. Section off one section with a butterfly clip.
4. Gather the other section of hair and place a hair band to secure the ponytail. Braid or make a two strand twist with the hair all the way to the end and then wrap the hair around the base of the ponytail and secure with hair pins.
5. Undo the butterfly clip from the other portion of hair and REPEAT step # 4 for this portion of hair.
6. PREPARING THE BRAIDING HAIR: Take out the braiding hair from one of the pack and proceed to braid the hair by following these steps.

If you don't have someone to hold the hair for you while you are braiding it, simply take a large hair pin and place it at the middle of the braiding hair to secure it. Next, find a draw open it a little bit and place the hair pin along with the braiding hair at the opening of the draw then close it so that the hair pin does not fall out.

Proceed to braid the hair. Start braiding the hair about 3 inches from the hair pin. (This will create the cup like shape you see in the picture). After you have form the cup like shape start braiding the hair more tightly but not too tight. Braid until you reach the end of the hair, and then secure the end with a small hair band.

Take the other pack of braiding hair from its package and proceed to prepare the hair for braiding the same way you just it for the previous hair.

7. Now take one of the braided hair and place the cup like shape part on your hair on top of the top bun (make sure that the braid is facing the right ear) and place hair pins around it to secure it in place. See picture.
8. Next take the other braided hair and place the cup like section of the hair on top of the bottom bun. This time facing the ground and then add hair pin to secure the hair in place.
9. STYLING THE BRAIDS: To create the style you see in the cover picture, the one on the bottom left hand corner. Simply take the top braid and wrap it around the head by placing it alongside the side of the head then go under the bottom braid and around the other side of the head. Then secure along the braid with hair pins.

10. Take the bottom braid and wrap this braid going the same direction you just wrap the top braid. This braid will end up somewhere around the front of the head. Secure with hair pins.

I had fun styling the braids when I had them in, as you can see in the picture. Just play around with it a little to come up with something unique and fun.

Fancy Side Swoop Braid

Fancy side swoop braid

For this hairstyle you might need the aid of a friend to help you create it. Since you'll be attaching and braiding the hair from the nape of the neck and braiding upwards to the front, this might be a little challenging if you are not accustom to braiding your own hair.

Items you'll need:

- ✓ 2 packs braiding hair (same texture as your own hair)
- ✓ Hair pins
- ✓ Soft brush
- ✓ Comb

Here's how to create the style:

1. Detangle the hair gently combing from ends to root.
2. Starting from the back of the head at the nape of the neck, attach the braiding hair to your hair and start doing an inverted French braid going all the way up to the front of the head. * *when braiding, stay in the in a straight line until you reach the front of the head then shift to one side a little bit**
3. Braid the hair to the end and secure with a small hair band.
4. Look at both sides of the head in the front to see which side has more space. Proceed to take the rest of the braided hair and place it on the side of the head that has more space. Lay the hair in a spiral pattern and place hair pins to anchor and secure the spiral into place.

Tip

If you find that the braided hair in the front has too little hair for your liking, pinch off some more hair from another pack of hair add and braid it in the then place it in a spiral pattern on the same side of the head filling in any gaps, and pin to secure it in place.

Here's another way to achieve the same look. If you have **really long hair** already and would like to do this style, proceed to braid your hair starting from the back of the head at the nape. Work your way up to the front (when you reach the front about 4 inches from the hair line slant the hair a little over to one side of the head and continue to braid the hair to the end.
Look at both sides and determine which side has more space. Take the remaining hair and make a spiral pattern with it at the side.

~If you would like to fill in the spiral to make it bigger do this~

Choose some braiding hair that is the same color and texture of your hair. Proceed to braid and secure the end with a small hair band. Be sure to braid the hair the same size as your real hair. Fill in the spiral on your head with the braiding hair, filling in any gaps. Secure with hair pins.

~Do you have short to medium hair? Here's a really quick way to create the hairstyle~

Starting from the back of the head at the nape of the neck, start creating a French roll going all the way up to the front of the head (as you work your way up to the front, place hair pins to secure the French roll in place).
Take the braiding hair from its package and pre braid the hair to the end. Place a small hair band at the end to secure it.
Place the bigger end of the braid at the bottom of the French twist/roll at the nape to cover and conceal it then secure it down with some hair pins.
Keep on placing the braided hair over the French roll and place hair pins to secure it in place as you work your way up to the front of the head. (As you approach the front slant the braided hair over to one side just a little then secure it and proceed to create a spiral pattern on the side front of the hair with more space).
Secure the spiral pattern into place with some hair pins.

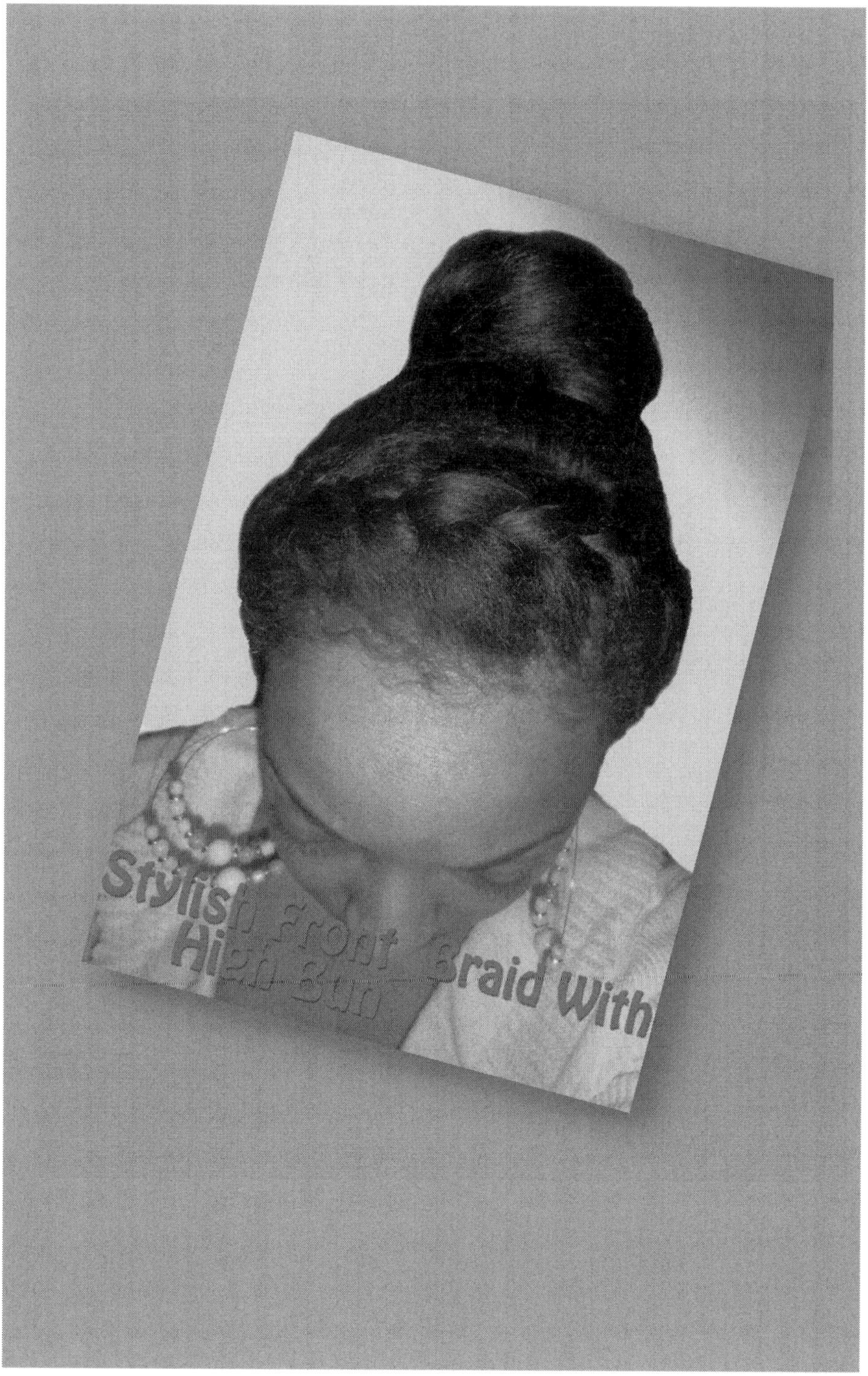
Stylish Front Braid With
High Bun

Stylish Front Braid With High Bun

Items you'll need:

- ✓ Comb
- ✓ Hair band
- ✓ Hair pins
- ✓ Butterfly clip
- ✓ Soft brush

Here's how to create the style:

1. First, gently comb through your hair to get rid of any tangles.
2. Starting from one side of the head make a part going across the head to the other side from ear to ear. This part should be parallel to the front hair line and the width should be about two inches.
3. Section off the back portion of hair and place a butterfly clip until later.
4. Now starting from the side of the head start doing an inverted cornrow just like you see in the picture until you get to the other side of the head. Keep on braiding the hair until you get to the very end. Now tuck the braid under itself to hide it, and place some hair pins to secure it.
5. *If you have longer hair and you are unable to tuck the braid under itself, wait until you get to the back of the head to make the high bun to include the left over hair with that portion of hair.*
6. Ok, now go to the back of the head and undo the butterfly clip. Gather all the hair up into one close to where the braid in the front is and brush to smooth out perimeter of the hair.
7. Take the loose hair from the braid in the front and include it with the ponytail in the back.
8. Place a hair band around the base of the ponytail to secure it in place.
9. Proceed to make a bun with the loose hair and use hair pins to secure it in place.

Tip

If you find that the hair from the ponytail is not sufficient or enough proceed to braid or do a two strand twist with the ponytail and wrap it around the base of the ponytail. Secure the twist or braid with hair pins.

Choose a drawstring ponytail that is the same color and texture as your own hair, length depends on your preference.
Place the drawstring ponytail over the bun you created earlier and adjust the combs into place. Draw the drawstring to tighten the ponytail.
Wrap the string around the base of the ponytail (you can place a hair pin so that it stays in place).
Now wrap the ponytail around its base, start to secure it in place with some hair pins.

The
Triple
Tuck

The Triple Tuck

Items you'll need:

- ✓ Comb
- ✓ Soft brush
- ✓ Hair pins
- ✓ Butterfly clip

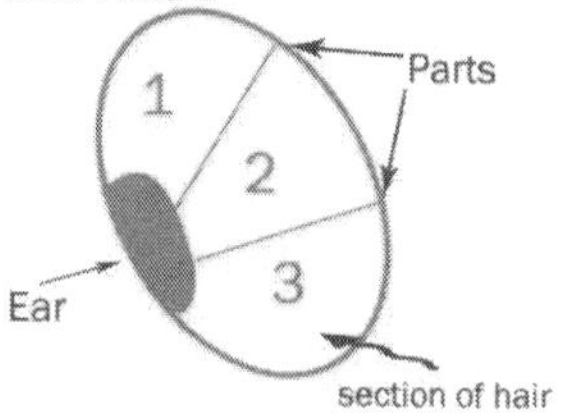

Here's how to create the style:

1. Comb through and detangle hair gently.
2. Make a part at the front of the head starting from the side and going across to the other side. *(The width of this section of hair should be about 2 inches).*
3. Take the butterfly clip and section off the back portion of hair for later.
4. Now take the comb and comb through the front section of hair gently. Hold the hair straight up from the head and start to tuck the ends of the hair under facing the back of your head. Roll and tuck the hair until you reach the head, then use the hair pins to secure the hair in place.
5. Undo the butterfly clip from the back portion of hair. Place the comb at the side of the head about an inch from the first part. Part the hair going across the head horizontally until you reach the other side of the head.
6. Section off the bottom portion of hair with the butterfly clip. Follow step # 4 for this portion of loose hair.
7. Undo the butterfly clip from the bottom and last portion of hair, and follow step #4 again.
8. Use the brush to brush up the edges of your hair.

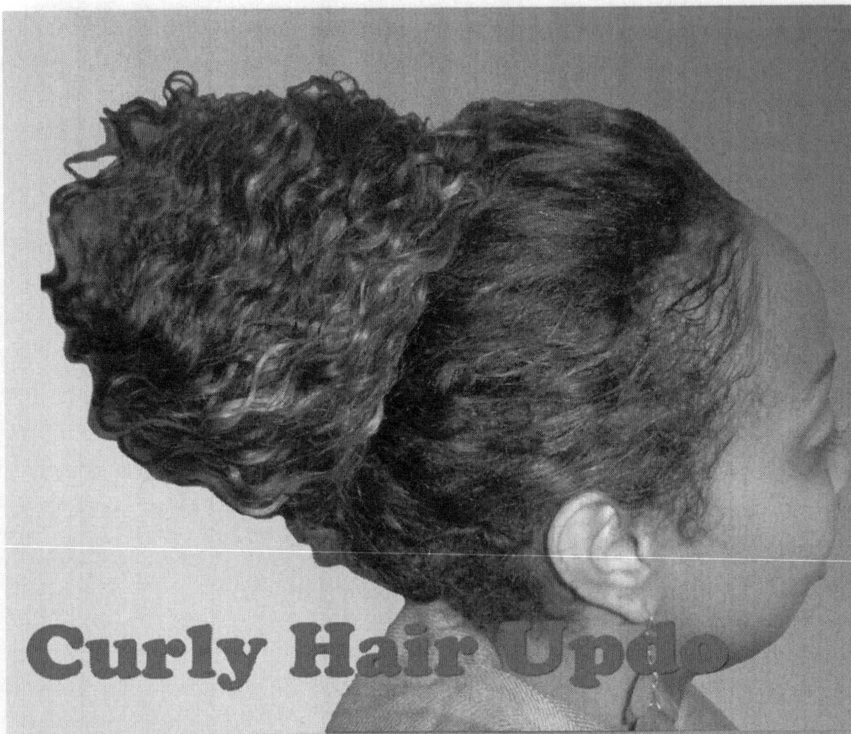
Curly Hair

Curly Hair Updo

This hairstyle was achieved by doing a braid out on the hair. That being said you will need to have some time available to allow the braids to set and form the curls.
Items you'll need:

- ✓ Comb
- ✓ Hair pins
- ✓ Curly drawstring clip on ponytail
- ✓ Hair band
- ✓ Hair mousse
- ✓ Coconut oil
- ✓ Silk / satin scarf

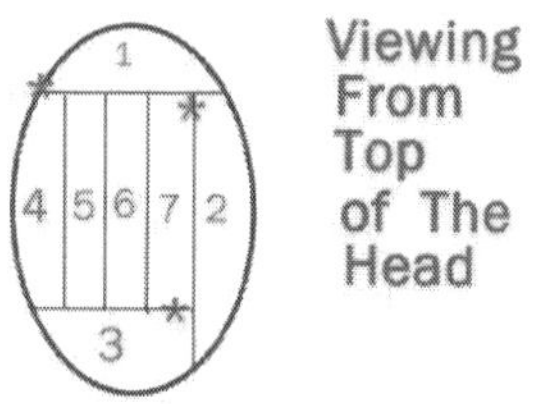

Here's how to create the style:

Preparing the braids

1. Take the comb and make a part going horizontally across the front of the head. *The thickness of the section you just parted should be about 1 ½ inches wide.* Now proceed to braid the hair to the end.
2. Below the top braid you just made, put the comb below that braid and about 2 inches from the side hair line make a part hair going down. Proceed to braid that portion of hair.
3. Make another braid going horizontally across the bottom portion of the head. *This section should be the same width as the other braids*. Proceed to braid the hair to the end.
4. Next go to the other side of the head and make a part below the top braid about 2 inches from the side hair line. Proceed to braid the hair to the end.
5. At this point, continue parting the hair vertically and braiding the hair to the end.
6. When the entire hair is braided. Take the hair mousse and squirt some in your hand and apply it all over the head, even to the ends.
7. Take the ends of the braids and tuck them away by securing them on the head with hair pins. Place a silk/satin scarf over the head and tie it. Let the hair dry and set. This process may vary from individual to individual depending on the length, and thickness of their hair. *(Hair can also be braided while wet as well. If you have natural hair just add some type of hair butter to the hair before braiding it).*
8. AFTER THE HAIR IS DRIED AND SET: Take off the scarf and take out the hair pins. Proceed to undo all the braids. *(TIP: put some coconut oil in the palm of your hands but not too much and rub together, when*

undoing the braids the coconut oil in the palm of your hand will add some shine to the hair and reduce frizz.)

9. After you undo the braids, take your fingers and gently rake through the hair a couple of times.
10. Now proceed to gather all the hair up into one and place a hair band to the base of the hair to secure it.
11. Take the ponytail and braid it then wrap it around the base of the hair. Secure with a hair pin.
12. Take the drawstring curly ponytail place it over the bun you just created. Draw the drawstring into place.
13. Take the hair from the ponytail and wrap it around itself, as you do so make sure to place hair pins to secure the hair in place.

Flat Twist Tuck

This hairstyle works best with medium to longer hair. However, if you have shorter hair and would like to do this style on your hair, you can try adding hair to the flat twists and also clip-in hair pieces in the back to give it length and volume.

Items you'll need:

- ✓ Comb
- ✓ Small black hair bands
- ✓ Butterfly clip
- ✓ Gel

Here's how to create the style:

1. Comb through hair gently to get rid of any tangles.
2. About 2 to 3 inches from the nape of the neck part the hair horizontally across the head. Section off the bottom portion of hair with the butterfly clip.
3. Go to the top of the hair and place the comb right at the front hair line and about ½ inch to 1 inch from the side of the head, make a part going straight to the back. Section off the rest of the hair with a butterfly clip for later. Place a small amount of gel to the smaller section of hair you just parted and proceed to do a flat twist.
4. When there's no more hair to flat twist, take a small hair band and secure the base of the flat twist.
5. Undo the butterfly clip from the bigger section of hair and make another part for another flat twist next to the one you just made. Add some gel to the hair. Do another flat twist to this section of hair. REPEAT step #5. Keep on doing this process until there's no more hair to flat twist for this section of hair.
6. After you have completed the entire flat twists for this top section, proceed to the bottom section of hair and undo the butterfly clip then merge the remaining hair from the top section with the bottom section of hair then comb through so that it is nice and neat then tuck the hair underneath itself.
7. Secure the hair with hair pins.

Simple Bun
Side
Double
High

Simple Bun

The BUN is one of the simplest protective hairstyles. It's quick and easy to do and look so put together. Great if you're on the go. You can wear it the traditional way (to the back) to the side or way up high.

Items you'll need:

Bun Maker

- ✓ Comb
- ✓ Soft brush
- ✓ Hair band
- ✓ Hair pins
- ✓ Bun maker
- ✓ Decorative pin

Here's how to create the style:

1. Comb through the hair gently.
2. Gather all the hair into a ponytail, take the soft brush to brush around the perimeter of hair to smooth it out.
3. Place the hair band around the base of the ponytail to secure it in place.
4. Take the bun maker and place the ponytail through the hole of the bun maker and slid it down to the base of the ponytail.
5. Fan out the ponytail over the bun maker, start wrapping the ponytail over the bun maker covering it. Work your way around it until it's completely covered and the ends of the hair are tucked under the bun maker (as you do so make sure to place hair pins around the bun make to secure the hair in place).
6. If you like, you can place a decorative pin in the center of the bun.

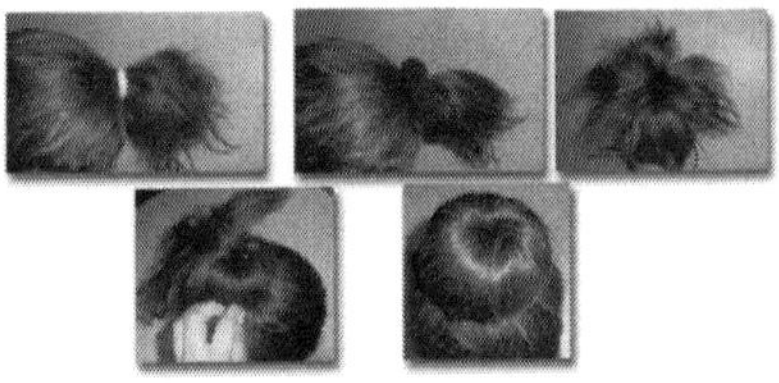

Simple Wrap
Special
Occasion
Updo

Simple Wrap Special Occasion Updo

Items you'll need:

- ✓ Comb
- ✓ Hair pins
- ✓ Butterfly clips
- ✓ Soft brush

Here's how to create the style:

1. Gently comb through hair to get rid of any tangles.
2. Go to the front of the head where the hair line is, place the comb at the middle. Make a part going back about 1 inch to an inch and a half.
3. Turn the comb to the right of the head and continue to part the hair. Part the hair alongside the head *(IMPORTANT: when making this part it should be parallel to the hair line in front of the head and at the side of the head*) stop parting when you reach about 2 inches from the nape of the neck. Take a butterfly clip and section off this portion of hair for later.
4. REPEAT step #3 for the other side (instead of going right go left) section off that portion of hair for later with a butterfly clip. At his point you should have 2 sections of hair sectioned off in the front.
5. Proceed to the back of the head. Part the hair into 2 equal parts horizontally (going across the head).
6. Section off both of them separately with butterfly clips.
7. At this point you should have the whole head sectioned off into 4 parts, 2 in the front and 2 in the back. *See picture above.*
8. Ok. Proceed to the back of the head. Undo the butterfly clip from the portion of hair at the bottom.
9. Gently comb through it, and then hold the hair 90 degrees of the head, go ahead and gently back comb the roots of the hair (this will create some volume) take the soft brush and smooth the front part of the hair.
10. Start to roll the hair under itself loosely until you reach the head. Use the hair pins to secure the hair in place. (*make sure that the sides are pin down as well*)
11. Undo the butterfly clip from the portion of hair that's directly on top of the bottom one. REPEAT steps # 8 & 9 for this section of hair.
12. **On to the 2 portions of hair in the front.** Undo the butterfly clip from the portion of hair from the front right side.
13. Take the soft brush and brush to smooth out the hair on the side so that it is laying on the side of the head neatly. Lay the hair so that it is covering the part. Take a small hair pin that is the color of your hair and place it neatly on the side of the hair right where the ear is to secure it in place.

14. Take the left over hair and swoop or bring it across the middle section of the head where the part and gap is. Extended the hair to the other side of the head. When you reach to the other side of the head bend any excess hair under itself (if you don't have any excess hair to bend under that's fine). Now pin the hair where you see the **horizontal part** on the side.
15. Go to the other side and take out the butterfly clip from the front portion of hair (last portion of hair) REPEAT steps #13 & 14.

* Use clip-in hair pieces where you see fit if you have shorter hair to achieve this look.

Messy Inverted Braid Ponytail

Items you'll need:

- ✓ Comb
- ✓ Soft brush
- ✓ Edge control
- ✓ Large hair pins
- ✓ Drawstring clip on ponytail (the color and texture of your hair)
- ✓ Hair band

Here's how to create the style:

1. Comb through and detangle hair gently.
2. Gather all the hair together in one and place a hair band around the base of the hair to secure it.
3. Make a braid or a two strand twist with the ponytail and then wrap it around the base. Secure it with hair pins.
4. Now place the drawstring clip on ponytail over the bun. Adjust the combs in place and then draw on the drawstring to tighten (not too tight).
5. BRAIDING THE PONYTAIL: when braiding the ponytail you're not going to do a normal braid. Instead you will be creating a cornrow on the ponytail.
6. Ok. First, start from the top of the ponytail grab three pieces of hair and proceed to do an inverted cornrow going all the way down to the very end of the hair.
7. Place a small hair band at the end to secure it.
8. Now starting from the top of the ponytail, just tug on the sides of the hair a little just to fluff out the cornrow.
9. Next take the end of the braid and do a pin curl with the end a couple of times then proceed to secure it on the head with hair pins.
10. Take some small hair pins and secure the hair onto the head alongside the braid on both sides.

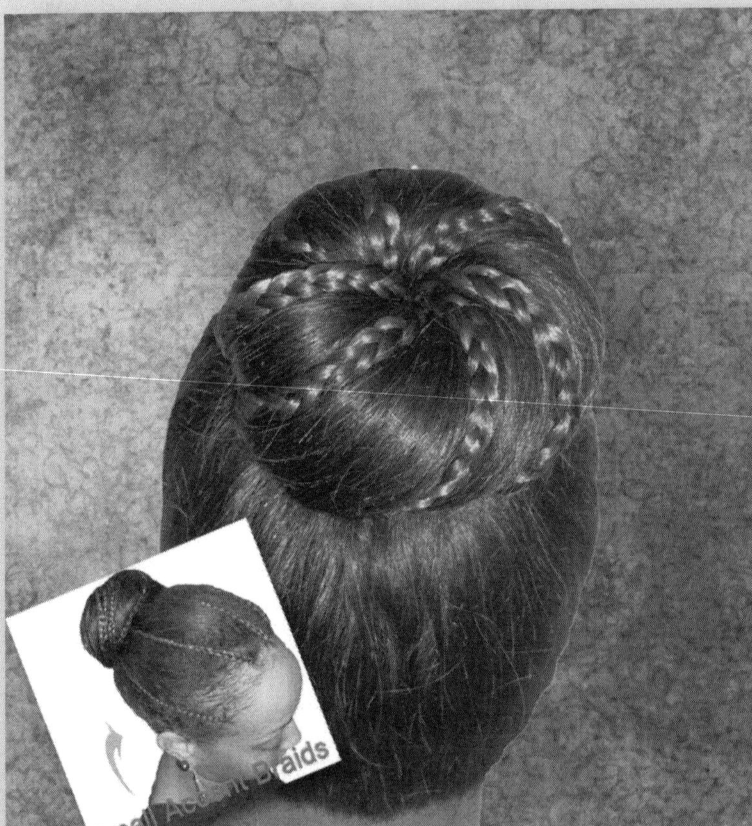
Small Accent Braids

Cinnamon Swirl Textured Bun

Items you'll need:

- ✓ Comb
- ✓ Soft brush
- ✓ Bun maker
- ✓ Hair pins
- ✓ Braiding hair butterfly clip (for holding the braiding hair while braiding)

Here's how to create the style:

With Braid-in Braids

1. Comb hair gently to get rid of any tangles.
2. Spread out the hair so that you can access the center of the head.
3. Take small pieces of braiding hair about the length of your hair. About 7 pieces.
4. Begin to attach the braiding hair one by one to the hair that is in the center, and braid all the way to the end.
5. After you have completed attaching and braiding all the hair. Proceed to gather all of your hair into one including the braids.
6. Place a hair band around the base of the ponytail to secure the hair into place.
7. Place the ponytail through the hole of the bun maker and slide it all the way to the base of the ponytail.
8. Now fan the hair out over the bun maker and proceed to fold the hair over it so that it can be hidden by the hair. Work your way around the bun maker until there is no more hair left.
9. Take the pieces of braids that are in the middle and arrange them neatly around the bun maker. Tuck each one under the bun maker and secure with hair pins.
10. Check under bun maker just to make sure nothing is sticking out from underneath it.

With detachable Braids

If you don't want to or just can't braid the extension hair on top of your head. Try pre braiding the hair and then place small hair pins through the loop of the braids at the end, and then placing the braids in the center of the head along with the hair pins. Then follow steps 5-10 above.

With Small Accent Braids

Want to try the small accent braids you see the picture? Ok- well simply pinch off small pieces of braiding hair (be sure to measure the hair and cut to the desired length) start attaching the extension hair along the hair line in the front of the head at equal distance. (About 5 braids will do) then gather all braids along with the loose hair in to a ponytail and proceed to create a bun.

OR

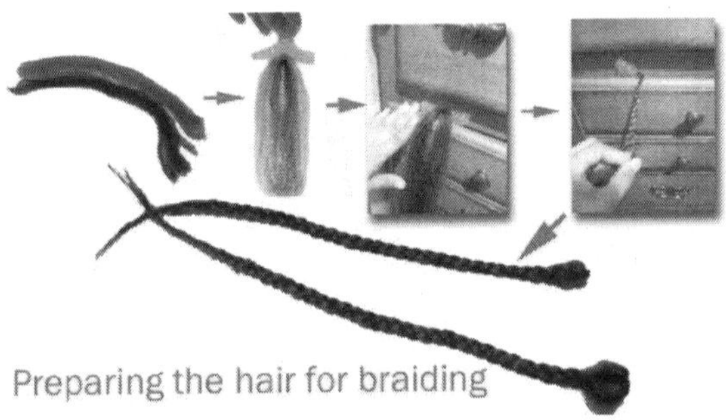

Preparing the hair for braiding

Simple French Roll

Simple French Roll

Items you'll need:

- ✓ Comb
- ✓ Soft brush
- ✓ Hair pins
- ✓ Decorative clip
- ✓ Braiding hair *(for stuffing the French roll)* same color as your own)
- ✓ Gel *(optional)*

Here's how to create the style:

1. Comb through hair gently to get rid of any tangles.
2. Comb the hair over to one side of the head in the back.
3. Take the braiding hair and fold it into a log shape and place it vertically in the back center of the head. Use the hair pins to secure the hair in place on the head.
4. Next, take the comb and comb the hair from the side over to cover the braiding hair.
5. Begin to tuck the remaining hair under the braiding and use the hair pins to secure the hair in place.
6. Apply some gel on the edges of your hair and then use the soft brush to brush and smooth out the edges of the hair on the front, the sides and the nape of the neck.
7. Lastly take the decorative clip and place it alongside the French roll.

Simple Tuck Under Style

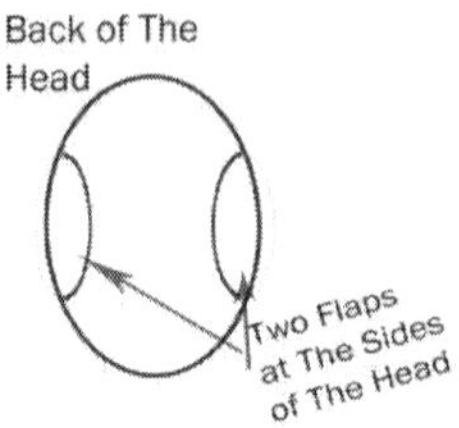

Items you'll need:

- ✓ Comb
- ✓ Soft brush
- ✓ Hair pins
- ✓ Butterfly clips *(for sectioning off hair)*
- ✓ Hair spray *(to hold the hair in place. Optional)*

Here's how to create the style:

1. Comb through the hair to get rid of any tangles. Make sure to comb all the hair back towards the back of the head.
2. At each side of the head pinch off too flaps of hair about 4 inches long in length and about an inch and a half wide. *See diagram.*
3. Section off each flaps with butterfly clips.
4. Gently comb through and smooth out the middle section of hair starting from the front of the head working your way to the back.
5. Begin to fold the hair under itself at the nape of the neck. (*Fold the hair as if you are about to do a raised pin curl*). Now use the hair pins to secure the hair in place.
6. CROSSING OVER THE FLAPS: undo one of the butterfly clips at the side of the head. Take the comb and comb through the hair, now cross that flap of hair over the middle portion of the head and tuck the ends of the hair under the bottom of **tucked hair** you created earlier. (*If you have longer hair just keep wrapping the hair around the base of the tucked hair until you have no more hair).* Now spray some hair spray so that the hair stays in place.
7. Undo the butterfly clip on the other side of the head REPEAT step # 6 for this flap.

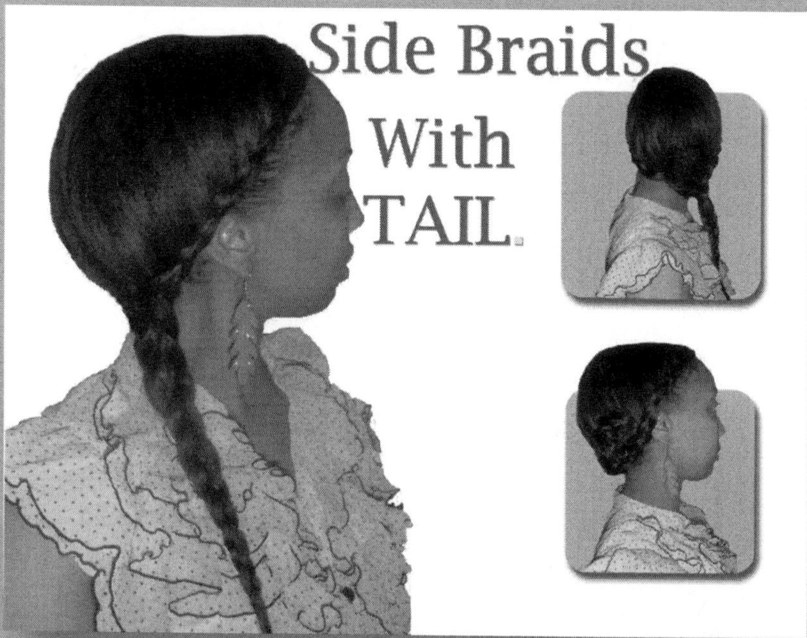
Side Braids
With
TAIL.

Side Braids With Tail.

Items you'll need:

- ✓ Comb
- ✓ Soft brush
- ✓ Small hair band
- ✓ Butterfly clip *(for sectioning off the hair)*

Here's how to create the style:

1. Gently detangle the hair.
2. Comb and arrange the hair so that the hair at the sides of the head are covering the sides of your face.
3. Make a small part at the front of one side of the head about one inch back.
4. Choose the side of the head with the most hair. Start at the point where the part is at the front and begin to braid only the perimeter of the hair line. Braid until you reach the side of the neck and STOP. Take a butterfly clip to hold that point of the hair for now.
5. Proceed to the other side of the head. Locate the *part* again and begin to braid the hair around the perimeter of the hair line, work your way along the side towards the back of the head until you meet the other braid with butterfly clip.
6. Remove the butterfly clip and merge the two sets of hair together and proceed to braid the loose hair as one, do so all the way to the end of the hair. Fold the tip of the hair under once and secure the end with a small hair band.
7. Take a soft brush to lightly brush and smooth down the hair.
8. You can leave the hair as it is right now as you can see in the picture, or you can make a spiral pattern against the side of the head. Secure the spiral with hair pins.

   **For longer length, add some braiding hair to your hair while braiding. Remember to feather out or make the ends of the braiding hair uneven for a more natural look.*

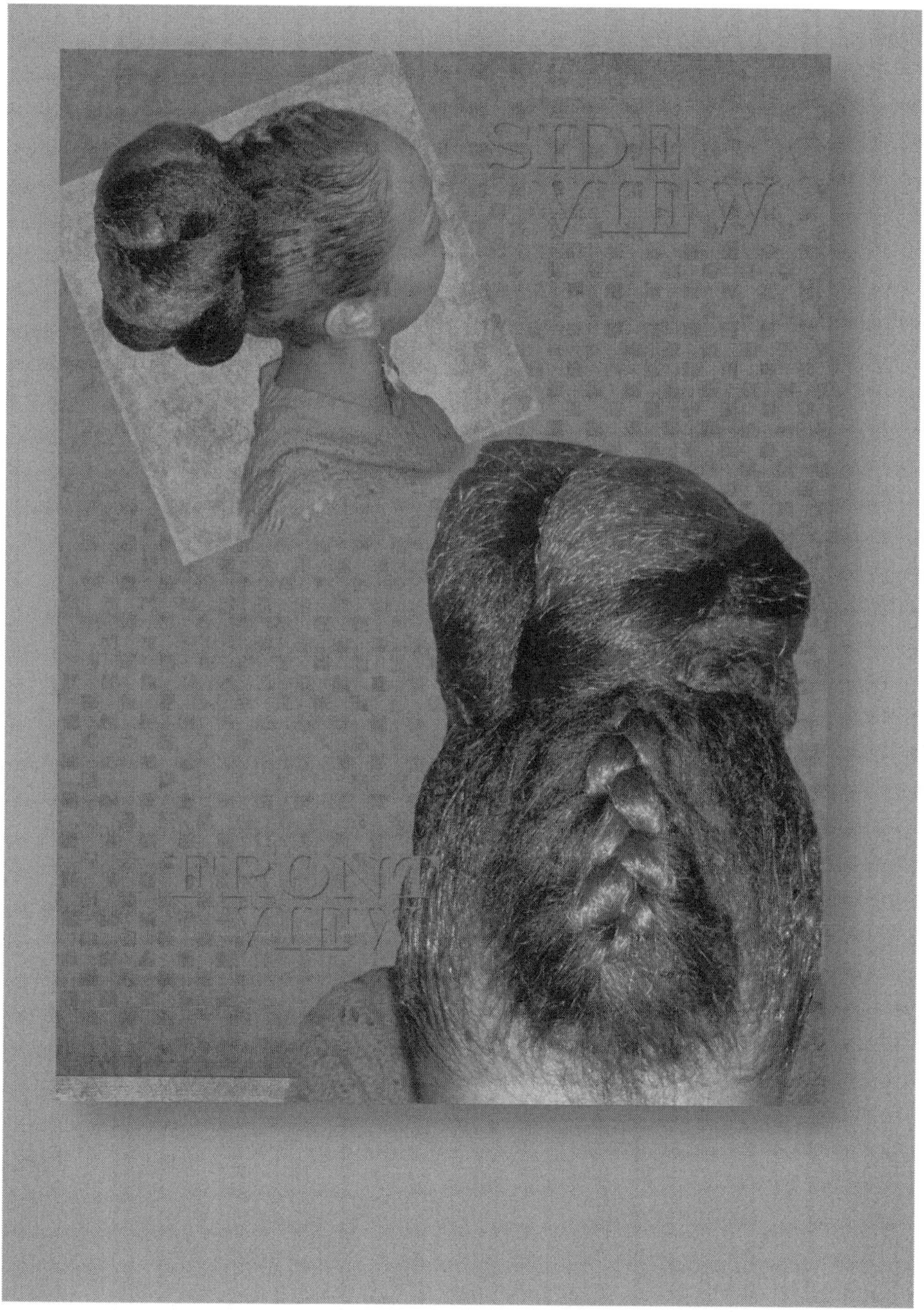
SIDE VIEW
FRONT VIEW

Highlighted Front Braid with Big Puffy Bun

Items you'll need:

- ✓ 2 different color braiding hair *(one that's the same color as your own hair and a lighter color)*
- ✓ Comb
- ✓ Soft brush
- ✓ Gel
- ✓ Hair pins
- ✓ Small hair bands
- ✓ Butterfly clip *(for sectioning of the hair)*

Here's how to create the style:

1. Comb through hair gently to get rid of any tangles.
2. Make a "U" shape part at the front of the head. About 2 inches wide and 4 inches long.
3. Section off the back portion of hair with a butterfly clip.
4. Pinch off a small amount of braiding hair from the pack *(make sure that it is the same length as your real hair*) and attach it to the front of the "U" shape part close to the hair line. Begin to do an inverted cornrow until you reach the end of this section of hair continue to braid the hair to the end until there is no more hair to braid. Secure the end with a hair band if you find the ends unraveling.
5. Undo the butterfly clip from the back section of hair. Place some gel around the perimeter of the hair and use the soft brush to brush and smooth the edges.
6. Now gather up all the hair in one into a high ponytail, (*including the braid from the front*) secure the base of the hair with a hair band.
7. CREATING THE BIG PUFFY BUN*: (mixing two colors together)* take the braiding hair that is the same color as your own hair add some of the lighter color hair to it.
8. Proceed to the ponytail and attach the braiding hair to the ponytail by start braiding the hair from the base of the pony tail. When you reach about 4 inches of braid convert to a two strand twist, and twist the braiding hair all the way to the end. Secure with a small hair band.
9. Now start to wrap the twist around the base of the ponytail until there is no more hair left to wrap, and then secure the end around the bun with hair pins.

The High Bun

The High Bun

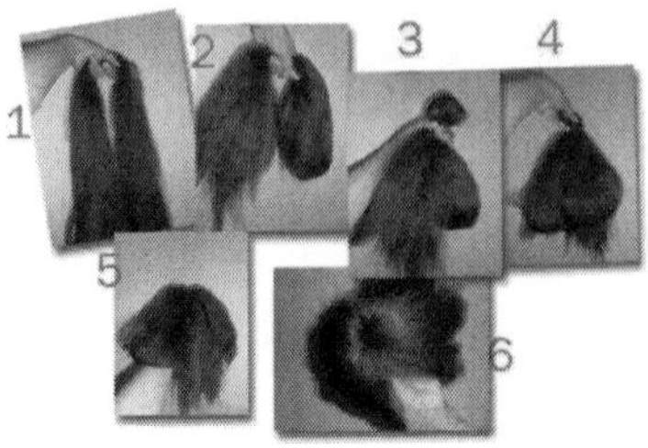

Items you'll need:

- ✓ Comb
- ✓ Soft brush
- ✓ Gel
- ✓ Hair pins
- ✓ 2 different color braiding hair *(one the same color as your own hair & the other a little lighter than your own hair)*

Here's how to create the style:

1. Detangle the hair gently.
2. Place some gel around the perimeter of the hair then use the soft brush to brush and smooth the edges of the hair.
3. Gather all the hair at the front of the head and to the side just a little.
4. Place a hair band at the base of the ponytail to secure it.
5. Now create a braid or a two strand twist with the ponytail.
6. Wrap the twist or braid around the base of the hair and secure with hair pins.
7. PREPARING THE BRAIDING HAIR TO PLACE ON TOP OF THE BUN: Take the braiding hair that is the same color as your hair and add some of the lighter color to it.
8. Hold the braiding hair at the middle so that it is hanging (in pic. # 1) hold the middle of that hair like in pic # 2. Move your hand and re grasp the hair to hold it like pic # 3. Place a small hair band around the section of hair to hold it in place. See pic. #4 now hold the tip of the hair and flip the hair over like a mop. See pic. #5.
9. Now take the hair and sit it on top of the bun in front of your head and secure with hair pins. Begin to arrange the braiding hair just like you see in the picture by making sure that you have the split in the middle and the highlights are on both sides. Then tuck away the ends and secure with hair pins.

Top View
Under Handed French
Braids With
Continuous Braid

Inverted Cornrows With Continuous Braid

Items you'll need:

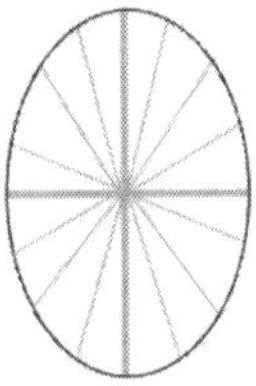

- ✓ Comb
- ✓ 5 butterfly clips
- ✓ Hair pins

Here's how to create the style:

1. Comb through hair gently to get rid of tangles.
2. Next part the hair into four equal sections and section off each section with a butterfly clip.
3. **PREPARING THE SECTIONS OF HAIR FOR BRAIDING**.
4. Choose one section of hair and locate the middle of the head then place the comb right in the center. Make a part from this point going all the way down to the hair line. *(This part should be straight and dividing the hair into two equal parts, further divide these 2 sections into 2 more equal parts each. Now you should have 4 equal parts within this section. Proceed to create inverted cornrows with each small section of hair one at a time starting from the smallest point of the section to the biggest part of the section of hair (which would be where the hair line is) and **STOP**. Place a hair pin right where the hair line is to hold the hair for later. See demonstration.*
5. Undo the butterfly clip from the other section of hair that is right next to the one you just cornrowed and repeat step # 4 for this section and the remaining sections.
6. Finally start from any cornrow. Undo the hair pins as you go and cornrow the hair at the hairline going around the head.
7. When you meet back where you started the cornrow, just braid the hair to the end and tuck the tail of the braid under the cornrow right at the hairline and secure with a couple of hair pins.

The hairstyle is complete!

Twist & Tuck

Twist & Tuck

Items you'll need:

- ✓ Comb
- ✓ Hair pins
- ✓ 2 Decorative combs
- ✓ 2 hair bands
- ✓ Butterfly clip

Here's how to create the style:

1. Detangle hair gently.
2. Start from the front of the head and place the comb at the hair line in the middle.
3. Start making a part going towards the back of the head until you reach the nape of the neck. *(At this point you should have two equal parts of hair)* section off one section of hair with the butterfly clip.
4. With the other section of hair start from the front of the head right where the part is and start making one big twist against the head. Place hair pins along the twist to secure it *(be sure to stay in the center area within the part when working your way down with the twist*).
5. When you reach a couple of inches from the nape of the neck place a small hair band around the base of the hair to secure it.

6. Take the left over hair and create a two strand twist with it then place a small hair band around the end of the hair to stop it from unraveling.

7. Undo the butterfly clip from the other side and follow steps 4-6 for this section.

8. Now take the twisted hair from the right side of the head and cross it over to the left side. At this point you are going to tuck some of the twisted hair under the big flat twist. *(If you have to undo some of the hair pins that are securing the flat twist into place, go ahead and do so. Just remember to secure the hair back into place)*

9. Do the same thing to the left side. After you are done place the 2 decorative combs on both sides of the head just like you see in the picture.

10. If you happen to have longer hair and you want to try this style. Just arrange the two strand twist hair in the back a little different.
11. Instead of tucking it, just place the two strand twist into a bun.

Side Ponytail

Side Ponytail

Items you'll need:

- ✓ 10 inch straight drawstring ponytail *(same as your hair color)*
- ✓ Comb
- ✓ Soft brush
- ✓ Gel
- ✓ Hair band

Here's how to create the style:

1. Gently comb through and detangle the hair.
2. Apply some gel to the perimeter of the hair and proceed to smooth out the hair by using the soft brush.
3. Gather all the hair up into a high ponytail in the front of the head about an inch back from the front hair line.
4. Place a hair band around the base of the hair to secure it in place.
5. Make a braid or twist with the ponytail, and then wrap it around the base of the hair. Use hair pins to secure it in place.
6. Now take the drawstring ponytail and place it over the bun *(be sure to have the drawstring hanging from the side of your head)* adjust the combs in your hair and then draw the drawstring to tighten but not too tight.
7. If you like you could spray some hair spray on the ponytail so that it stays into place a little.

The "S" Braid

The "S" Braid

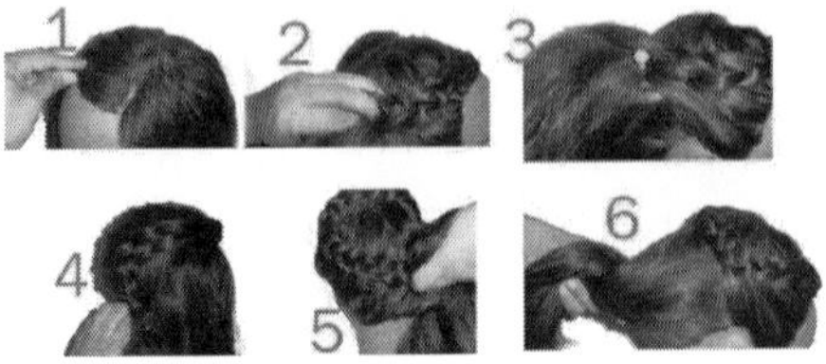

Items you'll need:

- ✓ Braiding hair
- ✓ Comb
- ✓ Hair pins

Here's how to create the style:

1. Comb through the hair gently to get rid of any tangles.
2. Make a side part in the front just like you see in the picture above.
3. Take out the braiding hair from its package and divide it into two equal portions.
4. Use one portion of the braiding hair and prepare it into 3 equal sections. Proceed to attach the braiding hair to your own hair in the front of the head on the side with the most hair. Now begin to braid your hair and the braiding hair together.
5. When you braid about 4 inches down the hair line begin to braid away from the hair line. *When you reach the back of the head use your hand to roughly section off the hair into 2 top and bottom.*
6. Continue braiding the hair so that the braid is going towards the back horizontally across the head.
7. When you reach about an inch from the hair line, start braiding the hair going down (*remember you are only braiding the perimeter of one side of the head when braiding down, not the whole section*).
8. When you reach about an inch from the nape of the neck curve the direction of the hair and continue braiding alongside the nape of the neck, about an inch above it.
9. STOP when you reach about half way.
10. Gather all the remaining hair into one and make one big braid. Secure the end with a small hair band.
11. Wrap the braid into a tight spiral shape and place it on your head in the empty space at the side of your head. Use hair pins to secure the hair in place.
12. Braid the other piece of braiding hair and add it to the spiral shape braid on the side of your head to fill and make it bigger. Place hair pins to secure as you go.

Stylish Jumbo Twist

Stylish Jumbo Twists

Items you need:

- ✓ Highlighted braiding hair
- ✓ Butterfly clips
- ✓ Hair pins
- ✓ Comb
- ✓ 3 regular size hair bands
- ✓ 3 small hair bands

Here's how to create the style:

1. First comb through hair gently to make sure that it is detangled.
2. Make a triangle shape part going from front to back. Start from the front-right at the hair line in the middle. Then move the comb over to the right a little about an inch and proceed to part the hair going all the way to the nape of the neck. *See the position of the part in the demo.*
3. Place a butterfly clip on this portion of hair *(right side)*
4. Go back to the front of the head and locate the hair line, place the comb 2 inches from the previous part you made earlier *(within the hair line)* and proceed to part the hair in the same manner in which you did on the right side.

Tip

When you reach the nape of the neck, check between the two parts to make sure that they are about 3 inches apart. (The bottom parts should be wider than the top parts) ***see diagram below***

Section off 2 sections of hair separately with a butterfly clips.

1. INCLUDING THE BRAIDING HAIR WITH YOUR HAIR. Divide the highlighted braiding hair from the pack into 1/3 s. pick up one piece.
2. Attach the braiding hair to your real hair by picking up two small sections of hair from the front of the head *(within the part of one section of hair)* attach the braiding to the two pieces of hair as if you're about to do a Senegalese twist. After you attach the hair, start to twist the hair in - do so about 2 times.
3. Now lay the twist flat against the head and transition into a two strand flat twist. Continue to do a two strand flat twist from this point all the way the back (stop when you reach about 1 ½ inch from the nape of the neck.
4. Place a hair band around the base of the twist to secure it in place
5. Continue to twist the hair all the way to the end. Then place a small hair band around the end to stop it from unraveling.
6. Undo the butterfly clip from the other section of hair. Pick up the next piece of braiding hair FOLLOW STEPS 2-5 to complete this side.

7. Undo the butterfly clip from the **last section of hair**. Pick up the next piece of braiding hair FOLLOW STEPS 2-5 to complete this side.
8. All three sections of hair should be twisted at this point. Take the two strand twist from the middle section of hair and wrap it around the base of itself. Secure with hair pins.
9. Take the two strand twist from the left side and wrap it around the base of the two strand twist you just wrap in the middle. Secure with hair pins. Do the same for the right side.

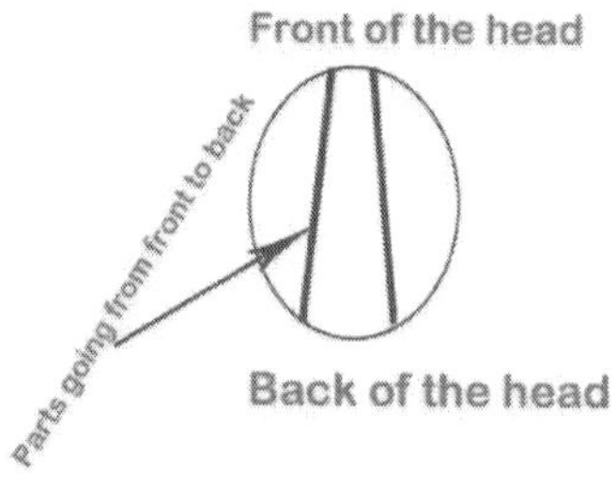

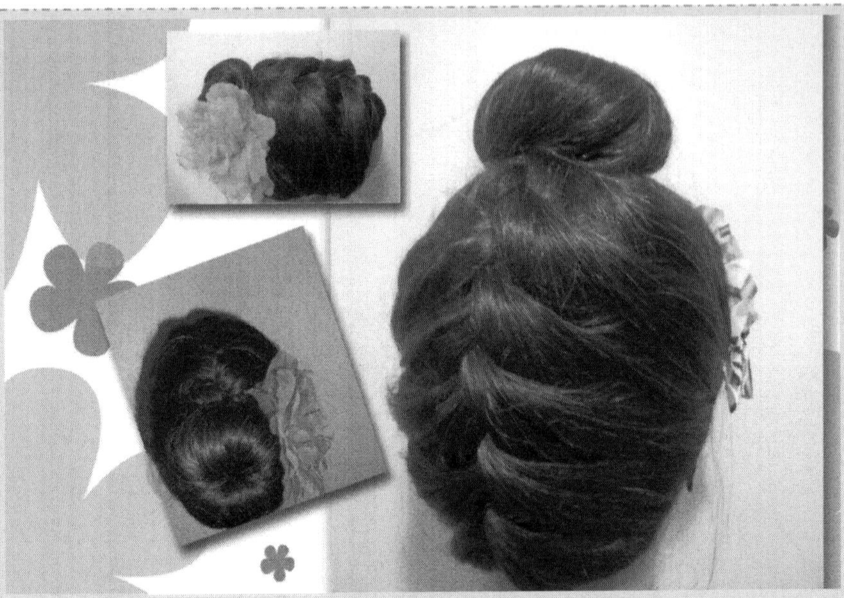

Upside Down Cornrow With Bun

Items you'll need:

- ✓ Hair pins
- ✓ Comb
- ✓ Hair band
- ✓ Bun maker
- ✓ Butterfly clip

Here's how to create the style:

1. Detangle the hair gently from ends to root.
2. Take the comb and part the hair from one ear to the other. You should now have two sections of hair *(one small section in the front and a large one in the back)* section off the small one in the front for later.
3. *You might need a friend to help with this part.* Pick up three small sections of hair from the nape of the neck and proceed to do an underhand braid/ inverted cornrow. (As you work your way up be sure to stay within the center of this section of hair.) STOP when you reach the part that separates the bottom portion of hair and the top portion of hair.
4. While holding the base of the braid with one hand, take the other hand and undo the butterfly clip from the top portion of hair.
5. Now merge the two portions of hair together. Use the comb to comb through the front of the hair so that it is nice and smooth.
6. Place a hair band around the base of the hair and gathered all the hair.
7. Now take the bun maker and place the ponytail through the hole of the bun maker so that the bun maker can sit at the base of the ponytail.
8. Fan the ponytail hair out over the bun maker and start to cover it with the hair by tucking the ends under it. Then use the hair pins to secure the bun in place. (**this is the look you see on the right in the picture**)
9. If you want to try the look you see on the left, simply reverse the styling process by making the front part of the hair the larger portion and then start the cornrow from front to back.
10. Make the bottom portion the smaller one and place the bun in the back. Add a flower to the side of the bun if you like.

Senegalese Twist

Senegalese Twist
Puffy Top
Senegalese
Twist
Senegalese
Twist
Knoted
Ponytail
Textured
Braiding
Hair
Senegalese Twist
Bun
Braided
Twist

Senegalese Twist Oversize Bun

To do the oversize bun style, simply bent over forward so that your head is kind of upside down so that the twist are hanging off your head.
While your head is still hanging down, gather all the twist together in one and start to wrap it around itself at the base. Use really big jumbo size hair pins to secure the bun in place.

Braided Twist

Bend your head down and forward so that the twist are hanging down. Grab three small sections of twist from the back and begin to braid/cornrow your hair. Work your way up to the front of the head. Once you reach the front continue to braid the twist all the way to the end and secure with a small hair band. Now proceed to tuck the braid that's in the front under itself. Secure the braid with hair pins.

Senegalese Twist Puffy Top

Bend your head forward and down so that the twist are dangling down. Reach to the back of the head right at the nape of the neck and pick up two sections of twist. Proceed to do a two strand flat twist. Work your way up to the front until you reach the ears, STOP. Then use a couple of big hair pins to secure the twist at this point. Gather the rest of the twist together and hold it up off the head about 90 degrees. Start from the ends of the twist and roll the hair down facing the back. When you reach the head, take some large hair pins and secure the hair in place.

Senegalese Twist Knotted Ponytail

For this hairstyle, arrange the twist so that they are all in the back. Take a section of twist from the bottom side of the head and wrap it around the rest of the hair, keep on wrapping until there is about 2 to 3 inches of hair left then tuck it within the wrap. Place a couple of hair pins where you tuck the hair to secure it in place.

Senegalese Front Bun

To create the **Senegalese twists front bun** simply bend your head over forward and down so that the hair is hanging. Next, gather all the hair together in the front of the head and adjust it so that it is place to the side of the head a little. Now place a hair band around the base of the hair. Proceed to fan the hair out so that you can see the center, then tuck the ends under itself so that you can't see them. Now place hair pins to secure the bun in place.

Please see "Tips before styling" section to learn how to do Senegalese twist

3 Ways To Style A Side Braid

Circle Braid

Circle Braid

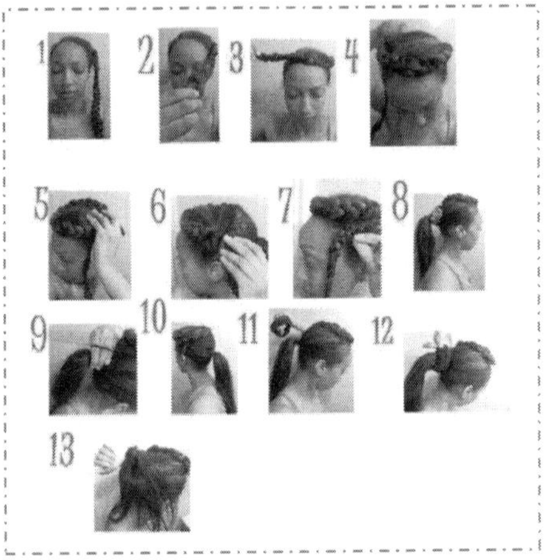

Items you'll need:

- ✓ Braiding hair
- ✓ Hair pins
- ✓ Comb
- ✓ Soft brush
- ✓ Hair band
- ✓ Edge control or gel
- ✓ Bun maker/sock bun
- ✓ Butterfly clip (for sectioning off the hair)

Here's how to create the style:

1. Comb through the hair gently to get rid of any tangles.
2. Make a side part on the right side of the head going back about 3 inches then stop.
3. Turn the comb to the left and make another part going down the side of the head *(towards the left ear)*
4. Use the butterfly clip to section off the back section of hair for now.
5. **Braiding the front section of hair.** Take the braiding hair from the package and divide it into half. Take ½ of the braiding hair and arrange it into 3 even sections. Set it to one side for a moment.
6. Apply some gel to the edges of the hair and use the soft brush to brush and smooth out the hair. Now gather all the hair into one like a ponytail.
7. Pick up the braiding hair you arrange into 3 even sections and begin to attach it to the front portion of hair at the side. Like this.

   Braid the hair down to the end. Start to lay the braid down on the head by first bringing the braid around to the front, to the other side of the head covering the **part,** continue around to the back covering the **part** as well. When you come back to where the braid originally started, begin to tuck the remaining hair under the braid. (Remember, as you bring the hair around use the hair pins to secure the hair in place (*see steps 2-7 in picture above to see how to lay the braid down*).
8. Next, remove the butterfly clip from the back section of hair and apply some gel on the edges. Use the brush and smooth out the hair. Gather the hair into a high ponytail and use the hair band to secure the hair in place. Take the bun maker or sock bun and place the hair from the ponytail through the hole of the bun maker. Slide it all the way down to the base of the ponytail.

9. Fan the hair evenly over the bun maker and begin to tuck the excess hair under it then use the hair pins to secure the hair in place.

Swirl Front Braid

Swirl Front Braid

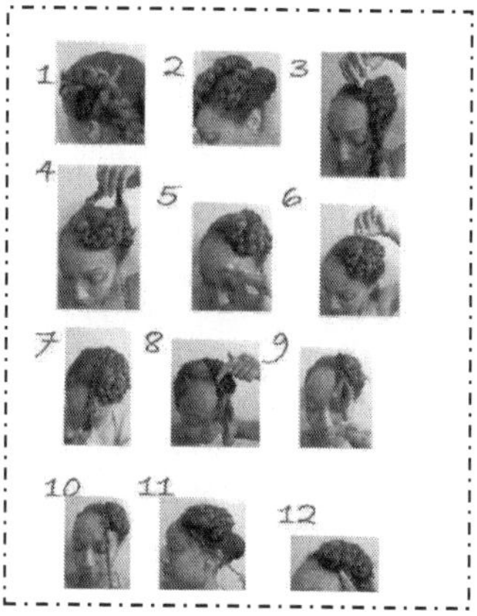

Items you'll need:

- ✓ Comb
- ✓ Soft brush
- ✓ Braiding hair
- ✓ Hair pins
- ✓ Bun maker
- ✓ Hair band
- ✓ Gel
- ✓ Butterfly clip (*for sectioning off the hair*)

Here's how to create the hairstyle:

1. Comb through the hair gently to get rid of any tangles.
2. Make a side part on the right side of the head going back about 3 inches then stop.
3. Turn the comb to the left and make another part going down the side of the head (*towards the left ear)*
4. Use the butterfly clip to section off the back section of hair for now.
5. **Braiding the front section of hair.** Take the braiding hair from the package and divide it into half. Take the other section of hair and arrange it into 3 even sections. Set it aside for a moment.
6. Apply some gel to the edges of the hair and use the soft brush to brush and smooth out the hair. Now gather all the hair into one like a ponytail.
7. Pick up the braiding hair you arranged into 3 even sections and begin to attach it to the front portion of hair at the side. Braid the hair all the way to the end and secure with a hair band.
8. Once the braiding hair is attach to your own hair, begin to pin the braid down on the head in a zig zag pattern going down the side of the head and secure with hair pins as you go (*be sure that there's no gap in between the braids*). *Please see demo above.*

9. **Making the bun in the back**. Next, remove the butterfly clip from the back section of hair and apply some gel on the edges. Use the brush and smooth out the hair. Gather the hair into a high ponytail and use the hair band to secure the hair in place. Take the bun maker or sock bun and place the hair from the ponytail through the hole of the bun maker. Slide it all the way down to the base of the ponytail.
10. Fan the hair evenly over the bun maker and begin to tuck the excess hair under it then use the hair pins to secure the hair in place.

Wrap Around Side Braid

Wrap around side Braid

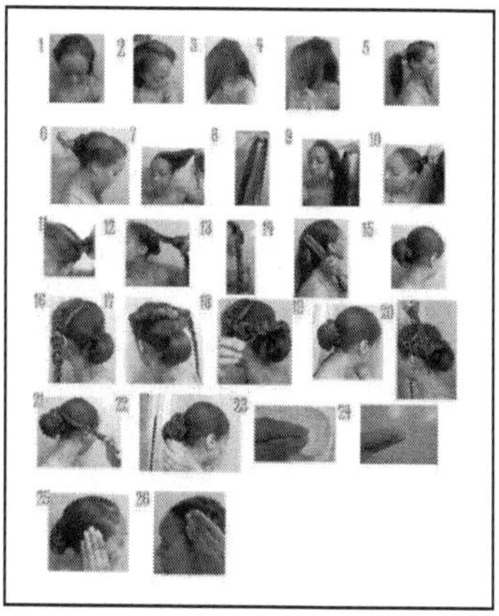

Items you'll need:

- ✓ Comb
- ✓ Soft brush
- ✓ Braiding hair
- ✓ Hair pins
- ✓ Bun maker
- ✓ Hair band
- ✓ Gel
- ✓ Butterfly clip (*for sectioning off the hair*)

Here's how to create the hairstyle:

1. Comb through the hair gently to get rid of any tangles.
2. Make a side part on the right side of the head going back about 3 inches then stop.
3. Turn the comb to the left and make another part going down the side of the head *(towards the left ear).*
4. Use the butterfly clip to section off the back section of hair for now.
5. **Braiding the front section of hair.** Take the braiding hair from the package and divide it into half. Take the other section of hair and arrange it into 3 even sections. Set it to one side for a moment.
6. Apply some gel to the edges of the hair and use the soft brush to brush and smooth out the hair. Now gather all the hair into a ponytail.
7. Pick up the braiding hair you arrange into 3 even sections and begin to attach it to the front portion of hair at the side, braid the hair all the way to the end and secure with a small hair band.
8. **Making the bun in the back**. Next, remove the butterfly clip from the back section of hair and apply some gel on the edges. Use the brush and smooth out the hair. Gather the hair into a high ponytail and use the hair band to secure the hair in place. Take the bun maker or sock bun and place the hair from the ponytail through the hole of the bun maker. Slide it all the way down to the base of the ponytail.
9. Fan the hair evenly over the bun maker and begin to tuck the excess hair under it then use the hair pins to secure the hair in place.
10. Take the braided hair from the front and lay it on the side of your head, use hair pins to secure it. Then continue to bring the braid to the back and wrap it around the base of the bun. Use the hair pins to secure the braid around the hair.

Back Accent Braid

Back Accent Braid

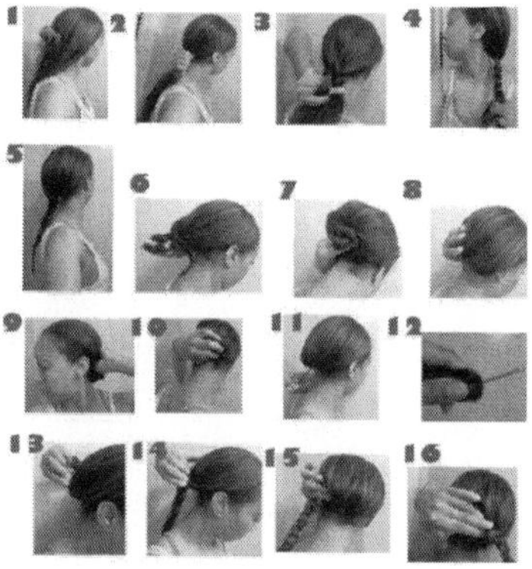

Items you'll need:

- ✓ Comb
- ✓ Soft brush
- ✓ Braiding hair
- ✓ Decorative hair clip
- ✓ Hair jam

Here's how to create the hairstyle:

1. Comb through the hair gently to get rid of any tangles.
2. Comb all the hair to the back.
3. Apply some hair jam on the edges and on your hair then proceed to brush the hair to smooth it out.
4. Take the rest of the hair and proceed to braid and tuck it under itself and then use the hair pin to secure the tuck hair.
5. **Preparing the braiding hair for attachment**. Take the braiding hair from the package and remove about ¼ to ½ of it. Start to braid the braiding hair. When the braiding hair is completely braided, take one end of it and place it at the bottom of the head where the nape of the neck is at the corner (*please see photo # 14 above*). Take the hair pin and secure the hair in place.
6. Take the braid and bring it across the bottom of the head (*on the nape of the neck, photo # 15*) and use a couple hair pins to secure the hair braid in place.
7. Take the braid and bring it horizontally across the bottom of the head again but going the opposite direction. Place it above the previous braid without any gaps between them and use the hair pins to secure the braid in place.
8. Continue to go back and forth with the braid and securing it on the head with hair pins until there's no more hair to pin.
9. Take the decorative hair clip and place it on the side of the head where the braid is.

Multi Braid Pin Up

Multi Braid Pin Up

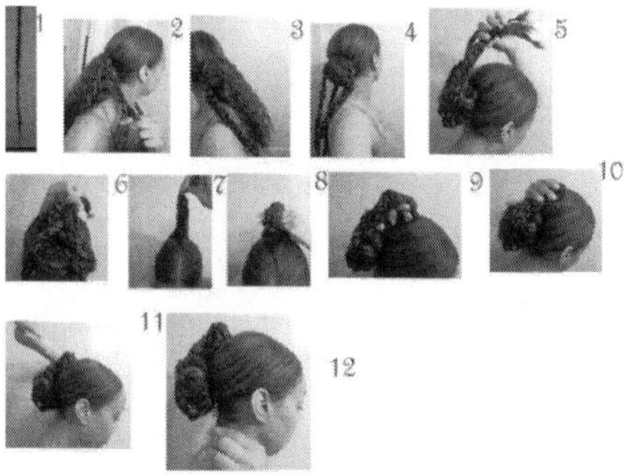

Items you'll need:

- ✓ Comb
- ✓ Soft brush
- ✓ Hair pins
- ✓ Hair jam
- ✓ Curly clip on ponytail

Here's how to create the hairstyle:

1. Comb through the hair gently to get rid of any knots.
2. Make a part at the front of the head in the middle. Comb the hair out on both sides of the part.
3. Apply a little hair jam on the edges of the hair, include the back as well. Now take the soft brush and begin to brush the hair to smooth it out.
4. Proceed to gather all the hair into a low ponytail and secure with a hair band. Twist or braid the rest of the hair and wrap it around the base of the ponytail then secure the hair with hair pins.
5. **Braiding the clip on ponytail hair**. To make it easy for you. Take the clip on hair and place it on the bun on your head *temporarily. Place the top comb in the root of the hair so that it stays put while you are braiding the hair.* Ok begin to take small sections of hair and braid them, when you have completed all the braids gather the ends together and then take a small hair band and place it on the ends of the braids to hold them together. Remove the clip on ponytail from your hair and place it back on your hair. This time place it **upside down.** Secure the combs from the clip on ponytail into the hair and pull the drawstring to tighten and secure.
6. Fold the ends of the hair under itself, enough to hide the ends and the hair band around it. Take the hair pins and begin to secure the hair in place against the back of the head.

Cascading
Curly Bang

Cascading Curly Bang

Items you'll need:

- ✓ Flexi rods
- ✓ Setting lotion or hair mousse
- ✓ Spray bottle w/ some water
- ✓ Hair pins
- ✓ Gel
- ✓ Soft brush
- ✓ Time

Here's how to create the hairstyle:

1. Detangle the hair completely and gently.
2. Make a "U" shape part in the front part of the head. (About *4 inches wide and 5 inches going back*) section off this portion of hair with a butterfly clip for later.
3. Comb through the bottom section of hair. Take some gel in the palm of your hands and apply it to the hair against your head in a downward motion.
4. Next, use the soft brush and gently brush and smooth the hair that you just apply the gel to.
5. Starting from the side of the head right where the ear is begin to twist the hair under and against the head alongside the hair line. Do so until you reach the other side of the head. When you can't twist any more, use a couple of large hair pins to secure the twist against the head. Leave the ends of the hair out from this twist (*remember to place hair pins as you go to secure the twist in place*)
6. Undo the butterfly clip from the top portion of hair.
7. Gently comb through this portion of hair. Then take the water bottle and spray the hair to dampen it a little.
8. Apply mousse to the hair *(the front section only)*
9. Take a small section of hair from the front of the hair, comb to smooth it out and place the end of the hair on the end of the flexi rod (about inch away from the end of the flexi rod) begin to roll the flexi rod so that the hair rolls unto it). Continue with this motion until all the hair is rolled unto the flexi rod.
10. Bend the ends of the flexi rods in opposite direction so that the rod can stay in place.
11. Continue to take up small pieces of hair within this section and roll it on the flexi rod then secure the rod by bending the ends in opposite directions to secure (be sure to include the loose hair from the end of the twist).
12. After the hair is completely dry, remove the flexi rods by undoing the ends and gently unroll the hair from the rod down to the end. (Don't rush this process because you will snag and possibly cause breakage to your hair).
13. Now fluff out the curls to your liking and arrange them how you like.

Continuous
Braid With
Beautiful
Center
Curls

Continuous Braid with Beautiful Center Curls

Items you'll need:

- ✓ Comb
- ✓ Butterfly clip
- ✓ Lots of hair pins
- ✓ Flexi rods
- ✓ Setting lotion

Here's how to create the hairstyle:

1. Gently comb through the hair to get rid of any tangles.
2. Take the comb and place it right at the hair line at the front of the head. Make a part going straight back about 2 inches. STOP, turn the comb to the right and make a part going all the way around the head *(stay parallel to hair line at all times)*, continue parting until you reach back to the front where you started.
3. Section off the middle portion of hair with a butterfly clip.
4. Locate the spot where you made the part in the front going back, pick up 3 small equal portion of hair right at the part and start doing an inverted cornrow. Do so all the way around the head until you're back where you first started. Continue to braid the hair to the end.
5. Take the braid and roll it into a spiral shape, place it against the head and secure it with a small hair pin.
6. CURLING THE MIDDLE:

Undo the butterfly clip from the middle portion of hair. Pick up a small piece of hair. Spray some setting lotion on it. Take the end of the hair and place it on the end of the flexi rod about 1 inch from the tip. Start rolling the rod so the hair can roll on it.

When all the hair is on the rod, secure the ends of the rod by bending them in opposite directions.

7. Continue this process throughout the middle of the head, picking up small sections of hair, spraying setting lotion on it, and rolling it on the flexi rod.
8. AFTER THE HAIR IS COMPLETLTLY DRY: Remove the flexi rods from the middle portion of hair by unfolding the ends and unraveling the hair off the rod. Do so until all rods are out of the hair.
9. Fluff out the curls with your fingers. Arrange the curls to your liking. Now begin to pin the curls in place.

Tip

For extra hold, you can try spraying some hair spray on the curls.

Need more length and volume? Try adding clip in hair pieces.

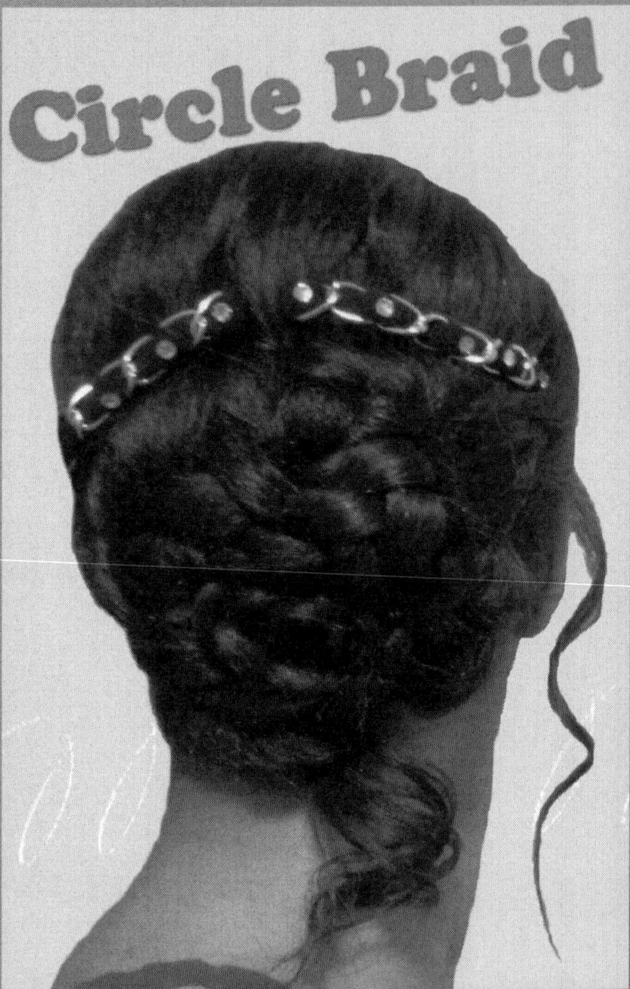
Circle Braid

Circle Braid

Items you'll need:

- ✓ Comb
- ✓ Hair pins
- ✓ Setting lotion
- ✓ 3 Small flexi rod
- ✓ Decorative combs
- ✓ Butterfly clip

Here's how to create the hairstyle:

1. Comb through hair gently to get rid of any tangles.
2. Then comb the hair back so all the hair is laying in the back. Pick up 2 small pieces of hair from the temple of your head on both sides. Spray setting lotion on the 2 pieces of hair and roll the hair unto the flexi rod. Secure both sides of the flexi rod by bending the ends in opposite directions.
3. Part off a small portion of hair at the nape of the neck, spray some setting lotion on it and roll it on the flexi rod.
4. Picture in your head an imaginary line going across the middle of the head in the back horizontally. Start from the side of the head about an inch and begin to do an inverted cornrow along the imaginary line. When you reach to the other side of the head *(an inch from the hair line)* start cornrowing down 1 inch parallel from the hair line.
5. When you reach about 2 inches from the nape of the neck continue to cornrow the hair across the lower part of the head. When you get the other side of the head *(about an inch)* cornrow the hair going up, staying an inch away from the side of the head.
6. At this point continue to cornrow the hair into a spiral shape.
7. When there is no more hair to cornrow. Finish braiding the hair to the end. Finish off the spiral by rolling the braided hair unto itself and nestle it in the middle. Secure with hair pins *(you just created a spiral shape inverted cornrow).*
8. Remove the flexi rods from both sides of the head when it is completely set and dry *(this will give two spiral curls at both sides of the head).*
9. Remove the flexi rod from the back also *(for another curl)* bring the curl up a little so that it is not passing the shoulders, place it against your head and place hair pins to secure it in place.
10. OPTIONAL: Take the 2 decorative combs and place them above but close to the spiral cornrow.

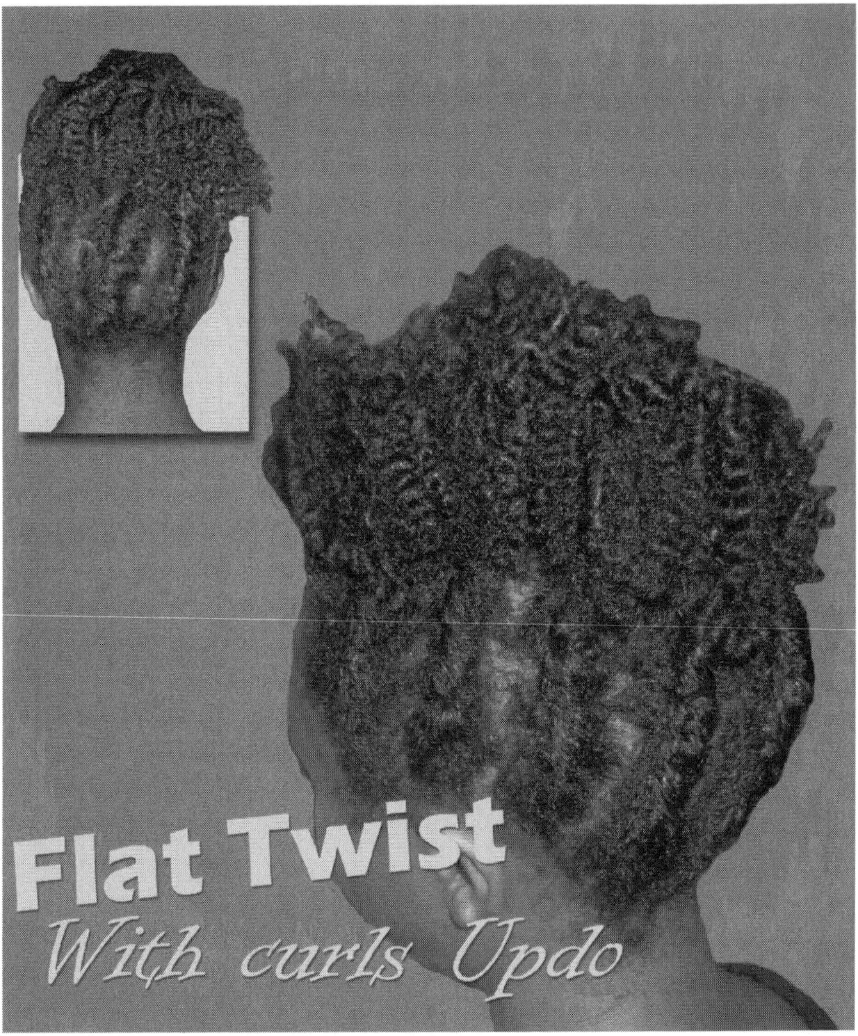
Flat Twist
With curls Updo

Flat Twists With Curls Updo

Items you'll need:

- ✓ Large tooth comb
- ✓ Coconut oil
- ✓ 2 Butterfly clip
- ✓ Hair pins
- ✓ Moisturizer

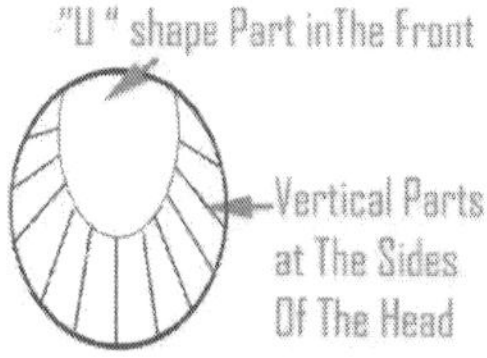

Here's how to create the hairstyle:

1. First I just want to make mention that this hairstyle is done from a two strand twist out on natural hair. So be sure to do two strand twists beforehand and let it set before attempting to do this style.
2. Place some moisturizer in the palm of your hands and then apply it to the whole head of twists.
3. Next, put some coconut oil in the palm of your hands then rub the hands together. *(Doing this will help to reduce frizzy hair while undoing the twist).*
4. Start to undo all the twist one by one. (If your hands need more coconut oil go ahead and apply some more. Remember not to add too much and overdo it).
5. DOING THE FLAT TWIST: Take the large tooth comb and gently make a "U" shape part at the front of the head. (*About 4 inches wide and 5 inches back. However, you can adjust the size of the part to your liking).* Gently section off this portion of hair with a butterfly clip until later.
6. Locate the side of the head in the front. Make a vertical part parallel to the hair line in the front. Take a butterfly clip and section off the rest of the hair for a moment. You should be left with a small section of hair at the side.
7. Take the small section of hair and grasp the bottom of it right at the roots and proceed do a flat twist going up, stop when your reach the **part** for the "U" shape **part.** Take the hair pin and secure the twist in place at the root of the hair.
8. Undo the butterfly clip from the bottom portion of hair and continue to make vertical parts (*parallel to the previous parts you made*) around the head. Section off any loose hair you are not working with while creating the flat twist. Be sure to always secure the flat twist with hair pins.
9. When you're completely done flat twisting the sides and back the head, remove the butterfly clip from the top portion of hair. Fluff the hair out with your fingers as well as the ends of the flat twist.

Two Strand
Twist On Natural Hair

Two Strand Twist on Natural Hair

This style can be done on either dry or wet hair.

Items you'll need:

- ✓ Decorative head band
- ✓ Comb
- ✓ Butterfly clips
- ✓ Leave-in conditioner or moisturizer

Here's how to create the hairstyle:

1. First detangle the hair gently.
2. Divide the hair into sections by; horizontally parting the hair across the head from ear to ear, *(you should have two sections of hair).* Take a butterfly clip and section off the bottom portion of hair for later.
3. Proceed to the front of the head and part the hair horizontally down the middle, now you should have two portions of hair. Section off one section of hair with a butterfly clip.
4. Before you start the twisting process apply some leave-in conditioner or a good moisturizer within the section of hair.

5. Now start creating the two strand twists within the portion of hair. Locate the side of the head and start doing the twists there, working your way up.

6. TWISTING THE HAIR. Part the hair in a half moon shape, *(like an arch)* take a butterfly clip and section off the hair you are not working with for now. Take the smaller section you just parted off and split the hair in two equal parts.

7. Grasp both sections separately with both hands right at the root and roll both sections of hair between the fingers in the same direction to the right. Then cross the two twists over each other. *(Take the twist that is in your right hand and cross it over to the left over the twist that is in you left hand. Now both twists are in different hands).*

8. Now roll both twists again between the fingers and cross them over each other again. Continue this process of rolling and twisting the hair until you reach to the end of the hair. Roll and twirl the end of the twist between your fingertips.

9. Undo the butterfly clip and make another half-moon shape or arch right next to the one you just created. REPEAT the process of rolling and twisting throughout the entire head of hair.

10. REMEMBER to moisturize before you twist, and make half-moons for your parts.

11. Allow the hair to dry and then place the head band if you like.

Tip

Before you go to bed, place a silk or satin scarf over the head so that the twist stays in place and to prevent the hair from getting frizzy.

Flexi Rod Curl Updo

Flexi Rod Curl Updo

Items you'll need:

- ✓ Flexi rods
- ✓ Mousse or setting lotion
- ✓ Hair pins
- ✓ Combs *(large tooth & medium teeth)*
- ✓ Shampoo & conditioner
- ✓ Water bottle with water
- ✓ Time *(to air dry)*
- ✓ Coconut oil
- ✓ Gel
- ✓ Soft brush

Here's how to create the hairstyle:

1. Wash hair with a moisturizing shampoo and condition with a moisturizing conditioner.
2. DETANGLE THE HAIR. Detangle the hair in small sections using the large tooth comb working your way up the hair length from ends to root. DON'T rush this process, because rushing will only result in premature breakage of hair.
3. After the detangling process is over. Start applying the flexi rod to the hair. To help manage the hair a bit, create a few sections of hair by making a couple parts going across the head horizontally and then place butterfly clips to secure them until you need to work with that section.
4. APPLYING THE FLEXI RODS: start from the back of the head right at the nape of the neck when you start applying your flexi rods.
5. Grab a small section of hair starting from the nape of neck *(a little bigger than a dime size)* use a medium size comb to comb through this section to smooth it out and to get rid of any tangles.
6. Apply some mousse to the section of hair. Take the hair and place it on the rod about ½ inch away from the end. Now begin to roll the rod so that the hair can start wrapping around it. When you reach the head and can no longer roll the rod, simply bend and curl the ends of the rod into a spiral shape in the opposite direction you were rolling it. Proceed to the other end of the rod and do the same thing.
7. Grab another section of hair a little bigger than the size of a quarter and REPEAT steps 5&6 throughout the whole head of hair.
8. AFTER HAIR IS COMPLETELY DRY: Remove the flexi rods from the hair by untwisting the ends of the rods and slowly unravel the hair from the rod.
9. Add a couple of drops of coconut oil in the palm of your hands and rub them together. Then begin to separate the curls into 2 or 3 smaller curls *(be careful not to create frizz to the curls)* while separating them.

Gently run your fingers down the strands of the hair to add the coconut oil from your hands.

10. CREATING AN UPDO WITH THE CURLS: Take the soft brush and smooth out the edges and sides of the head, then apply a small amount of gel to the section you just smooth out. Proceed to brush the hair to smooth again.
11. Go to the front of the head and loosely gather up a small portion of hair, take some hair pins and secure the hair at the roots on both sides.
12. Gather up another small portion of hair right below the one you just created and secure the hair at the roots on both sides again. Keep doing this until you reach the nape of the neck.
13. Fluff out the curls with your fingers some more if you desire more fullness.

> TIP: if you want to secure the roots of the hair Some more, try to place a few small hair combs right where you placed the hair pins.

Soft Fluffy Bantu knot Outs

Soft Fluffy Bantu Knot Outs

This Bantu knot out hairstyle can be done on wet or dry detangled natural, relaxed, or transitioning hair.

Items you'll need:

- ✓ Clip on flower
- ✓ Small cloth hair bands
- ✓ Comb
- ✓ Moisturizer or leave-in conditioner
- ✓ Coconut oil
- ✓ Time for drying

Here's how to create the hairstyle:

1. First detangle the hair. Be sure to start detangling starting from the ends of the hair working your way up to the roots.
2. Apply some moisturizer or leave in conditioner throughout the hair.
3. **Creating the Bantu knots**. You can choose to use a comb or your fingers at this point.
4. Grab a small section of hair at the front side of your head *(right in front of your ear about 1 ½ inch wide)*
5. Now begin to Bantu knot the hair, please refer back to the hairstyle on **how to *create Bantu knot*** *to complete this process.*
6. Continue to grab hair about 1 ½ to 2 inches in size all over the head, and create the Bantu knots. Remember to place the small cloth hair bands around the base of the Bantu knot to help it to stay in place. Allow the bantu knots to stay until they are set and completely dry
7. **Removing the Bantu knots after they are set**. Put a few drops of coconut oil in the palm of your hands and rub them together. Then start removing the Bantu knots by unraveling them. Do this by first removing the small cloth hair bands from the base of the Bantu knots and then undo the knots. Gently run your fingers down the length of the knot *(remember that the coconut oil is in the palm of your hands*) the oil will help to reduce the frizz while you're undoing the knots.
8. After all the knots are undone, just use your fingers to gently fluff out the hair a bit to create a fuller look.
9. Finally take the clip on flower and place it at the side of the hair.

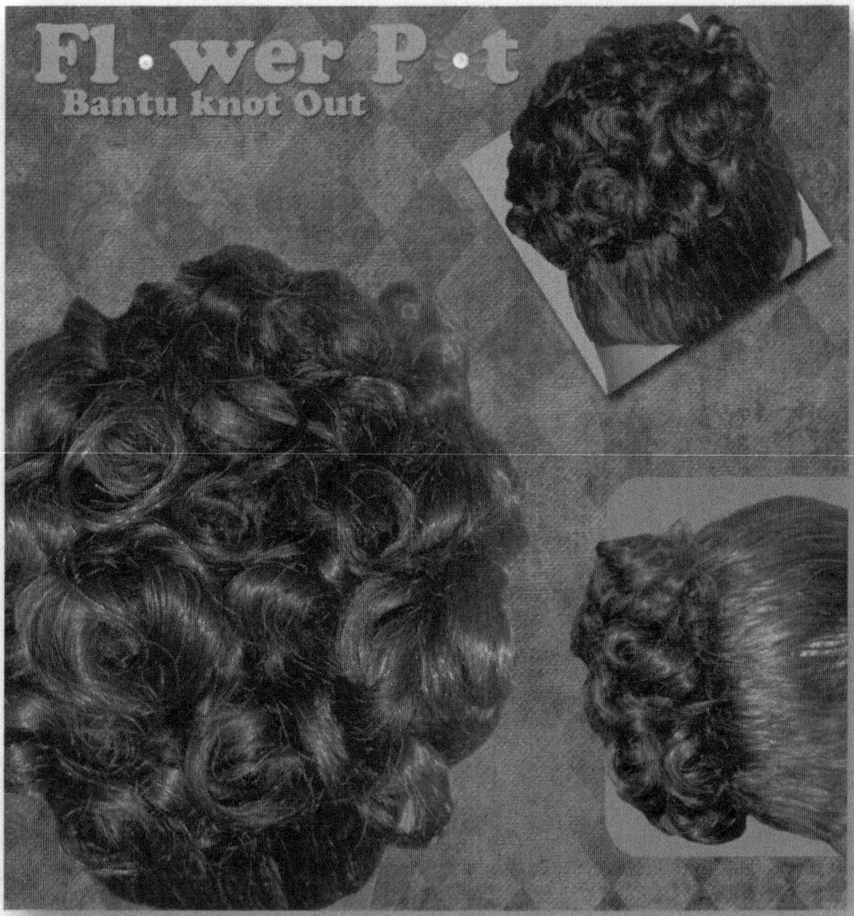
Fl•wer P•t
Bantu knot Out

Flower Pot Bantu Know Out

Items you'll need:

- ✓ Flexible comb
- ✓ 1 small hair band
- ✓ Several small cloth hair bands
- ✓ Small hair pins
- ✓ Moisturizer
- ✓ Setting lotion
- ✓ Coconut oil
- ✓ gel

Here's how to create the hairstyle:

1. Comb out hair so that it is tangle free.
2. Add some moisturizer to the hair; make sure to get the ends.
3. Apply some gel around the perimeter of the hair and gather all the hair into one and use the soft brush to brush around the edges. Then take the hair band and place it around the base of the hair creating a ponytail.
4. Take the flexible comb and place it around the base of the ponytail. This should be about three inches away from the ponytail. Go ahead and secure the flexi comb in place.
5. Now remove the hair band from the ponytail leaving the flexi comb in place.
6. Take a small portion of hair from within the flexi comb circle and proceed to do a two strand twist, and then spray some setting lotion along the twist.
7. With one hand grasp the root of the twist, and with the other hand wrap the twist around itself at the base until there's no more hair to wrap.
8. Place a small cloth hair band around the base of the Bantu knot. This is to keep it in place.
9. **Repeat steps 6-8** until you have complete Bantu knotting all the loose hair within the flexi comb circle. Allow to set and dry.
10. **Removing the Bantu knots for styling**: Place a few drops of coconut oil in the palms of your hands and rub them together start by removing the hair bands from the base of the Bantu knots. Then proceed to unravel them by unwrapping them from the base then undoing the *twists (separating the twist into two)* do this to all of the Bantu knots. Remember to lightly run your fingers down the twists with the coconut oil that's on the palm of your hands (*this process will help to reduce the frizz).*
11. You can go ahead and further separate each twist one more time to create more volume.
12. To keep the bantu outs close to the head and stationary use small hair pins to secure the Bantu knot outs in place against the head.

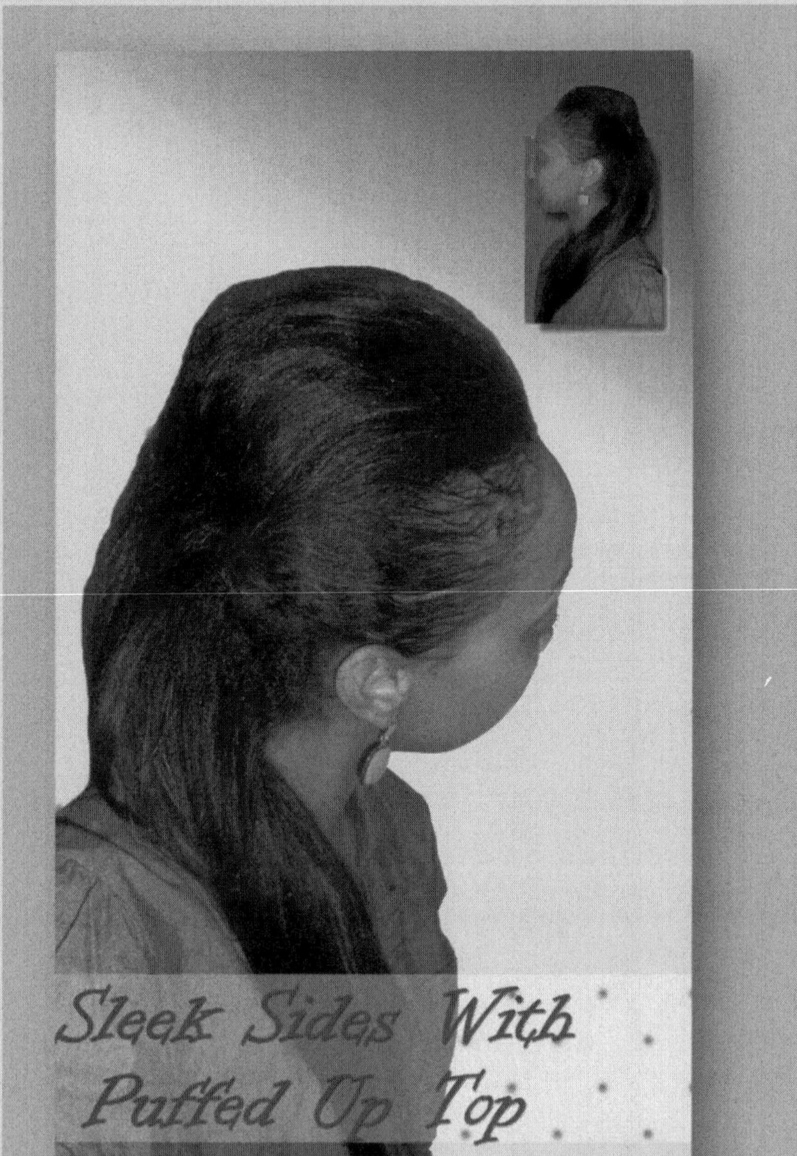
Sleek Sides With
Puffed Up Top

Sleek Sides with Puffed Up Top

This hairstyle is simple but sleek at the same time, looks great on medium to long hair. I love it because it is so quick to style and look so put together. **If you have natural hair, wet roller set your hair. Be sure that the ends are place nice and straight on the roller and the hair is rolled with tension, allow to dry. Then remove the rollers, add some oil moisturizer and serum to the length of the hair, then comb through the hair and criss cross wrap the hair. Place a silk or satin scarf on the head overnight. The purpose of this process is to relaxed and, straighten some of the curl pattern to achieve the sleek look for this style. Keep in mind that the hair will not go bone straight, however it will produce some straightness which is fine.*

Items you'll need:

- ✓ Comb
- ✓ Soft brush
- ✓ Double push combs
- ✓ Edge control or gel
- ✓ 2 Butterfly clip
- ✓ Hair spray (optional)

Here's how to create the hairstyle:

**Before you begin to style the hair, be sure to wrap your hair overnight so that the hair can be straight when you are ready to style it.*

1. Take the comb and gently comb through the hair from ends to root while detangling it. Use the soft brush to brush and smooth the whole head of hair going back.
2. Next make a "U" shape part at the front of the head (*this should be about 4 inches wide and 4 inches going back adjust this size to your liking). Place a butterfly clip to secure for now.*
3. Make another part, this time going across the head horizontally. Start this part about 2 to 3 inches above the nape of the neck. Then use the butterfly clip to section off this bottom portion of hair for now.
4. Now you are left with a section of hair in the middle of the head. At this point take some gel or edge control and apply some at the edges and sides of the hair. Gather the section of hair in one and use the soft brush to brush the sides to smooth it out.
5. Take the double push comb and proceed to secure this portion of hair. Do so by placing the double comb on top of the *gathered hair* (both combs should be on either side of the hair) just slip both combs in the root of the hair towards each other to secure the hair in place.

6. Now, take the butterfly clip from the bottom portion of hair and use the comb to gently comb through the hair *(comb so that it is nice and smooth)* blend the loose hair from the middle section of hair into the bottom portion of hair also.
7. Next proceed to the top of the hair and undo the butterfly clip from that portion of hair. Comb through the hair gently and then hold it up from the head about 90 degrees. Use the comb to gently back comb the roots. This will add some volume to the hair.
8. Now place/ lay the hair down towards the back over the middle portion of hair you placed double push comb. Try to cover it the best you can with the hair.
9. To allow the hair stay in place, secure it over the middle portion of hair with some small hair pins.
10. Now use the comb or brush to smooth the loose hair. At this point you can spray some hair spray along the hair so that it stays in place (optional).

Pin Curl & Braid Out
updo

Pin Curl & Braid Out Updo

Items you'll need:

- ✓ Comb
- ✓ Soft brush
- ✓ Hair pins
- ✓ Few small hair bands
- ✓ Setting lotion or mousse
- ✓ 3 Butterfly clips
- ✓ Silk scarf
- ✓ Gel
- ✓ Coconut oil
- ✓ Hair spray
- ✓ Time

Here's how to create the hairstyle:

1. First, gently detangle the hair from ends to roots.
2. Make a part in the back of the head horizontally going across the head *(this should be about 3 inches above the nape of the neck)* then use the butterfly clip to secure the top portion of hair for later.
3. **Creating wave pattern for back section of hair**: start by making a vertical part about 1 inch away from the side hair line. Use the butterfly clip to section off the bigger portion of hair for later.
4. Take the smaller portion of hair and proceed to do a cornrow with it. Braid it all the way to the very end; place a small hair band around the end of the hair to keep it from unraveling. *Be very careful not secure the hair band too tight on the ends as this will cause unwanted breakage*.
5. Continue to make vertical parts about 1 inch away from the previous part. Then create your cornrows and secure the ends of the cornrows with small hair bands.
6. After you have completed all the cornrows on the bottom portion of hair. Take the setting lotion or mousse and evenly distribute it all over the cornrows from top to bottom. Now gather all the ends of the cornrows and make one braid. Secure the end with a small hair band. Loosely wrap the braid unto itself and place it against the head, take a few hair pins and secure against the head.
7. Undo the butterfly clip from the top portion of hair. Use the comb to gently comb through the hair and then use the soft brush to brush and smooth out the edges.
8. Secure this portion of hair by doing a criss cross wrap and secure the hair against the head with hair pins.
9. At this point take a silk or satin scarf and tie your hair. Wait until the next morning for the braids to completely set and dry so that you can style the hair.

10. **It's time to style the hair!** Remove the scarf from the head and undo the criss cross wrap from the top portion of hair and gently comb through the hair.
11. Make a side part at the front left side of the head about 1 ½ inches back. Turn the comb to the right and start parting the hair towards the ear (*make sure to stay parallel to the front hair line*) when you reach to the ear use one of the butterfly clip to section off this front portion of hair. Go back to the **side part** and place the comb right at the end of the part and begin to part the hair going towards the **left side of the head**, staying parallel to the hair line. Section off hair for now.
12. **It's time to style the hair!** Remove the scarf from the head and undo the criss cross wrap. Section off this portion of hair with a butterfly clip until later.
13. Take the middle portion of hair and section off with a butterfly clip as well. *See diagram for this style below: your parts and sections should resemble the diagram.*
14. **Sleeking Down The Two Front Sections Of hair.** Remove the butterfly clip from the right front side of hair, proceed to comb the hair so that it is laying nice and flat against the head then add some gel on this portion of hair. Take the soft brush and smooth out the gel on the hair. Do the same for left front side of hair.

(Take a look at the photo to get an idea of what I'm saying)

15. **Doing the pin curls**: Remove the butterfly clip from the middle portion of hair and gently comb through it to get rid of any tangles.
16. Start from the perimeter of the middle portion of hair and start grabbing small portions of hair and make a raised pin curl with each one. Do this by starting at the end of each small portion of hair that you grab, and start rolling the hair under itself until you reach the scalp. Then secure with a hair pin. *(Be sure to include the loose ends of the gel down hair, this should be at the side of the head. Also alternate the direction in which you roll the pin curls.)*
17. Lastly, undo the braids in the back. Place a few drops of coconut oil in the palm of your hand and them rub both hands together. (*When you are undoing the cornrows the coconut oil that's on the palm of your hands will help to keep the frizz down and also add some shine to the hair.)*

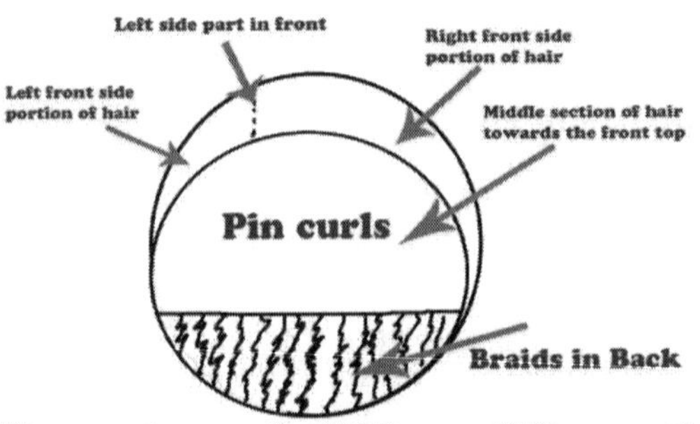

Back of The Head

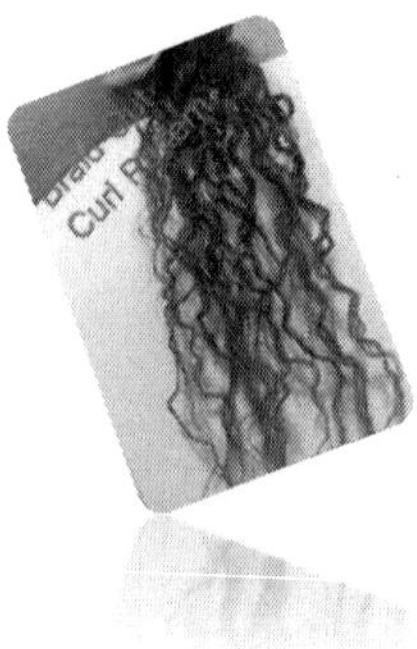

Starting with wet hair. *When starting out with wet hair simply braid the back while wet and roller set the top portion in different directions while wet also. Try wrapping a scarf around the perimeter of the hair and allow to dry overnight. When hair is completely dry remove the braids and the rollers and proceed with styling step # 10.*

Easy updo combo

Easy Updo Combo

This hairstyle requires the back of your hair to be braided and set for a while, perhaps overnight. Then undo the braids so that it has a textured look.)
I love this hairstyle so much because it has that messy look to it but it looks put together at the same time.

Items you'll need:

- ✓ Decorative flower clip
- ✓ Comb
- ✓ Hair pins
- ✓ 1 Butterfly clip
- ✓ Setting lotion
- ✓ Silk scarf
- ✓ Time
- ✓ Small hair bands
- ✓ Coconut oil
- ✓ Hair spray

Here's how to create the hairstyle:

1. First, make a part in the back across the head horizontally. This should be about 3 inches up from the nape of the neck.
2. Take the butterfly clip and secure the top portion of hair for later.
3. Take the comb and make a part vertically from top to bottom *(about 1 inch away from the side hair line).* Section off the larger portion of hair for a moment and proceed to cornrow the smaller portion of hair to the end then secure with a small hair band.
4. Undo the butterfly clip from the larger portion of hair (within the bottom section of hair) and make another vertical part and then proceed to make another cornrow. Continue this process of parting and cornrowing until you get to the other side of the neck. **the whole bottom portion of hair should be occupied with cornrows going across** Now gather the ends of the cornrows together and proceed to make one big braid. At this point, spray some setting lotion along the length of the braids. This will give it some hold.
5. **Set aside the top portion of hair properly** until the cornrows at the bottom are completely dry and you are ready to style the rest of the hair. *(Do this by undoing the butterfly clip from the top portion of hair. Use the comb to gently comb through the hair and then use the soft brush to brush and smooth out the edges. Secure this portion of hair by doing a criss cross wrap and secure the hair against the head with hair pins. Cover hair with a silk scarf.)*
6. **Ready to style? Let's go…**after the braids are set and dried, take the silk scarf off your head. Place a couple drops of coconut oil in the palm of your hands, and then rub then together (*this will eliminate some the*

frizz while undoing the cornrows). Proceed to start undoing the cornrows. Do so by starting from the ends of the hair and gently work your way up to the roots. When you're all done undoing all the cornrows, use your fingers to gently fluff the braid out hair. Take the butterfly clip and section off this portion of hair for now.

7. Proceed to the front of the head. Make a side part on the left side of the head going back about 2 inches. Comb out the hair on both sides of the **part**.
8. Start braiding the hair along the hair line on both sides of the **part**, starting from where the **part** is. STOP braiding the hair when you meet the **part** that is separating the top and bottom section of hair. Take a small hair pin and secure the cornrow right where the **part** is. When you've completed the cornrows on both sides of the head...go to the next step.
9. Lift up the top portion of hair *(90 degrees off the scalp)* and proceed to gently back comb the hair. This will create some volume.
10. Spray some hair spray on the roots of the hair and then place the hair down on the scalp *(*NOTE* the hair should resemble the shape of the top of a mountain*). Place a couple of hair pins to secure the hair in place right where the part separates the top & bottom sections of hair.
11. Remove the butterfly clip from the bottom section of hair (*the braid out hair*). Now hold the hair 90 degrees from the scalp. Next, gather any loose hair you see on the sides (*hair from the end of the 2 side braids and loose hair from the top section of hair) gather everything into one and begin to roll the hair as if you are about to do a raised pin curl. Roll the hair upwards, when you reach the scalp use the hair pins to secure the hair against the head (right where the part is, and then place the decorative flower on the side of the head).*

Side Braid
With Spiral
Curls

Side Braids with Spiral Curls

Items you'll need:

- ✓ Comb
- ✓ Soft brush
- ✓ Flexi rods *(select the size according to the length of your hair & also the size of the desired curl)*
- ✓ Setting lotion or mousse
- ✓ Hair pins
- ✓ Small hair band
- ✓ Silk scarf
- ✓ Time

Here's how to create the hairstyle:

1. First detangle hair completely and gently staring from ends to root.
2. Next, comb the entire head of hair to one side of the head.
3. Then, locate the front of the head right where you just comb over the hair. Start doing an inverted cornrow. When you reach about 2 inches of cornrowing, pull out a piece of hair *(make sure that it is hanging/falling naturally)*. After that, continue with the inverted cornrow. When you reach about 2 inches again, pull out another small piece of hair. Continue this process until you can no longer do an inverted cornrow.
4. At this point, braid the remaining hair to the end. Place a small hair band at the end of the braid so that it does not unravel.
5. Now coil or make a spiral pattern with the braided hair against the head right where the end of the inverted cornrow ends. Then secure the pattern with a hair pin. *See picture.*
6. For each one of the small sections of hair that you pulled out earlier, spray some setting lotion or place some mousse on it. Take the flexi rod and place the end of the hair you want to curl about ½ inch away from the end of the flexi rod. Roll the flexi rod about twice to secure the end of the hair. Continue to roll the flexi rod so that the hair can wrap around the rod, as you roll the rod the hair should be making a spiral pattern going upward to the root of the hair. When you reach about ½ inch from the other end of the flexi rod, simply bend and curve the end of the rod to secure it in place. Do the same to the other end. Place the silk scarf on your head to hold everything in place until the next morning.
7. When the hair is completely set and dried, start taking out the flexi rods by first undoing the ends of the rods then unravel the hair from the rod slowly.

Simple
Tuck & Curl

Simple Tuck & Curl

Items you'll need:

- ✓ Comb
- ✓ Soft brush
- ✓ Hair pins
- ✓ 2 butterfly clips
- ✓ Setting lotion or mousse
- ✓ Flexi rod
- ✓ Coconut oil
- ✓ Silk scarf
- ✓ Edge control (optional)
- ✓ Time

Here's how to create the hairstyle:

1. Be sure to gently detangle the hair from ends to roots.
2. Start about 3 inches away from the front hair line and start parting the hair horizontally across the head from ear to ear. Use the butterfly clip to section off the top portion of hair for a moment.
3. Start grabbing small sections of hair from the back portion of hair and comb through the hair to get rid of any tangles. Add some setting lotion or mousse to the hair and start to wrap the hair around the flexi rod. Secure the rod by bending each ends. Do this for each section of hair until you've completed the entire back section.
4. Undo the butterfly clip from the top section of hair and proceed to do a criss cross wrap with it and secure with a few hair pins. Place a silk scarf on the head and let the braids dry and set over night.
5. When the hair is dry completely, remove the silk scarf and undo the criss cross wrap.
6. **Styling the front top section of hair**. Make a part at the side of the head going back (*tip: use your eye as a maker to determine where to make the part*). You should now have a small section and big section of hair in the front. Section off the bigger section of hair with a butterfly clip for a moment.
7. Take the small section of hair and gently comb through the hair, take some edge control and apply some at the edges of the hair. Next brush the edges smooth. Now take the hair and begin to tuck the hair under itself. *(When tucking the hair remember to tuck in the back)*. Use the hair pins to secure the hair in place.
8. Undo the butterfly clip from the bigger section of hair and repeat the same steps.
9. **Styling the back section of hair**: Ok time for back! Remove the flexi rods from the back section of hair. (*Remember to unbend the ends of the flexi rods and then slowly unravel the hair from the rods*). Add some coconut oil in the palm of your hands then rub then together. Now separate each curl by splitting it into two and at the same time lightly and

gently run your fingers down the curl *(the coconut oil in the palms of your hands will help to keep the frizz down).*

If for some reason you do not want your hair out like that in the back, you can simply tuck the curled up section of hair under itself and then use hair pins to secure the hair in place.

If you have **natural hair** or you just simply **want a different curl pattern** in the back, try doing a two strand twist out, Bantu knot out, straw set or braid out for the desired look.

*Just add some moisturizer to the sections of hair then some setting lotion before twisting, braiding, or bantu knotting.

Accent Rope Braid With Curls

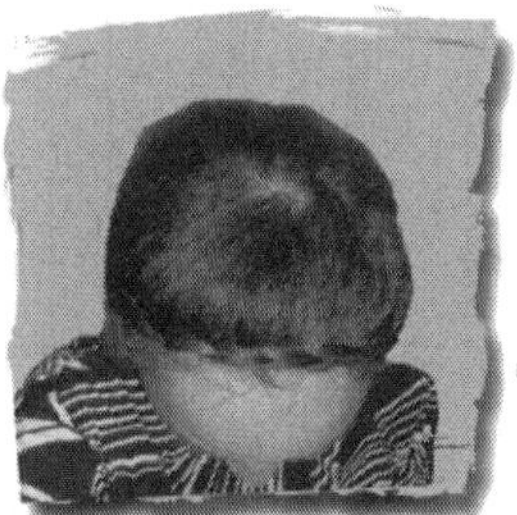

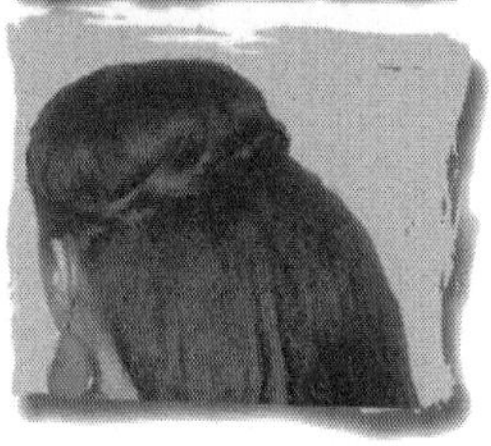

Accent Rope Braid with Curls

Items you'll need:

- ✓ Comb
- ✓ Hair pin
- ✓ Butterfly clip
- ✓ Flexi rods (*choose the size of the flexi rod according to the size of the curl you want to have*)
- ✓ Oil moisturizer
- ✓ Setting lotion or mousse
- ✓ Coconut oil
- ✓ Time

Here's how to create the hairstyle:

1. First detangle the hair gently.
2. Next part the hair in half, horizontally going across from ear to ear. Section off the bottom portion of hair for a moment with a butterfly clip.
3. Proceed to the top of the head and fan out the top portion of hair from the center. Use the comb to comb through the hair and smooth it out in the direction that you just fan the hair out.
4. Take a small section of hair from the side of the head close to the back of the head and begin cornrowing the hair. (*TIP: when cornrowing the hair, be sure to cover the PART that is separating the top section and bottom section of hair.*) Continue to cornrow the hair until you meet right back where you first begin the cornrow.
5. When you can't cornrow any more, just braid the remaining hair to the very end and secure the braid underneath the cornrow and then use a hair pin to secure the braid.
6. **Curling the back**: you have a few options when it comes to curling the back. Flexi rods, Bantu knot outs, braid outs, twist out, straw sets.

To achieve the spiral curl look, you can use flexi rods to curl the hair. Do so by first removing the butterfly clip from the bottom section of hair.

Then comb through the hair to detangle to it. Grab a small section of hair and apply a dab of moisturizer to the hair and then spray some setting lotion or add some mousse to the hair.

Place the end of the hair on the flexi rod about ½ inch to 1 inch away from the end of the rod. Roll the hair twice to secure it then begin to roll the hair in a spiral pattern on the rod, do so until there is no more hair to roll.

Bend both ends of the flexi rods in opposite directions to secure the rod.

Continue grabbing small sections of hair one at a time and rolling them on the rod then secure the rod in place by bending the ends in opposite directions. Be sure to secure the hair with a silk bonnet or scarf. Allow the hair to set and dry overnight.

TIP: when putting the flexi rods in your hair, starting from the bottom and work your way up (*it's easier and the rods won't get in the way as much*).

It's time to take out the flexi rods. First take off the silk scarf or bonnet, then take out the flexi rods one at a time. Remember to remove the rods slowly to avoid unwanted breakage.

Place a couple drops of coconut oil in the palm of your hands then rub your hands together *(this will keep the frizz down while separating the curls).*

Separate each curl into two curls to add more volume. While separating the curls run your fingers lightly down each one to apply a light coating of oil to the curl.

*For natural hair make sure the hair is saturated with water before applying the flexi rods.

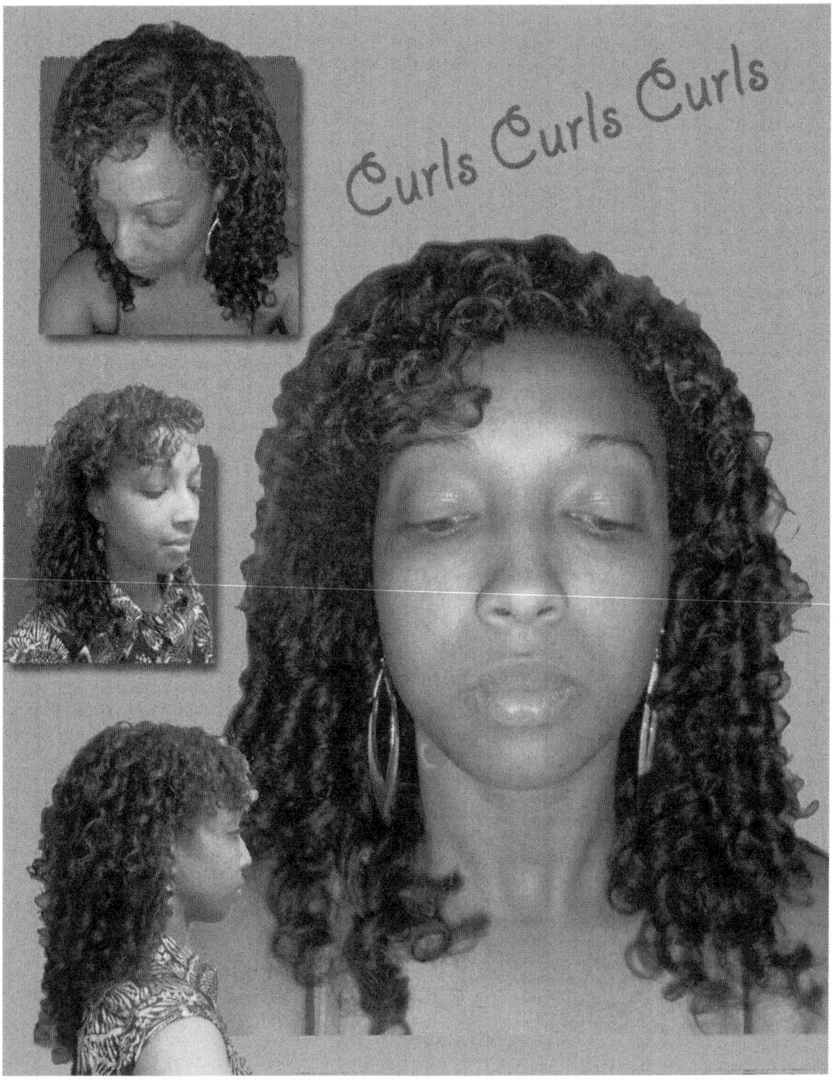
Curls Curls Curls

Flexi Rod Curls

Items needed:

- ✓ Flexi rod
- ✓ Butterfly clip
- ✓ Water spray bottle with water in it
- ✓ Mousse
- ✓ Comb
- ✓ Large satin or silk scarf
- ✓ Leave-in conditioner
- ✓ Coconut oil

Here's how to create the hairstyle:

1. First gently detangle the hair then wash the hair (*with detangling moisturizing shampoo and moisturizing conditioner*) in sections. Add some leave in conditioner to the hair after washing it.
2. Again gently detangle the hair and separate it in sections.
3. **Appling the flexi rods**. When applying the flexi rods start doing so from the nape of the neck. Just part a small section of hair and gently comb through it to smooth it out.
4. **Placing the hair on the flexi rod**. Please see "tips before styling" section at the beginning of this book.
5. Continue to make small parts and placing the hair on the flexi rod. As you work your way up to the front of the head spray some water on the section of hair that you are working with. This will help keep the hair wet and from drying out as you work your way up to the front. Also add the **mousse** to the hair before rolling the hair on the flexi rod.
6. When you reach to the front of the head, determine how you would like the hair to lay, *for instance, to the side, in the middle, or just going straight back),* parting the hair accordingly. Then continue to apply the hair on the flexi rod.
7. Place a large satin or silk scarf around the head and tie it. This will help to keep the flexi rods in place and also prevent any unwanted frizz.
8. **Removing the flexi rods**. Take the scarf off and put a pea size amount of coconut oil in the palm of your hand and lightly rub your hands together. *While removing the flexi rods and separating the curls the oil from your hand will help to keep the frizz down and plus add some sheen to your hair.*
9. If after removing the flexi rods from the hair you happen to like the curls the way they are, leave them just like that. However you if you would like a much fuller look, just gently separate each curls into two or three more. Be *careful not to create any frizz to the hair during this process.*

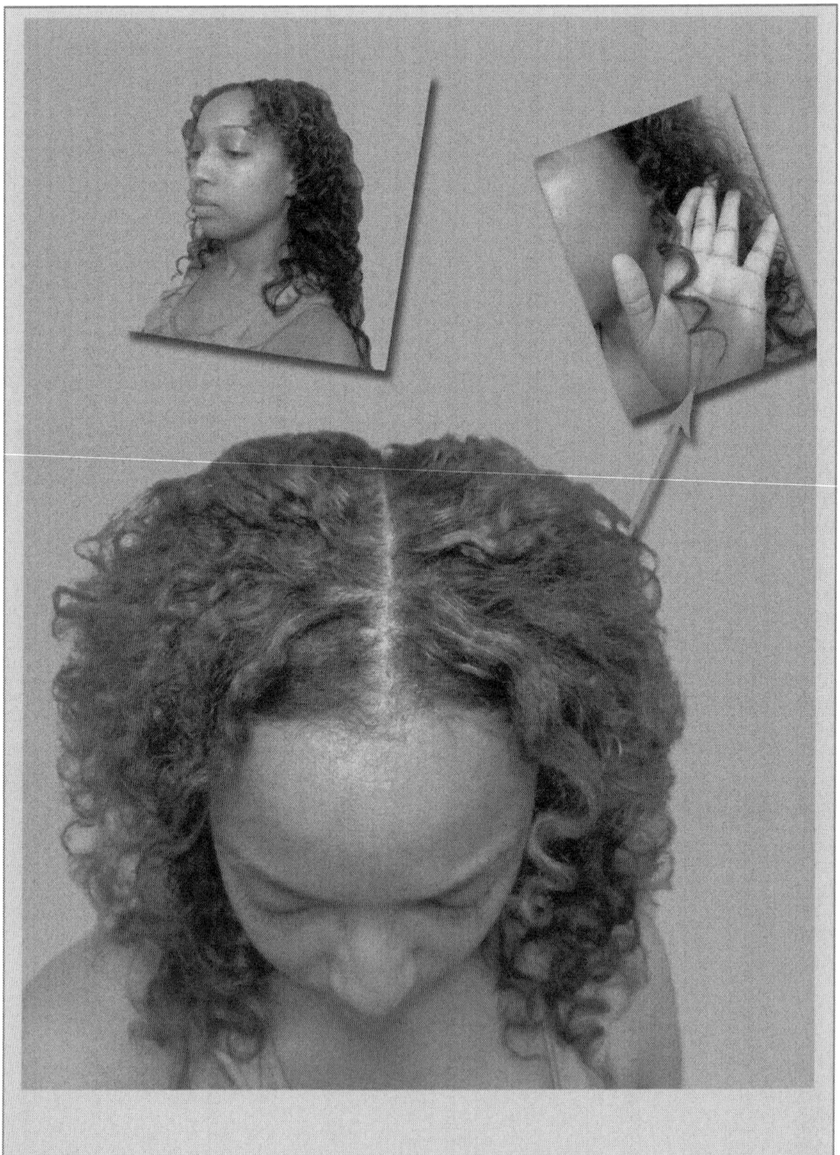

Braid Out And Bantu Knot Out Combo

This style can be done on wet or dry hair. I choose to set up the style on already dry hair.

Items you'll need:

- ✓ Comb
- ✓ Butterfly clip (s)
- ✓ Small cloth hair bands
- ✓ Setting lotion
- ✓ Coconut oil
- ✓ Moisturizer
- ✓ Silk scarf
- ✓ Time

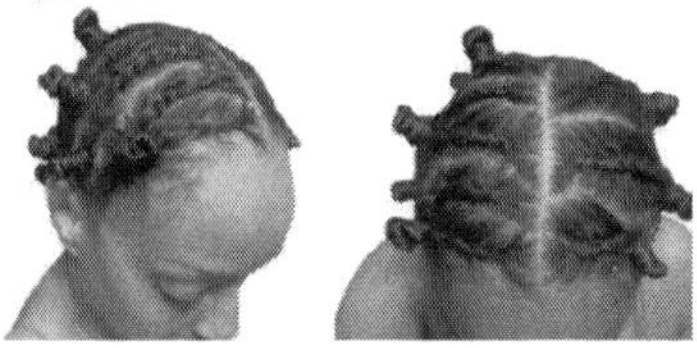

Here's how to create the hairstyle:

1. Gently comb through the hair to get rid of any tangles and then add moisturize to the hair.
2. Make a "U" shape part in the front middle of the head and section off the back section of hair with the butterfly clip(s)
3. Divide the "U" shape part into 2 two equal parts by parting the hair going back starting from the front of the head. Now you should have two equal parts. Take a butterfly clip and section off one half of the section for now.
4. Start to cornrow the hair into about 4 to 5 small section of hair and then at the end of each cornrow create a Bantu knot at each one.
5. Remove the butterfly clip from the other section of hair and follow step 4 for this section.
6. When the front is all braided. Proceed to the back section of hair remove the butterfly clip (s) and begin to make bantu knots
7. *use your hand not the comb to grab sections of hair to be Bantu knotted. All the Bantu knots should be the same size and randomly placed on the head. *This will give the Bantu knot out a more natural look to it when the style is completed. Also, after each Bantu knot, place a small hair band around the base of the Bantu knot to keep the hair from unraveling.*
8. For each section of hair that you grab, gently comb through the hair to smooth it out and spray a little setting lotion along the hair from root to end. Proceed with the Bantu knot. *See how to Bantu knot instructions in the "tips before styling section".*
9. Tie a silk scarf on the head until the next morning when the hair is completely dry.
10. **Styling the hair**. Start from the nape of the neck and start to undo all the Bantu knots one by one working your way up to the front of the head. (*after removing the cloth hair band from the bantu knot, simply twist the base of the knot the opposite direction you twist it to secure it*)
11. When all the Bantu knots are undone, undo the cornrows as well. Be careful not to cause frizz to the hair.

12. Simply adjust the hair to your liking and use your hair to cover over any parts you see.

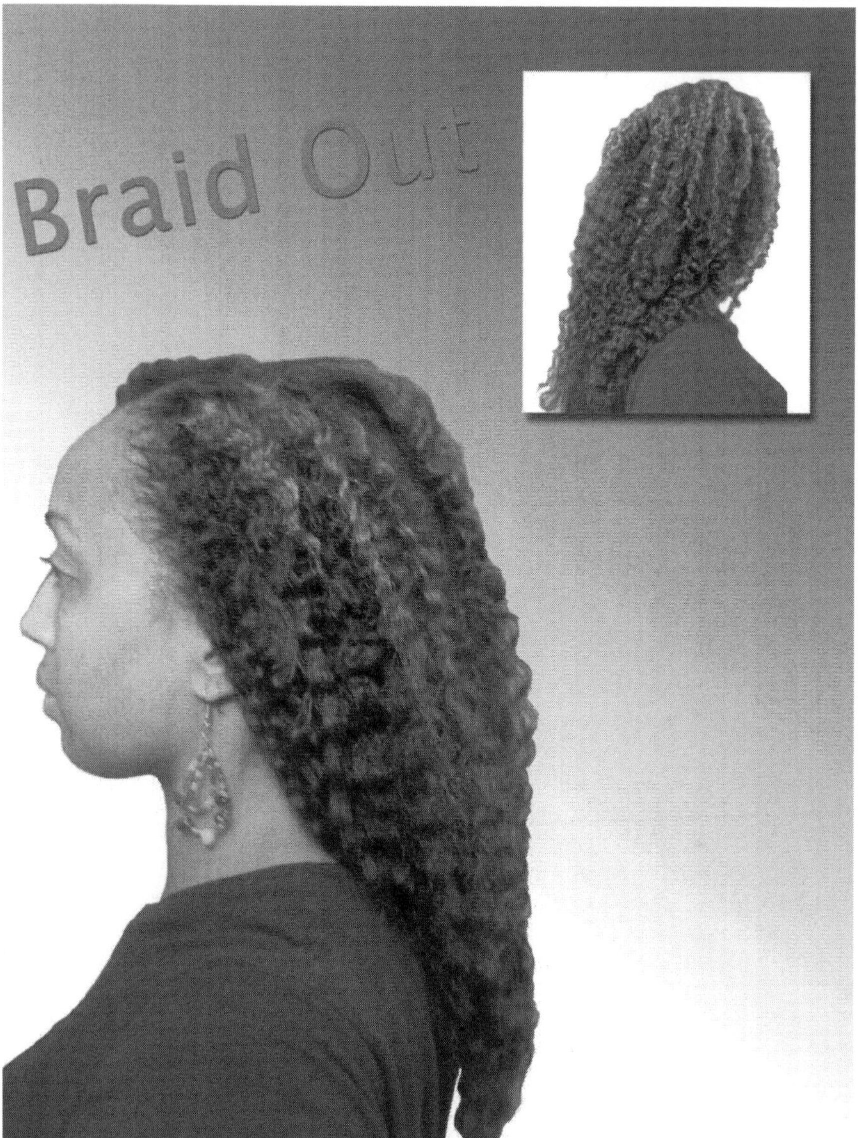
Braid Out

Braid Out

Items you'll need:

- ✓ Comb
- ✓ Coconut oil & olive oil
- ✓ Moisturizing shampoo
- ✓ Moisturizing conditioning
- ✓ Leave-in condition
- ✓ Setting lotion or mousse
- ✓ Spray water bottle water
- ✓ Silk scarf
- ✓ Butterfly clips
- ✓ Hair
- ✓ Shower cap
- ✓ Time

Here's how to create the hairstyle:

- **Before you begin, add some of the coconut oil and olive oil to the conditioner. This is good for extra conditioning for the hair.**

1. **Detangle the hair** gently and divide the hair into 4 sections, section off each section of hair with butterfly clips.
2. Go in the shower to wash the hair. (*When washing NEVER pill the hair on top of the head, this only encourage the hair to tangle and lead to breakage.*)
3. **First shampoo the hair**. While cleansing the hair with the shampoo grasp a section of hair at a time from the root and run your hands down the length of the hair a few times. Do this for the whole head in sections. After you are done with each section, just clip each section out of the way with butterfly clips.
4. **Conditioning the hair**. Follow step # 3 for conditioning the hair. Apply and leave the conditioner mixer in the hair and place the shower cap over the head. (*Optional: you can choose to go under a hooded dryer for about 30 min. if you choose are not choose to go under the dryer still leave the conditioner in the hair for 30 min.*) After the 30 min. are up take off the shower cap and rinse out the conditioner then wring out the excess water from the hair
5. Now apply the **leave in conditioner** to the hair.
6. **Braiding the hair**. Decide how you would like the braid out style to look. Would you like the hair to lay on the head going straight back? Or would you like a part at the side of the head or in the middle?
   Now part the hair accordingly. In the picture, I have my hair parted at the side so I'll be giving you instructions how to position the braids.

First **make smaller braids** or cornrow around the **perimeter of the hair** and around the **part.** This will give more definition around the hair line. After you braid or cornrow the perimeter of the hair start braiding the rest of the hair. **Before you braid each section of hair, make sure the hair is wet with water if not use the spray water bottle with water in it to wet the hair and then add some mousse or the setting lotion. Use the comb to comb and smooth out the hair before braiding it.** Don't bother to use the comb to part the hair for your sections, just use your free hand to take off sections of hair to make the braids. And also each row of braids should be layered like bricks, meaning that the braid above should be covering the **part** below (*this makes for a more natural look when the braids are taken out).*

Be sure to braid the hair all the way down to the ends so that ends can curl as well. Or place small perm rods at the ends

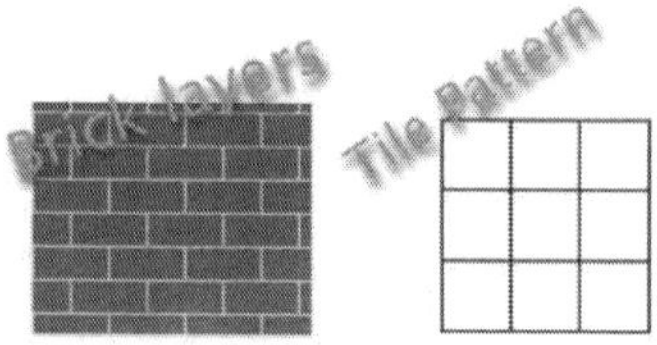

7. Secure the hair with a hair band or hair pins then place the silk scarf over the head. Wait over night until the hair is completely dry.
8. **Removing the braids**. Remove the silk scarf and anything else you placed in the hair. Apply a dab of coconut oil in the palm of your hand and lightly rub your hands together. Now begin to gently undo all the braids starting from the ends and work your way up to the root.
9. When all braids are completely undone gently fluff and arrange the hair to your liking.

Braid Out Updo

Braid Out Updo #1

For this hairstyle you must follow the instructions for the previous braid out hairstyle to achieve this particular textured look.

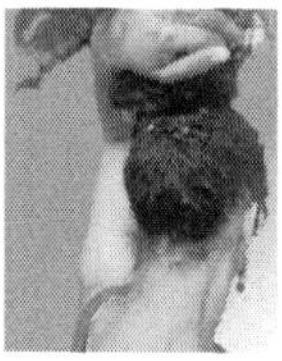

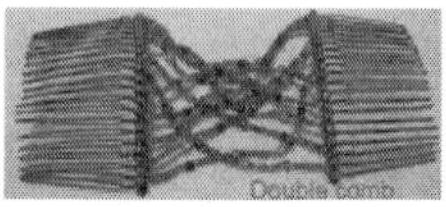

Items you'll need:

- ✓ Double comb clip
- ✓ Decorative flower clip
- ✓ Duck bill clip
- ✓ Hair pins
- ✓ Edge control or gel

Here's how to create the style:

1. First take out a piece of hair from the front of the head for the bang (optional) use the duck bill clip to section off the bang area for now.
2. Gather the hair like a ponytail and place it high up on the head.
3. Take the double comb clip place and secure it in the root of the hair under the base of the ponytail. One comb on each side. *See picture above.*
4. Let go of the hair so that the hair falls down. Gently fluff and fix the hair to your liking.
5. Use the hair pin to secure any hair that is sticking up.
6. Take the decorative clip and place it at the front of the ponytail right at the base.
7. Now undo the duck bill clip from the bang area and adjust it to your liking.

Braid Out Updo

Braid Out Updo #2
Again, for this hairstyle you must follow the instructions for the "Braid Out" hair style to achieve this particular texture.

Items you'll need:

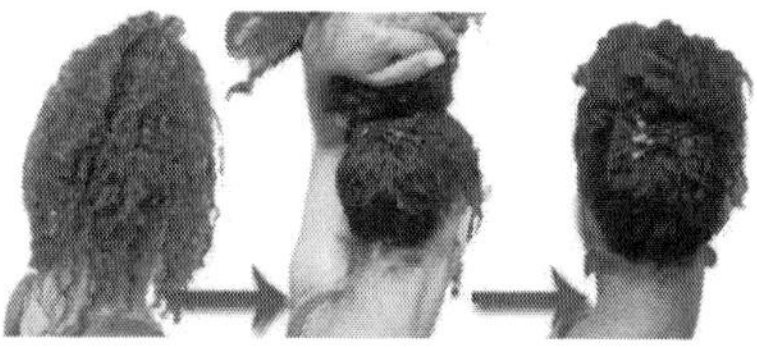

- ✓ Decorative double comb clip
- ✓ Hair pins
- ✓ Coconut oil
- ✓ Hair spray (optional)

Here's how to create the style:
1. After you have taken out all the braids put a dab of coconut oil in the palm of your hand and lightly rub your hands together.
2. Begin to fluff out the braids for a fuller look. (*Remember that the coconut oil is on the palm of your hand so this will help to keep the frizz down while handling the braid out. And also at the same time add some shine to the hair.*)
3. Gather all the hair into a high ponytail (*close to the front of the head*).
4. Take the decorative double comb clip and place it at the base of the ponytail in the back. Do so by securing the combs in the root of the hair one at a time on both sides. *Please see picture above for how the clips are placed.*
5. **Bringing the hair forward**. Look at the picture above again. Pick up the ponytail and bring it forward to the front of the head then adjust the hair so that it is place to the side a little.
6. Take the hair pins and start to pin and secure the loose hair down. Adjust the hair to your liking.
7. Optional: if you feel you need a little hold to the hair, try spraying a little hair spray on the hair. Be careful not to get the hair spray in your eyes and don't spray too much.

Swoop Around Cornrow With Stylish Side Bang

Items you'll need:

- ✓ Comb
- ✓ Soft brush
- ✓ Hair pin
- ✓ Butterfly clip
- ✓ Small hair band (optional)
- ✓ Moisturizer
- ✓ Edge control

Here's how to create the hairstyle:

1. First comb through the hair gently to get rid of any tangles.
2. Next, make a side part on the left side of the head in the front going back about 3 inches long. Then turn the comb towards the right ear and begin to make a part going towards the right ear. Take this front section of hair that you just parted off and section it off with a butterfly clip.
3. **Cornrowing the remaining portion of hair in the back**. Comb through this portion of hair, add some moisturizer to it from root to end. Locate the side front part of the head and begin to make an inverted cornrow to the hair. Work your way all way to the back and finish off the inverted cornrow on the other side in a downward direction.
4. Braid the remaining hair to the end and secure with a hair band.
5. Undo the butterfly clip from the front section of hair and comb it to smooth it out.
6. Hold the section of hair with a little tension from the end of the hair pointing down. Make a loop at the end and begin to roll the hair upward until you reach the scalp.
7. Take the hair pin and place it between the loop and secure it at the root of the hair against the scalp. Apply some edge control on the edges for a neater look. **(Optional) you can add braiding hair while braiding to add more length if you like.**

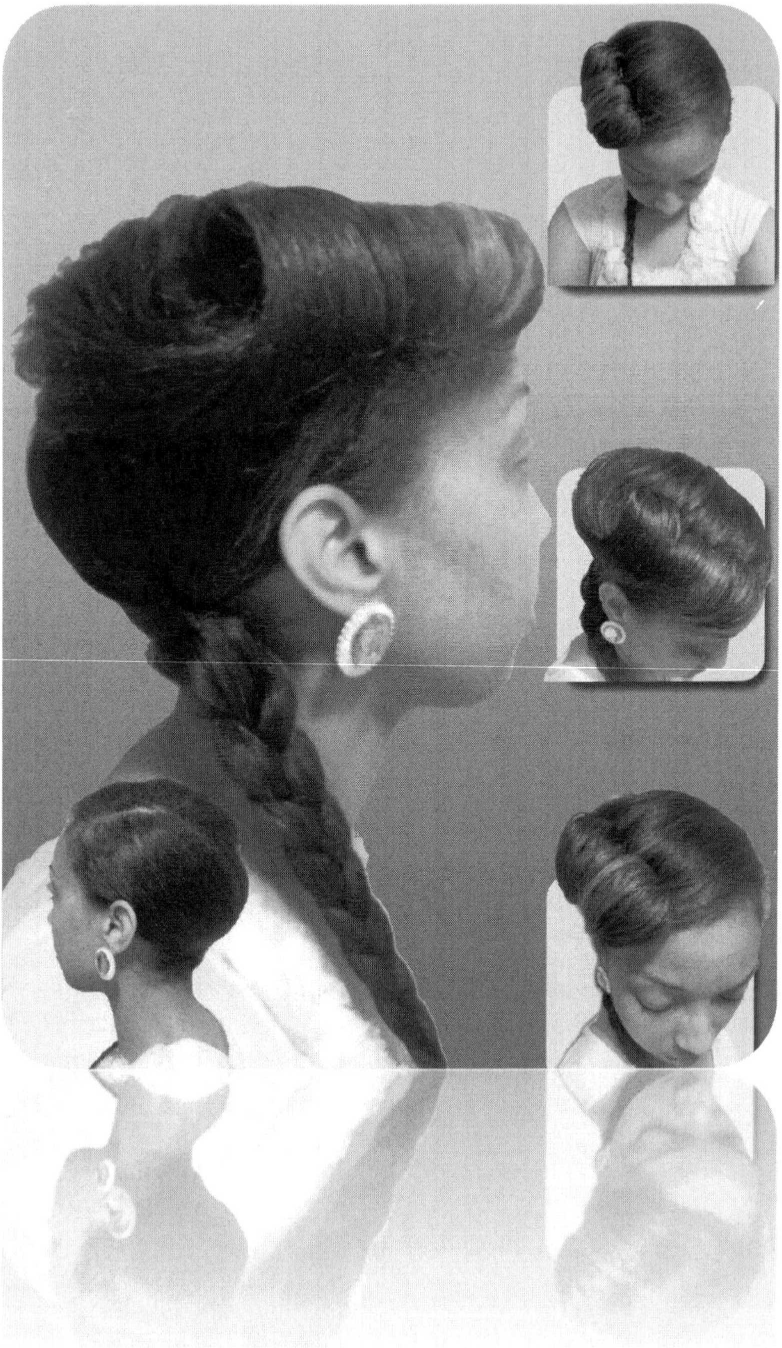

Side Braid With Oversize Side Pin Curl

This hairstyle is kind of similar to the previous style. The difference between the two hairstyles are that the bang area is bigger and the back portion of hair is swooped and braid in a side braid in this style.

Items you'll need:

- ✓ Comb
- ✓ Soft brush
- ✓ Large hair pins
- ✓ Butterfly clip
- ✓ 2 duck bill clips (for holding the hair)
- ✓ Small hair band (optional)
- ✓ Moisturizer
- ✓ Edge control
- ✓ Hair spray

Here's how to create the hairstyle:

1. Comb through the hair gently to get rid of any tangles.
2. Make a nice big "U" shape part at the front center of the head *(about 4 inches wide and 4 inches going back).* Section off this portion of hair with a butterfly clip for now.
3. Proceed to the back section of hair and gently comb through it. Apply some edge control to the edges and use the soft brush to smooth it out.
4. As you brush and smooth the hair simultaneously swoop it to one side of the head and braid the hair down to the end. (*If you have short or medium hair and would like to have more length to the braid, simply add some braiding hair and proceed with the braid.*)
5. Next, undo the butterfly clip from the top section of hair and gently comb and smooth out the hair.
6. Take a duck bill clip and slide it at the roots within this section of hair. Take another duck bill clip and do the very same thing to the opposite side of this section of hair. (*The clips will help to keep the hair in place while you are working with it.*)
7. Ok, now hold the hair from the ends with a little tension. Make a loop and begin to roll the hair upward to the scalp. When you reach to the scalp secure the loop or curl against the head by sliding a large hair pin between the loop and the root of the hair. Do the very same thing to the other side.
8. Now slide out the duck bill clips that were temporarily holding the hair in place.
9. If for some reason you feel the curl needs a little hold to it, simply spray a little hair spray on it.
10. Lastly, grasp the braid by the root or base and twist it upward once then secure it in this position with a hair pin.

Side Braid With A Twist

Side Braid with a Twist

Items you'll need:

- ✓ Comb
- ✓ Soft brush
- ✓ Butterfly clip
- ✓ Hair pins
- ✓ Gel or edge control

Here's how to create the hairstyle:

1. Comb through the hair gently to get rid of any tangles.
2. **Parting off the bang area**: Make a "U" shape part at center front section of the head, about 2 inches wide and 2 ½ inches going back. Use a duck bill clip to section off this hair for now.
3. Locate the left side of the head and begin to do an inverted cornrow. Cornrow the hair until you reach the back of the head then transition the cornrow to a 2 strand flat twist. Twist until you reach the ear then finish twisting the hair to the end.
4. Take the twisted hair and place it against the side of the head in the shape of a spiral. Use the hair pins to secure the hair in place.
5. Remove the butterfly clip from the bang area and use the comb to comb and smooth it out. Next swoop it to the side and use the hair pin(s) to secure it the hair on the side.

TIP: If you have shorter hair and would like to create this hairstyle, simply add some braiding hair that matches your own hair texture and color while braiding your hair around your head.

Pretty High Bang
With Two Oversize Bantu Knots

Pretty High Bang with Oversized Bantu Knots

Items you'll need:

- ✓ Comb
- ✓ Hair pins
- ✓ Gel or edge control
- ✓ Hair spray
- ✓ 2 hair bands
- ✓ Soft brush
- ✓ Butterfly clips
- ✓ Weaving hair (*same texture & Color as your own hair*)

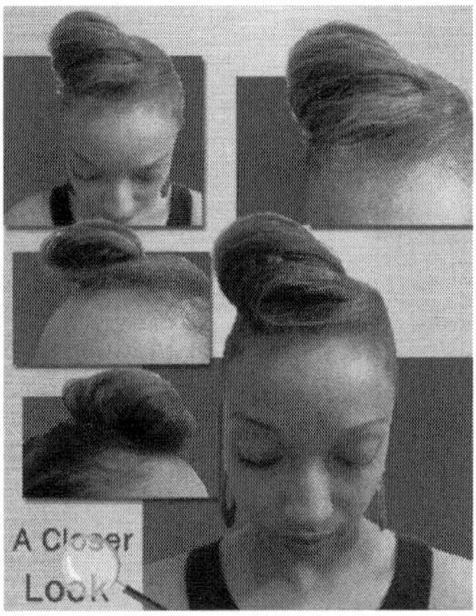

Here's how to create the hairstyle:

1. Gently comb through the hair and get rid of any tangles and knots you might have.
2. Make a "U" shape part at the front center of the head (*4 inches wide and 4 inches going back*). Use the butterfly clip to section off this section of hair for now.
3. **Parting the hair in the back**. You are going to divide the hair into 2 equal parts. Do this by start parting the hair from the side of the head. Then work your way to the back and around the other side of the head. After you're done parting the hair check to see if the part and section of hair are straight and even. Now section off one section of hair with the butterfly clip for now.
4. Gather the other section of hair into one; make sure that the edges are smooth. Place the hair band around the hair to secure the ponytail in place.
5. Take a piece of the weaving hair and wrap it around the base of the ponytail. Wrap the hair around the base until you have the desired thickness cut the weft then secure the hair with hair pins.
6. Make a two strand twist with the ponytail weave you just created then begin to wrap it around the base of the ponytail. When there is no more hair to wrap, simply secure the hair with hair pins.
7. Remove the butterfly clip from the other section of hair and repeat steps # 4-6
8. **Styling the bang/oversize pin curl**. Remove the butterfly clip from the bang area. Comb and smooth it out to the side. Use the soft brush to gently brush and smooth it out a little more.
9. Make a loop at the end of the hair and begin to roll the hair up towards the head. When you reach the scalp use large hair pins to secure the hair,

do so by placing hair pins through the loop and the root of the hair below. Do so to both sides of the pin curl.

10. Spray some of the hair spray on the pin curl you just created. The hair spray will help to keep the shape of the curl without making it too hard.

Double Side Tuck

Double Side Tuck

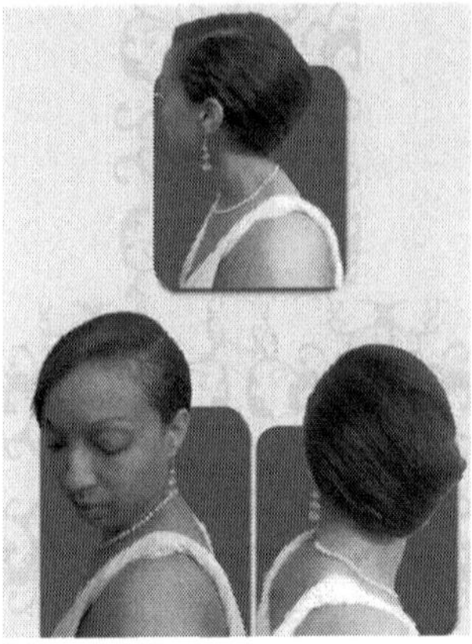

Items you'll need:

- ✓ Comb
- ✓ Soft brush
- ✓ Hair pins
- ✓ Butterfly clip
- ✓ Hair spray (optional)
- ✓ Gel or edge control

Here's how to create the style:

1. Comb through the hair gently to get rid of any tangles.
2. Make a side part on the left side of the head at the front going back about 4 inches. Stop then turn the comb to the right and continue to make a straight part going towards the ear, then stop. Section off the other portion of hair with the butterfly clip for now.
3. Take the front section of hair you just parted and take the comb to comb through the hair then use the soft brush to brush and smooth it out even more.
4. Next neatly roll and tuck the hair under itself close to the head *(see picture)*, and proceed to secure the hair with hair pins.
5. Now, undo the butterfly clip from bottom section of hair use, then comb and swoop it around the other side of the head, just where you tuck the other section of hair *(see picture)*.
6. Now begin to tuck this section of hair as well (horizontally) (*see picture*). Then secure the hair with hair pins.
7. At this point add some gel or edge control to the sides and edges of the hair then use the soft brush to brush the edges and sides to smooth.
8. Optional: You can use the hair spray to help tame those fly aways. Simply use the soft brush to first brush the hair that is sticking up then lightly spray the hair spray on it. Be careful not get the spray into your eyes.

Flat Twist
Pin Curls

Flat Twist Pin Curl

Items you'll need:

- ✓ Comb
- ✓ Soft brush
- ✓ Gel
- ✓ Hair pins
- ✓ Butterfly clips
- ✓ Decorative double comb
- ✓ Small hair pins
- ✓ Hair spray (optional)

Here's how to create the style:

1. Comb through the hair to get rid of any tangles.
2. Next start to make a part from the back of the ear going across the head horizontally; stop when you get to the other ear. Section off the back section of hair with a butterfly clip for now.
3. **Creating the flat twist**. Determine how wide you would like the flat twist to be and make a part accordingly (*If you would like the size of the flat twist to be 1 inch wide, then the first part should be 1 inch away from the hair line on the side.*) Make the part going back vertically. After you've made the part for the first flat twist, section off the rest of the hair with a butterfly clip for now.
4. Now take the small section of hair you are going to flat twist and add some gel to the root of the hair and along the length of the hair as well (*see the instruction for how to flat twist in the "tips before styling" section*)
5. **Creating the heatless curls in the back**. After you've completed all the flat twist, remove the butterfly clip from the back of the head. Comb through the hair again and gather all the hair into a high ponytail close to the flat twists.
6. Use the decorative double comb and place it underneath the ponytail right at the base. One comb at a time on both sides.
7. Begin to create pin curls alongside the flat twists. All pin curls should be facing the front of the head. (*please see how to do pin curls in the "tips before styling" section*)
8. Take a small amount of gel and place it in the palm of your hand, lightly rub your hands together then apply it to the nape of the neck, then use the soft brush to brush and smooth the hair.
9. Optional: you can use the hair spray to add a little hold to the pin curls.

Bread loaf Hair

Items you'll need:

- ✓ Comb
- ✓ Soft brush
- ✓ Hair pins
- ✓ Hair band
- ✓ Banana clip
- ✓ Hair spray
- ✓ Gel
- ✓ Butterfly clip

Here's how to create the styles:

1. Gently comb through the hair to get rid of any tangles you might have.
2. Make a part from ear to ear horizontally across the head (*the width of the part should be about 2 to 3 inches wide*) then section off the back section of hair for now.
3. Tuck the front section of hair under itself away from the face and secure with hair pins. Check to see if there is any hair sticking out. If not, go ahead and spray the hair spray on the front section of hair and then use the palm of your hands to further sculpt the hair into place.
4. Next undo the butterfly clip from the back section of hair. Gather the hair into a ponytail and place the hair band around the ponytail to hold the hair in place for now. Apply a small amount of gel around the hair line and use the soft brush to brush and smooth the hair.
5. Take the banana clip and place it horizontally around the base of the ponytail and clip it into place. Then remove the hair band from the base of the ponytail.
6. Fill up any gaps in the banana clip with your hair by gently pulling the hair by the root to both sides of the banana clip.
7. Now tuck the hair under itself and use the hair pins to secure the hair in place. Also cover the ends of the banana clip with your hair by adjusting the hair then secure the hair with hair pins as well.

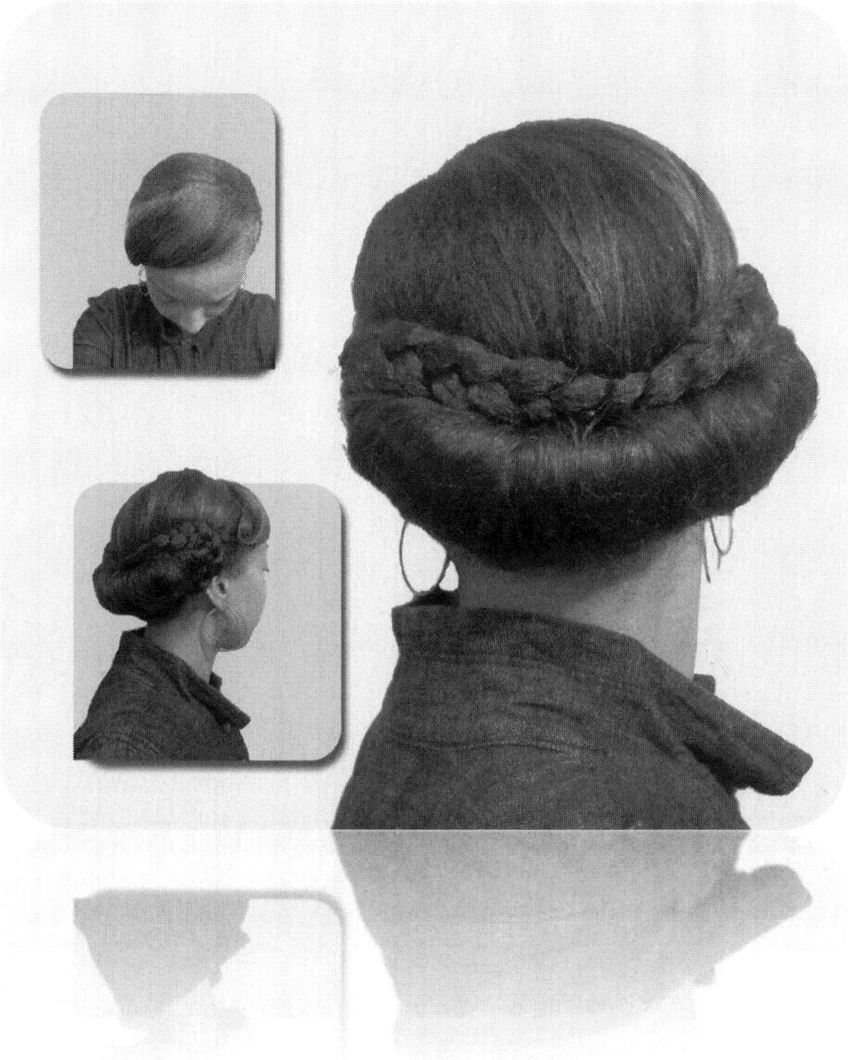

Roll with accent braid

Items you'll need:

- ✓ Comb
- ✓ Soft brush
- ✓ Lots of hair pins
- ✓ Butterfly clip
- ✓ Small hair bands (*the same color as your own hair*)
- ✓ Braiding hair (*same color and texture as your own hair hair*)

Here's how to create the hairstyle:

1. Comb through the hair gently to get rid of any tangles.
2. Part off a small section in the front of the hair for the bang and section off this section with a butterfly clip.
3. Take out the braiding hair from the package and divide it into two. Braid and secure the end with a small hair band and set it aside for now.
4. Take the other portion of braiding hair and make it into the shape of a log. (*By folding the hair into half three times then place small rubber bands around it to hold its shape in place. *make the size of the log according to the length and thickness of your own hair* if the log is too big and you have thin or shorter hair, your hair won't adequately cover the log.*)
5. Place the log horizontally against the head and use a few hair pins to secure the log onto the head.
6. Next, take the hair from underneath the log and bring it up and over the log to cover it entirely. Secure the hair that is covering the log with hair pins.
7. Take the pre braided hair you braided earlier and place it along and around the contour of the log. Again, use the hair pins to secure the braided hair in place.
8. Take the butterfly clip from the bang area and comb and smooth it out with the brush. Fold it under itself towards the face and lay it flat on its side and secure with a couple of hair pins.

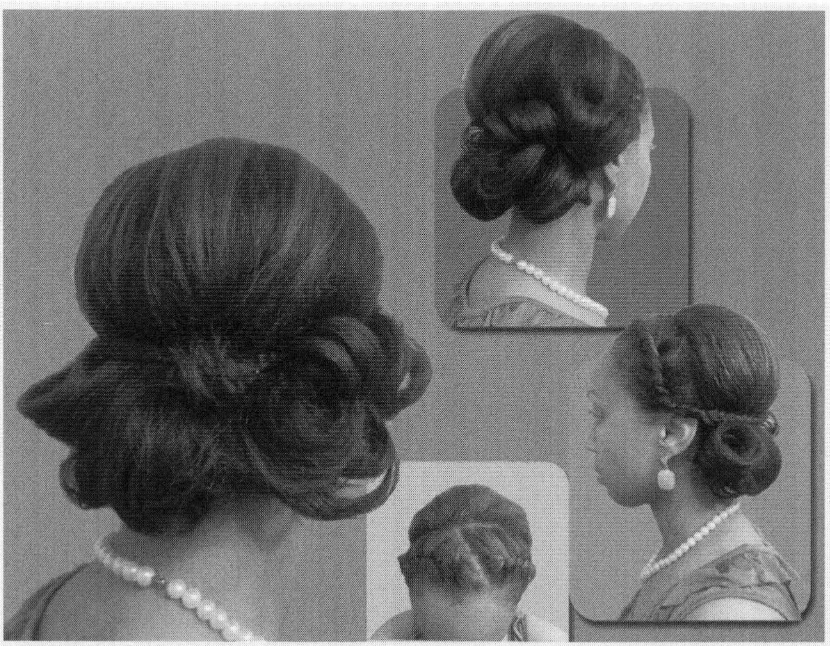

Flower Bottom

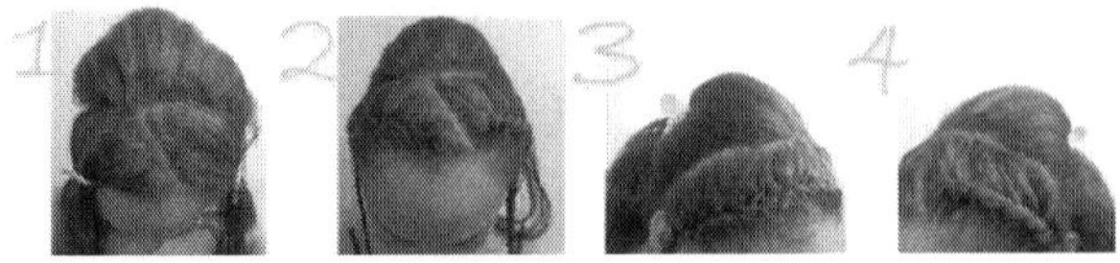

Items you'll need:

- ✓ Comb
- ✓ Hair pins
- ✓ Braiding hair
- ✓ Clip on hair pieces *(same color and texture as your own hair)*
- ✓ Hair spray *(optional)*
- ✓ Butterfly clips
- ✓ Soft brush
- ✓ Small hair band *(same color as your own hair)*

Here's how to create the hairstyle:

1. Gently comb through the hair to get rid of any tangles.
2. Make a part in front of the head from ear to ear horizontally about 2 to 3 inches wide. Section off the back portion of hair with the butterfly clip for now.
3. Make a diagonal part in the center of the front portion of hair. *Please see photo # 1 above*. And section off the left section of hair with a butterfly clip for now.
4. Take a small piece of braiding hair (*about 20 inches long*) and split it into 3 pieces, pick up 3 small pieces of hair right at the diagonal part within the right section of hair. Then line up the 3 pieces of braiding hair with 3 pieces from your OWN hair by placing the braiding hair on top and then proceed to do an inverted **cornrow**. Braid the hair all the way to the end.
5. Remove the butterfly clip from the left side of the head and take a small piece of braiding hair from the bunch of hair (*about 20 inches long*) pick up 2 small pieces of hair close to the diagonal part within the left section of hair, proceed to attach the braiding hair to the 2 small pieces of hair that you pick up earlier from your own hair and begin to create a Senegalese twist *(please see how to do Senegalese twist in the "tips before styling" section*). **Twist** the hair about 3 times and then lay it down within the section of hair and begin to do a 2 strand flat twist. Twist the hair to the end.
6. Proceed to the back section of hair and remove the butterfly clip. Add the clip-on hair pieces to the hair – amount depends on the volume and length you would like to achieve. Split the hair into 2 (top and bottom) for a moment and proceed to gently back comb the roots of the top section of hair, towards the back (this *will create some volume to the top*). Then use the hair spray to spray the hair where you just back comb. Lay the hair back down and gently brush the top with the soft brush to smooth out the hair (*be careful not to flatten down the hair*) then spray some hair spray on the top as well.
7. Take the comb and begin to comb through the rest of the hair gently to smooth it out.

8. Take the tail or the ends of the braided portion of the extension hair from the front and bring them around the sides to the back. Use the small hair band to secure them like a ponytail. Then create a pin curl with the rest of the braided hair and secure with a hair pin.
9. For the rest of the loose hair on the bottom, begin to pin curl the hair from little pieces of hair at a time and use the hair pins to secure. Remember when pin curling the hair, roll some towards the top and some towards the bottom. *See main photo.*

The "V" Braid

The "V" Braid

Items you'll need:

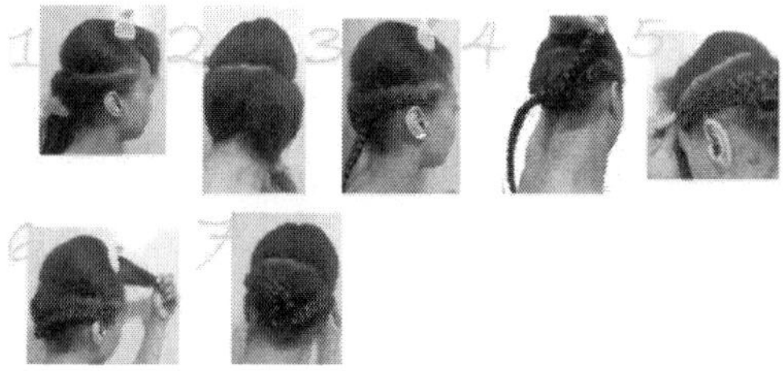

- ✓ Comb
- ✓ Soft brush
- ✓ 2 Butterfly clip
- ✓ Hair pins
- ✓ Hair band
- ✓ Hair spray (optional)
- ✓ Gel or edge control

Here's how to create the hairstyle:

1. First comb through the hair gently to get rid of any knots and tangles.
2. Next make a "U" shape part at the front of the head (*8 inches wide and 9 inches going back*) then section of this portion of hair with a butterfly clip for now.
3. Part the back section of hair into half (vertically). Section off the right section of hair with a butterfly clip.
4. Locate the front of the head and begin to cornrow the left section of hair. (*Stay close to the side hair line when cornrowing the hair.*) Braid the hair all the way to the end.
5. Proceed to the opposite side of the head (the right side) and remove the butterfly clip. REPEAT step # 4 for this section of hair.
6. Take both ends of the braids and criss cross them over each other and lay them above the cornrows on opposite sides. Use hair pins to secure the hair in place.
7. Proceed to the top portion of the hair and remove the butterfly clip and begin to gently comb through the hair to smooth it out.
8. Lift the hair about 90 degrees off the head and start to gently back comb the roots of the hair. (*This will create a little volume to the hair.*) Use the hair spray to spray the roots for a little hold.
9. Lay the hair back down and smooth out the top by gently brushing it with the soft brush. *(Be careful not to flatten the top, you want to have a little height.)*
10. Now take the hair band and secure the hair at the base. Create a bun from the rest of the loose hair and then secure the bun with hair pins. (*You can make a bun with the loose hair or you can 2 strand twist it and then wrap it around the base of the hair and then secure it with hair pins.*)
11. Take a small amount of gel or edge control and apply it to the edges of your hair in the front, and use the soft brush to smooth it out.
12. Look in the mirror and adjust the hair if anything is crooked.

TIP: If your hair is short, just add clip in hair extensions to the top section of hair and braiding hair to the sides while braiding.

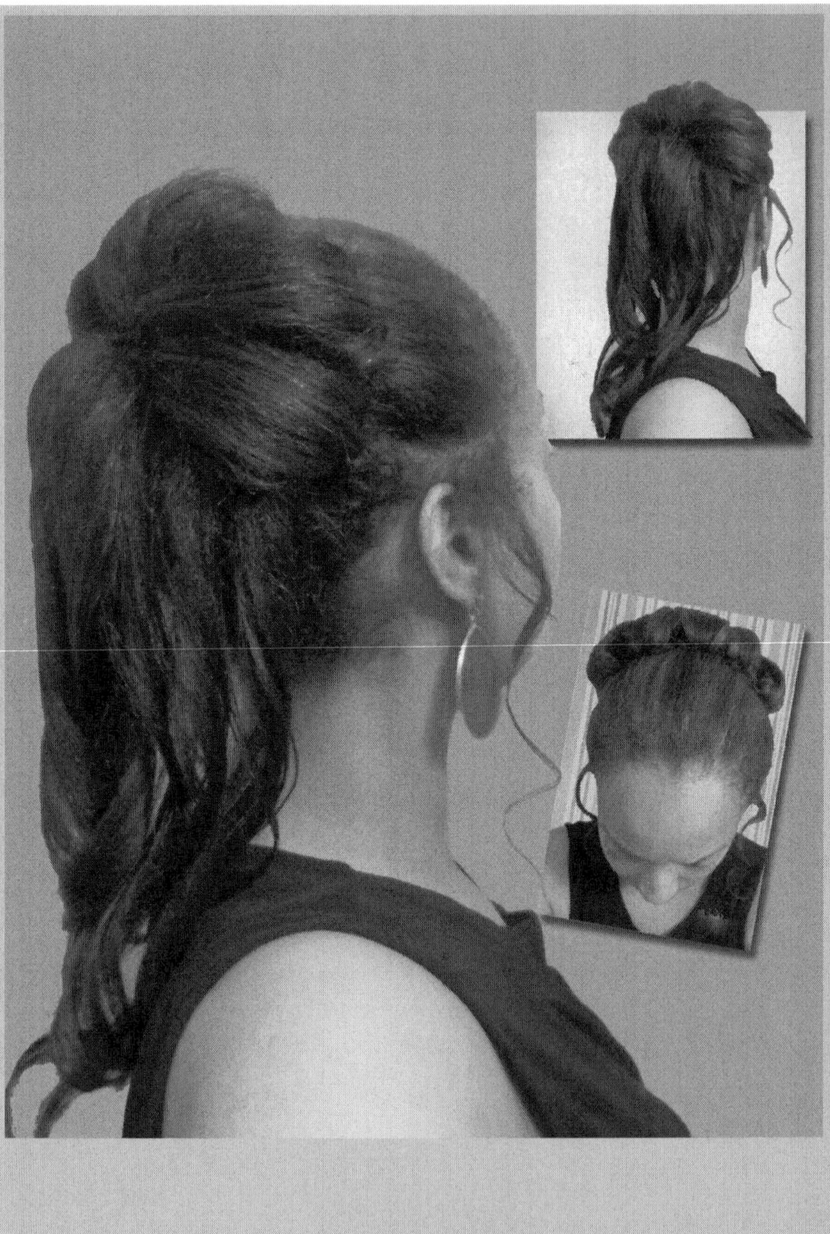

Cascading Curls

Items you'll need:

- ✓ 1 Banana clip
- ✓ Hair pins
- ✓ Flexi rods
- ✓ Mousse
- ✓ Gel
- ✓ Coconut oil
- ✓ Large silk or satin scarf
- ✓ Hair band
- ✓ Butterfly clip
- ✓ Comb
- ✓ Soft brush
- ✓ Time

Here's how to create the hairstyle:

1. Gently comb through the hair to get rid of any tangles.
2. Separate two small pieces of hair from the sides of your head right where the temples are. Use the butterfly clip to hold the rest of the hair out of the way for now.
3. **Curling the sides**: use the comb to comb and smooth out the hair then apply some mousse to it. Next, take a small flexi rod and begin to roll the hair on it in a spiral shape. When you reach the scalp, secure both ends of the flexi rod by bending and curling the ends. REPEAT step # 3 for the other side.
4. Remove the butterfly clip from the rest of the hair. Apply some gel around the perimeter of the hair. Use the soft brush to brush and smooth the edges, and proceed to gather the hair into a ponytail. Place a hair band around the base of the ponytail.
5. Take the banana clip and place it around the base of the ponytail horizontally and clip it into place. Remove the hair band from the base of the ponytail.
6. Evenly distribute the hair in the banana clip by gently pulling the roots of the hair to the ends of the banana clip on both sides.
7. Next, divide the hair within the banana clip into 2 equal parts top and bottom (horizontally). Just twist or braid the top portion of hair and tuck it away with a hair pin for now.
8. Divide the bottom portion of hair into 7 or 8 smaller sections and apply mousse to each section one at a time and then roll the hair separately on the flexi rods in a spiral shape. Secure the flexi rod in place by bending the ends.
9. **Setting the curls**. Place a large silk or satin scarf on the head and allow the hair to dry on the flexi rods overnight.
10. **When the curls are completely dry,** apply a dab of coconut oil to the palm of your hands and lightly rub them together, remove the scarf and

all the flexi rods from the hair. After removing the flexi rods lightly run your hands down the length of the curl and separate each one at a time for a fuller look. (*The oil from the coconut oil will add some shine and help to keep the frizz down.*)

11. **Pin curling the top portion of hair.** Undo the twist or braid from hair within the butterfly clip and begin to create pin curls around the contour of the top of the banana clip. Make sure that the pin curls are rolled towards the front of the head and then secure them with hair pins.

Tip: To add length, simply add a couple pieces of clip in hair pieces to the hair after step # 3. Add the pieces where you'll be placing the hair band.

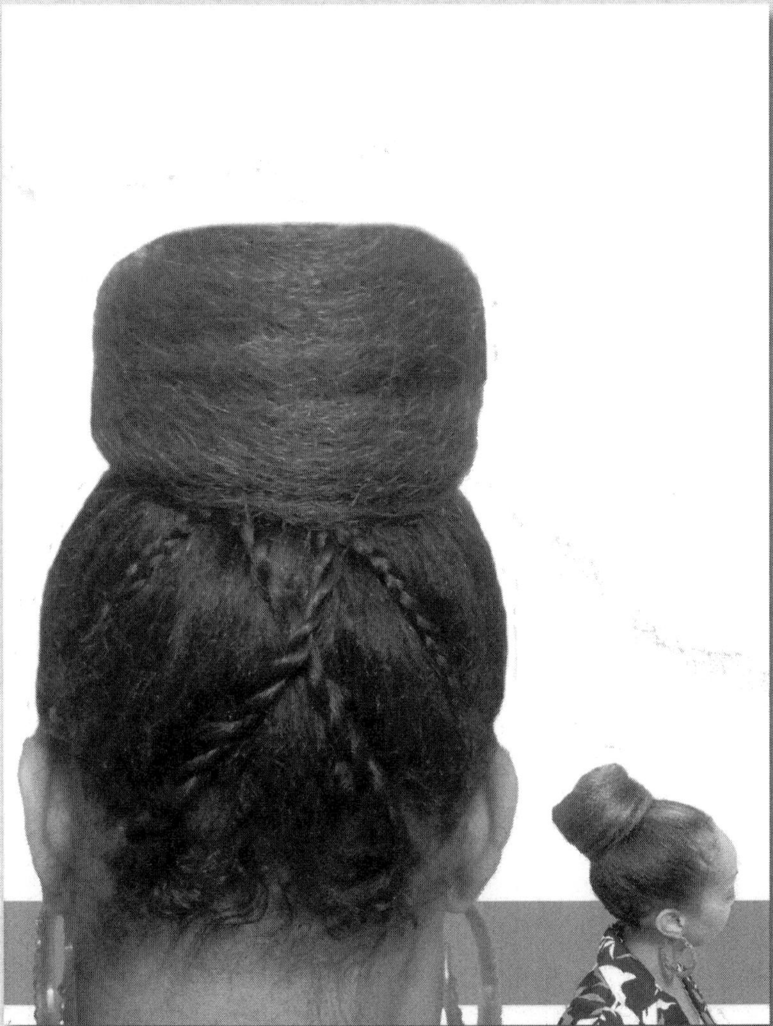

Criss Cross Twists & Braids

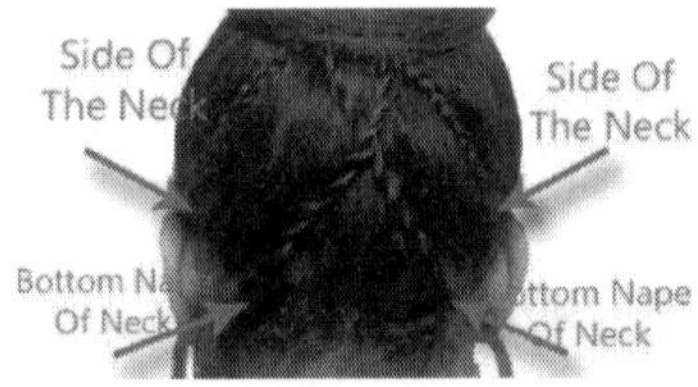

Items you'll need:

- ✓ Comb
- ✓ Soft brush
- ✓ Hair pins
- ✓ Gel
- ✓ Braiding hair (*same color & texture as your hair and also another with a highlighted color of your choice*)
- ✓ Hair band
- ✓ 4 Duckbill clips (*for sectioning off hair temporally*)

Here's how to create the hairstyle:

1. **Preparing the braiding hair**. Remove both colors of braiding hair from their package. And mix and blend them together. Set aside for now.
2. Comb through the hair gently to get rid of any knots and tangles.
3. Take out 2 small pieces of hair from the nape of the neck, about the size of a dime. And also 2 more small pieces from the sides right about where the ear is. Clip each one with the duckbill clips at the roots to keep them sectioned off from the rest of the hair.
4. Apply some gel around the perimeter of the rest of hair and proceed to smooth the edges of the hair by brushing it with the soft brush.
5. Gather all the hair into a high ponytail and place a hair band around the base of the ponytail. Twist or braid the remaining hair then wrap the hair around the base of the ponytail, secure with a hair pin.
6. **Adding extension hair in the back**. Pinch off 2 small amount of braiding hair from the pack of hair and proceed to create 2 separate Senegalese twists with the 2 small sections of hair at the bottom nape of the neck. Pinch off 2 more small pieces of braiding hair from the pack of hair and proceed to create two braids by adding the extension hair to the 2 small sections of hair at the sides of the neck.

Criss crossing the braids and twist. Start by taking one of the twists in the back and wrap it around the base of the ponytail bun you created earlier (*cross it over the other side of the head and continue to wrap the hair around the base until there is no more to wrap*). Do the same thing to the other twist. This should form a "X" shape.

Take the braids from the sides of the head and wrap each one around the base of the ponytail bun until there's no more hair to wrap.

7. Take the rest of the braiding hair from the package and fold it into ½ then place a hair pin that is the same color as the braiding hair and place it where the fold is.

Now place the hair pin along with the braiding hair in the center of the bun and begin to wrap the braiding hair around the bun. Use hair pins to secure the hair in place as you wrap the hair around.

French Roll with Pancake Bang

Items you need:

- ✓ Hair pins
- ✓ Comb
- ✓ Soft brush
- ✓ Hair spray
- ✓ Gel
- ✓ Decorative flowers
- ✓ Braiding hair
- ✓ Butterfly clip

Here's how to create the hairstyle:

1. Comb through the hair gently to get rid of any tangles.
2. Make a "U" shape part at the front center of the head (*2-3 inches wide and 3 inches going back*). Use the butterfly clip to section off this portion of hair for now.
3. Proceed to the back section of hair and apply some gel at the sides of the head and use the soft brush to smooth out the sides.
4. Take some braiding hair *(amount depends on the length of your hair and how big you would like the French roll to be*).
5. Comb the back section of hair over to the right side.
6. Shape the braiding hair in the shape of a log *(put a couple of hair bands around the log to hold it in place)* and then place it vertically on the back of the head in the center. Use a few hair pins to secure the log in place on the head.
7. Take the hair you comb to the side and use it to cover the log completely. *(Make sure that the hair you place over the log is place neatly and the ends are tucked under.)* Then proceed to secure the hair by placing hair pins in.
8. Remove the butterfly clip from the "U" shape part and comb the hair over to the left side. Begin to create a pin curl with the hair and roll the hair under itself. Secure the hair with hair pins when you reach to the scalp.
9. Now pull the pin curled hair from both sides *(front and back)* to stretch it out a little. Use the soft brush to brush and smooth out the top then proceed to spray some hair spray on the pin curled hair to give it a little hold.
10. Use the gel and apply some on the sides of the head and use the soft brush to brush and smooth out the hair.
11. Take the decorative flowers and place them alongside the French roll right where you placed the hair pins.

Sun Flower Pin Curls

Items you'll need:

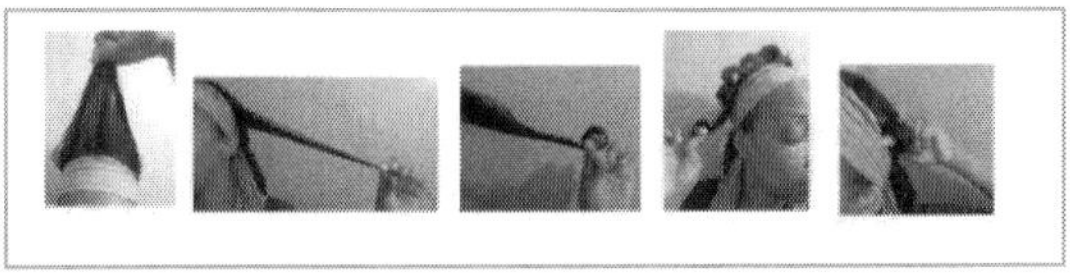

- ✓ Large head band
- ✓ Hair pins
- ✓ Hair spray (optional)
- ✓ Scarf
- ✓ Gel
- ✓ Butterfly clip or hair band (*for sectioning off the hair*)

Here's how to create the hairstyle:

1. Comb through the hair gently to get rid of any knots and tangles.
2. Make a part at the front of the head from ear to ear going horizontally across the head *(about 3 1/2 to 4 inches wide from to back*). Then section off the back portion of hair with the butterfly clip or hair band for now.
3. **Pin curling the front portion of hair**. Gently comb through the front of the hair again and apply some gel on the front only on the root area. Brush to smooth out the hair and then place the scarf only at the front of the hair (*leave about 1 inch of hair expose towards the back to be pin curl*) and then tie the scarf in place at the back of the head for now. *Please see photos above.*
4. Now begin to create raise pin curls from ear to ear going horizontally across the head. As you do each pin curl, be sure to place a hair pin to secure each one in place. Optional: if you would like to add a little hold to the pin curls, spray some hair spray on them.
5. Allow for the front of the hair to dry with the gel then remove the scarf. Take the large hair band and place it at the front of the head.
6. Remove the hair band or the butterfly clip from the back portion of hair and comb through the hair to smooth it out.

In the photo. I'm wearing the back straight, however if want to switch it up and do a braid out, twist out, bantu knot out, flexi rod etc., feel free to do so.

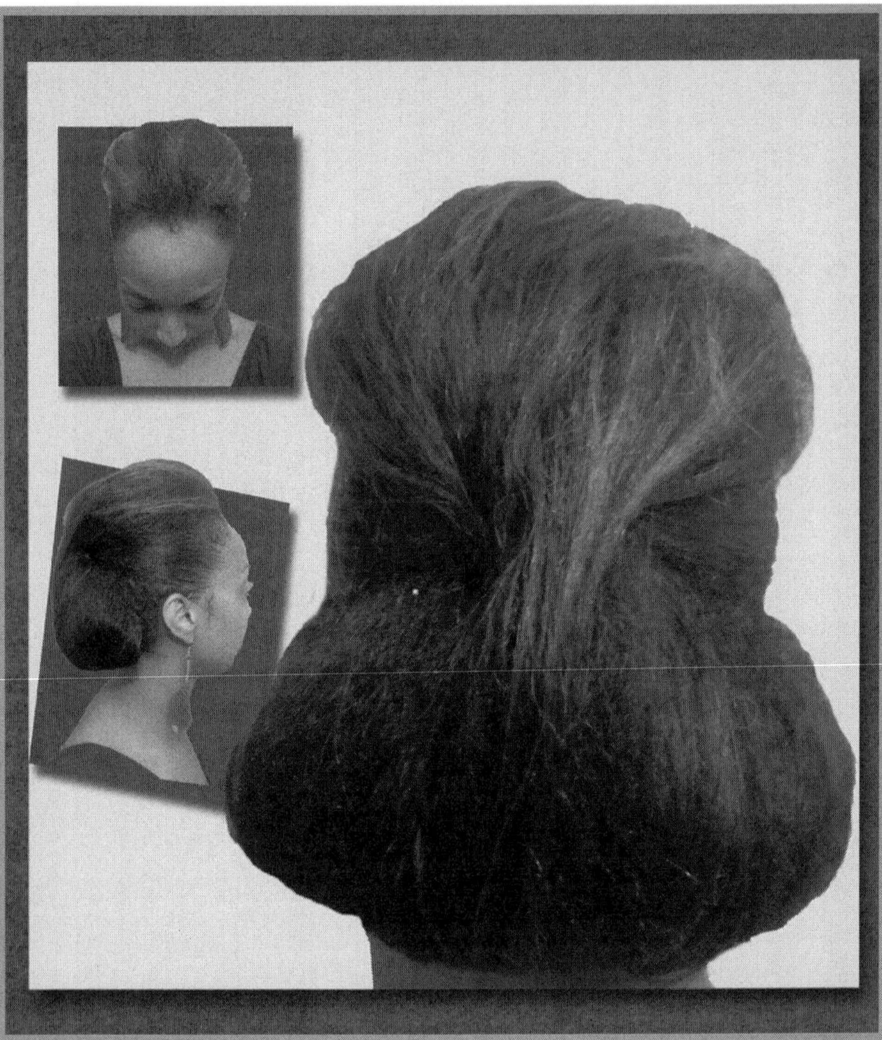

Hour Glass Hairdo

Items you'll need:

- ✓ Comb
- ✓ Soft brush
- ✓ Hair band *(same color as your hair)*
- ✓ Hair pins
- ✓ Hair spray
- ✓ 2 butterfly clips

Here's how to create the hairstyle:

1. Comb through hair gently to get rid of any knot and tangles.
2. Make a "U " shape part at the front center of the head (*4 inches wide & 4 inches going back*) and then section off this portion of hair for now with a butterfly clip.
3. Make a part at the back of the head going across the head horizontally from ear to ear (*this should be about 3 inches above the nape of the neck).* Take the butterfly clip and section off this portion of hair for now.
4. Now apply some gel on the sides of the hair within the middle section of hair. Use the soft brush to sleek down the sides and then gather all the hair in this middle section of hair into a ponytail and proceed to secure it with a hair band.
5. Remove the butterfly clip from the bottom section of hair and comb through the hair to smooth it out. Begin to fold and tuck the hair under itself (*while folding and tucking be sure to add the hair from the ponytail with the bottom section as well*) and secure the hair with a few hair pins.
6. Proceed to the top front section where the "U" shape part is and remove the butterfly clip. Comb through the hair to smooth it and then hold the hair up off the head about 90 degrees. Begin to back comb the hair at the roots gently. Spray the hair with a little hair spray at the roots then lay the hair back down *(don't force the hair down or else you'll flatten it*). Use the soft brush to gently brush the top of the hair to smooth it.
7. Make sure all the hair is in place and looks neat then proceed to use the hair spray to spray the top of the hair.
8. Adjust the lower portion of hair to cover over, mold and take the shape of the middle section of hair where the ponytail is. Once again use the hair spray to spray this section to hold it in place.
9. Blend and tuck any remaining hair from the top with the hair on the bottom.

Side roll

Items you'll need:

- ✓ Comb
- ✓ Soft brush
- ✓ Hair pins
- ✓ Braiding hair
- ✓ Gel or hair edge control
- ✓ Hair spray (optional)

Here's how to create the hairstyle:

1. Pinch off some hair from the pack of braiding hair. (The *thickness of the hair depends on the thickness of the roll in the hairstyle you would like to achieve.*) The length should be about 9 to 10 inches long.
2. Comb through the hair and swoop it to one side of the head.
3. Braid the braiding hair and place it on the side of the head where you just swoop the hair. (*The braided hair should lay parallel to the hair line on the side of the head.*)
4. Use the hair pins to pin the hair on the head. *Please see photo above.*
5. Starting from the back of the head, begin to place your loose hair over the braided hair and tuck it under the braided hair. As you tuck the hair use the hair pins to secure the hair in place. Continue to tuck the hair all the way to the front of the head. When you reach to the front, leave a little hair out from the bang area.
6. Use the hair from the bang area to create a pin curl (*roll the pin curl away from the face*) lean the pin curl to connect it to the roll you created earlier so that it appears seamless. Use the hair pin to secure the pin curl in place. Spray the hair spray on the bang area to add a little hold to it.
7. Apply some gel or edge control to the side of the head that is opposite the roll. And use the soft brush to smooth the side.

Peacock Style

Items you'll need:

- ✓ Comb
- ✓ Soft brush
- ✓ Hair pins
- ✓ 2 hair bands
- ✓ 2 Decorative combs
- ✓ Gel
- ✓ Hair spray (optional)
- ✓ 2 Medium/small size banana clips
- ✓ Butterfly clip (for sectioning off the hair temporally)

Here's how to create the hairstyle:

1. Comb through the hair gently to get rid of any knots and tangles.
2. Then divide the hair into 2 equal sections (top & bottom) section off the top section for now with the butterfly clip.
3. Take the bottom section of hair and apply gel on the edges and then use the soft brush to smooth the hair out. Gather the hair in a ponytail and place the hair band around the base to secure the hair in place for now.
4. Take the banana clip and place it around the base of the ponytail vertically and clip it into place. Now remove the hair band from the hair. Fill up the space of the banana clip with the hair that is in it by gently pulling the hair by the roots to both sides of the banana clip.
5. Remove the butterfly clip from the top portion of hair and REPEAT steps #'s 3 & 4 from applying the gel.
6. Go back to the bottom section of hair and begin to comb through the hair gently to smooth it out. Now tuck the hair under at the nape of the neck, just as you see in the photo. Place hair pin to secure the hair in place.
7. Proceed to the top portion of hair and begin to gently comb through the hair to smooth it out. Then separate the hair within the banana clip into 3 equal sections and then begin to pin curl each sections of hair one at a time. Use hair pins to secure the pin curls in place. In the photo, I have the 2 pin curls facing away from the face and the front pin curl facing the face. However, you can switch the pin curl in the front to the other direction if you like. Take the decorative combs and place them on the sides. (optional)

The Ribbon Wrap

Items you'll need:

- ✓ Comb
- ✓ Hair pins
- ✓ Butterfly clips

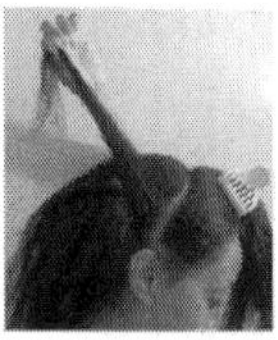

Here's how to create the hairstyle:

1. Comb through the hair gently to get rid of any knots and tangles.
2. Make a part from ear to ear going across the head horizontally *(this should be about 4 inches wide from front to back).* Section off the back portion of hair with a butterfly clip for now.
3. Divide the hair in the front into 2 equal parts by parting the hair from ear to ear and then create 2 separate inverted cornrows. At the end of the inverted cornrows, join the loose hair from both inverted cornrows together, comb through the hair to smooth it out and then proceed to create a pin curl. (*When rolling the pin curl, roll it in a upward direction and then secure the pin curl against the head with a couple hair pins.*)
4. **Styling the back**. Remove the butterfly clip from the back section of hair and comb through it to smooth it out.
5. Begin to create the wrap style in the back by first taking a small section of hair from the side, say… the left side *(about 1 inch from the part that is separating the top and back section of hair*) and bring it over and across horizontally to the right side of the head and lay the hair flat with the rest of the hair hanging down, secure the hair on the hair beneath it (*about ¼ inch from the hair line*) with hair pin.
6. Next, Pick up a small piece of hair from the hair line right below where you just place the hair pin and bring it across the head horizontally and lay it flat on the head with the rest of the hair hanging down, then use the hair pin to secure the hair in place.
7. Continue doing this method back and forth by following steps #'s 5 & 6. Be sure to lay the hair close to one another to prevent any gaps.
8. **Options**: when you reach to the nape of the neck you have 2 options of finishing off the hairstyle.

A). Continue to bring the hair back and forth horizontally across the head until there's no more hair to bring across. *This will create a seamless finish.*

Or

B). Finish off the hairstyle just like the one in the picture. Do this by simply leaving out a small portion of hair at the bottom of the head (*at the nape of the neck*). Comb through the hair gently to smooth it out and then bring the hair over to the side of the head (*horizontally and at the same side of the pin curl in the front).* Begin to tuck the hair underneath it self and secure the hair with hair pins.

Side
Curls

Side Pin Curls

Items you'll need:

- ✓ Comb
- ✓ Soft brush
- ✓ Hair pins
- ✓ Hair band (*to hold the hair temporally*)
- ✓ Banana clip
- ✓ Butterfly clip (*for holding the hair temporally*)
- ✓ Gel or hair jam
- ✓ A couple duck bill clips (*optional*)

Here's how to create the hairstyle:

1. Start by combing through the hair gently to get rid of any knots and tangles.
2. Next, make a part on the left side of the head in the front (go back about 5 inches) stop, turn the comb to the right and continue to part the hair straight down to the right ear. Use the butterfly clip to section off the back portion of hair for now.
3. **Styling the front**. Comb through the front section of hair gently (to the right side of the head) and begin to create a pin curl. Do this by rolling the hair upward, and then secure the hair with hair pins. To create the double pin curl you see in the photo, simply create 2 separate pin curls one up and the other down and pin them close to each other (*TIP: to help with the pin curling process try placing a couple of duck bill clips on both sides of the section of hair to help the hair stay in place during the pin curling process. Just remove them when you are done*)
4. **Styling the back**. Remove the butterfly clip from the back and gently comb through the hair to smooth it out.
5. Apply a small amount of hair gel or hair jam on the edges of the hair and then use the soft brush to brush and smooth out the hair. While brushing the hair swoop it to the left side of the head and then gather all the hair into one. Place the hair band in the hair to create a temporary ponytail.
6. Next, take the banana clip and place it horizontally at the base of the ponytail and then clip it to secure it in place.
7. Remove the hair band from the hair and then proceed to fill up the banana clip with hair by gently pulling the hair by the roots to both sides of the banana clip.
8. Divide the hair into 2 equal parts (*top and bottom*) and use a duck bill clip or the butterfly clip to hold the bottom portion of hair for a moment.
9. Start to **create pin curls** with small sections of hair. Create the pin curls by rolling the hair upward and then secure them with hair pins alongside the contour of the top of the banana clip. *(The hair should be covering the banana clip.)*
10. Remove the butterfly clip or the duck bill clip from the bottom portion of hair and REPEAT step # 9 for this portion of hair.

Casual Dressy Updo

Items you'll need:

- ✓ Comb
- ✓ 2 Butterfly clips
- ✓ Soft brush
- ✓ Gel or hair jam
- ✓ Hair spray
- ✓ Hair pins
- ✓ Hair band
- ✓ Clip on ponytail

Here's how to create the hairstyle:

1. First comb through the hair gently to get rid of any tangles and knots.
2. Make a part from ear to ear horizontally across the head (*the front portion of hair can be a tad smaller than the back portion*). Section off the back section of hair with a butterfly clip for now.
3. Make 2 parallel parts going back, at the front center of the head and section off this middle section with a butterfly clip for now.
4. **Cornrowing the sides of the head**. Part the hair into 3 equal parts at one side of the head and proceed to cornrow each one going back one at a time. Next connect all 3 ends of the cornrow together by cornrowing the base of the braids *(starting from the last one going up*). Please, see photo.
5. Proceed to the opposite side of the head and follow step # 4 for that side.
6. Now that both sides of the head are braided, connect both sides by twisting the remaining hair from both sides to the end then fold it under itself and secure with a hair pin.
7. **Styling the middle front section**. Remove the butterfly clip from front section of hair and comb through it to smooth it out. Hold the hair up off the head about 90 degrees and proceed to gently back comb the roots of the hair in the back (*this will create some volume*). Use the hair spray to spray the area where you just back comb then gently lay down the hair. Use the soft brush to gently brush and smooth out the front and top of the hair and again use the hair spray to spray the top of the hair. Now proceed to gather all the hair in the back and fold and tuck the hair under itself, then secure the hair with a few hair pins. (*Be sure the ends of the cornrows are hidden under the fold and tuck.*) See photo.
8. **Styling the back of the head**. Remove the butterfly clip from the back section of the hair and comb through it to smooth it out. Apply some gel or hair jam around the edges of the hair and use the hair brush to brush and smooth out the nape of the neck and the edges.
9. Gather all the hair into a high ponytail and secure with a hair band. Braid or make a 2 strand twist with the hair from the ponytail and wrap it around the base of the ponytail then secure with a couple hair pins. Now you have a bun.

10. Take the clip-on ponytail piece and place the ponytail over the bun (*the combs on the ponytail hair should be placed in the roots of the hair close to the bun*). Now pull on the drawstring to tighten the clip-on ponytail. Just comb through the ponytail to smooth it out.

Two Hair Styles In
One

Two Hairstyles in One

Items you'll need:

- ✓ Comb
- ✓ Soft brush
- ✓ Braiding hair
- ✓ Hair pins
- ✓ 2 Butterfly clips

Here's how to create the hairstyle:

1. Comb through the hair gently to get rid of any knots and tangles.
2. Make a straight part from front to back separating the hair into about 2 equal parts. Section off the left section of hair with the butterfly clip for now.
3. Proceed to the right side of the head and begin to make **2 strand flat twists** going up along the side of the head. For each 2 strand flat twist place a small hair pin at the end of the 2 strand flat twist right at the roots to secure it in place.
4. Proceed to the left side of the head and remove the butterfly clip from the hair. Begin to comb through the hair to smooth it out, use the soft brush to brush and smooth the hair as well (**The hair should be laying on the side and the loose hair from the 2 strand flat twist should be included in this section of hair in a seamless appearance.*)
5. **Large 2 strand flat twist**. Pinch off a small section of the braiding hair and hold the hair in the middle, locate the front of the head where the loose hair starts and pick up 2 small pieces of hair, begin to attach the braiding hair to the 2 strands of hair to create a Senegalese twist. (*Please see "*Tips before styling*" section of this book to see how.) Twist the hair about 2 to 3 times and then lay it flat against the head right at the hair line and begin to do a 2 strand flat twist along the hair line.
6. When you reach to the back of the head and there's no more hair to 2 strand flat twist, just twist the rest of the hair down to the ends. Take the single twist and place it in the middle of the head where there is the separation between the two styles on both sides of the head. Now place a few hair pins to secure the twist hair in place.

TIP: If the twist hair is too long when you lay it down, just simply fold excess hair back on itself and use the hair pins to secure the hair in place.

Fake
Bang
Piece

Fake Bang Piece

Items you'll need:

- ✓ Comb
- ✓ Soft brush
- ✓ Hair pins
- ✓ Weft/ weaving hair (*the color and texture as your own hair*)
- ✓ A pair of scissors
- ✓ 2 Hair band
- ✓ Gel or hair jam
- ✓ Hair spray *(optional)*
- ✓ Flat iron (*for the fake bangs*)

Here's how to create the hairstyle:

1. First comb through the hair to get rid of any potential tangles.
2. Apply some gel or hair jam around the perimeter of the hair and use the soft brush to brush and smooth out the edges of the hair.
3. Gather all the hair into one high ponytail (*about 5 inches away from the hair line in front of the head*) and secure the hair with a hair band. Braid the remaining hair from the ponytail and wrap it around the base of the hair, then secure with a hair pin or two.
4. **Making the fake bang piece**. Cut off a piece of weft/weaving hair about 12 inches long. Fold it into half and place it at the front of the head against the base of the ponytail bun. Use the small hair pins to secure it.
5. Take a small piece of hair from both sides of the bang and begin to wrap the around the base of the ponytail bun. Use hair pin to secure the hair in place.
6. Next, use the pair of scissors to cut and shape the bangs to a desired length. Use the flat iron to curl the bang.
7. **Making the bun**. Take the remaining weaving hair and fold it into half. Place a hair pin in the fold of the hair and then place the hair pin along with the weaving hair in the middle of the ponytail bun. Now begin to wrap the weaving hair around the base of the ponytail bun until there's no more weaving hair left to wrap around. (*As you wrap the hair around, add hair pins to secure the hair in place.*)
8. Comb through the ponytail weave to smooth it out. Take the hair band and place the ponytail weave through it, slide the hair band down the hair and stop when you feel the bun from your own hair through the ponytail weave. Proceed to wrap the hair band around the ponytail weave (*right above the bun from your real hair*).
9. Now fan out the ponytail weave with the comb and proceed to wrap the hair around the base of the ponytail. Use hair pins to secure as you go.
10. Take the hair spray and spray the bun and the bang.

Side Swept Curls
With
Side Braid

Side Swept Curls With Stylish Side Braid

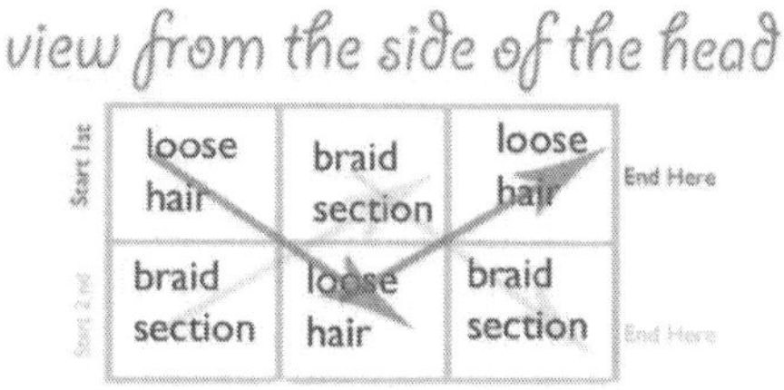

Items you'll need:

- ✓ Comb
- ✓ Soft brush
- ✓ Hair pins
- ✓ Flexi rods
- ✓ Silk or satin scarf
- ✓ Mousse
- ✓ Butterfly clip (*for sectioning off the hair temporally*)
- ✓ Coconut oil
- ✓ Time

Here's how to create the hairstyle:

1. First comb through the hair to get rid any tangles.
2. Part off a square shape at the side of the head in the front (4 inches by 4 inches). Section off the rest of the hair with the butterfly clip for now.
3. **Cornrowing the side**. Divide the side portion of hair into 2 equal parts by making a part at the side of the head, starting from front to back. You will be dividing those 2 sections of hair further, into 3 more sections each. So all together you should have 6 small sections of hair to work with.

   To create the stylish cornrow pattern, you must section off some of the boxes while others stay loose. Do this by starting from the **top row**. Simply braid the middle box so that it stays out of the way. **Bottom row** should have the 2 end boxes braided so they can also stay out of the way.

   Now begin to cornrow the hair starting from the front of the head. Cornrow all the loose hair you see by following the direction of the arrow. When you get to the end of the cornrow simply use a small hair pin to secure the hair at the roots and leave the rest of the hair loose. Undo the braids from the rest of the small boxes and begin to cornrow the remaining loose hair starting from front to back. And then secure the hair at the root with a small hair pin and leave the remaining hair loose. See photo.

4. **Styling the rest of the hair with curls**. Ok comb and swoop the rest of the hair to the opposite side of the head where the stylish cornrows are. Begin to take small sections of hair and roll them in a spiral motion on the flexi rods one at a time. *Remember to first comb through each section to smooth it out and then apply the mousse before you roll the hair on the flexi rod.*
5. When you've completed all the flexi rods and there's no more hair left out. Take the soft brush and brush the hair to smooth down the top of the

hair. Then place the silk or satin scarf on your head. Allow the curls to set and dry overnight.

6. When all the curls are completely dry, take a dab of coconut oil and rub it into your hands. (*The coconut oil will help to keep the frizz down and also add shine to the hair while removing and working with the curls.*) Start to remove the flexi rods from the hair.
7. When all the flexi rods are removed, begin to gently divide all the curls into 2 (*this will create some volume to the hair*).

Do you have natural hair? Try doing a braid out instead of a flexi rod set.

Wavy Bang

Wavy Bang

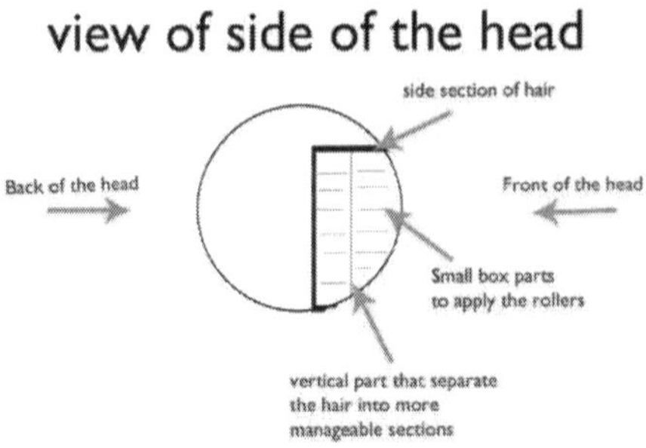

Items you'll need:

- ✓ Comb
- ✓ Soft brush
- ✓ Hair pins
- ✓ Hair band
- ✓ Butterfly clips
- ✓ Gel or hair jam
- ✓ Coconut oil
- ✓ Spray bottle w/ water
- ✓ Weaving hair (optional) same color and texture as your own
- ✓ Small plastic rollers with the cover
- ✓ Time

Here's how to create the hairstyle:

1. Comb through the hair to get rid of any tangles.
2. Part off the front section of hair by first making a part on the left side of the head (the *part should be about 4 to 5 inches going back*). Stop, turn the comb to the right and continue to part the hair down to the right ear. Take the butterfly clip and section off the back section of hair for now.
3. **Curling the front section of hair**. There are 2 ways you can go about curling the front. **1). Using the rollers** or **2). Doing a braid out**.
4. Using the roller method. Take the front section of hair and use the water bottle to saturate the hair with water. Divide the side section of hair into 2 manageable sections by parting the hair vertically and then use the butterfly clip to section off the other section for now.
5. Begin to make small parts starting from the top within this section of hair (*just like you see in the diagram below*). Part the hair about ½ to 1 inch from the top. Take that small section of hair and comb through it then apply some mousse to the hair.
6. Hold the hair up off the head about 90 degrees off the head with a little tension and take the plastic roller and place it underneath the hair horizontally at the root and then lay the hair down on the roller. Take the roller cover and place it on top of the roller with the hair still on top of the roller.
7. Make another horizontal part about ½ to 1 inch away from the roller. Take that small section of hair along with the hair on top from the previous roller set, comb through it, apply some mousse to the hair, hold the hair up off the head about 90 degrees and proceed to place another roller underneath the hair at the root. Lay the hair down on the roller and take the roller cover and place it on top of the roller to secure the hair. **If*

*you feel as if the hair is starting to dry out as you set the hair, simply spray the hair with some more water.** Continue this process to this front section of hair. When you've completed applying the rollers to the front section of hair proceed to the back.

8. Ok, remove the butterfly clip from the back section of hair. Apply some gel or hair jam on the edges and take the soft brush to brush and smooth out the edges of the hair.
9. Gather all the hair into a ponytail and secure with a hair band. Proceed to make a bun with your own hair or add weaving hair to create the bun. If you are using weaving hair simply braid and wrap your own hair around the base and then secure with hair pins. Take the weaving hair and begin to wrap the weft/ weaving hair around the base of the ponytail bun. As you wrap the hair around, remember to secure the weaving hair with hair pins.
10. Comb through the ponytail weave and begin to wrap it around the base of the hair and also secure the hair with hair pins.
11. Take the silk or satin scarf and tie your head overnight with it.
12. **Removing the rollers** from the front section of hair. When the hair is completely dry, begin to remove the rollers from the hair one at a time.
13. Apply some coconut oil to your hands and rub them together. Now begin to gently fluff out the hair with your fingers or with a large tooth comb **be careful not frizz the hair during this process.** Next, tuck the excess hair under itself and use hair pins to secure the hair in place. Please see photo.

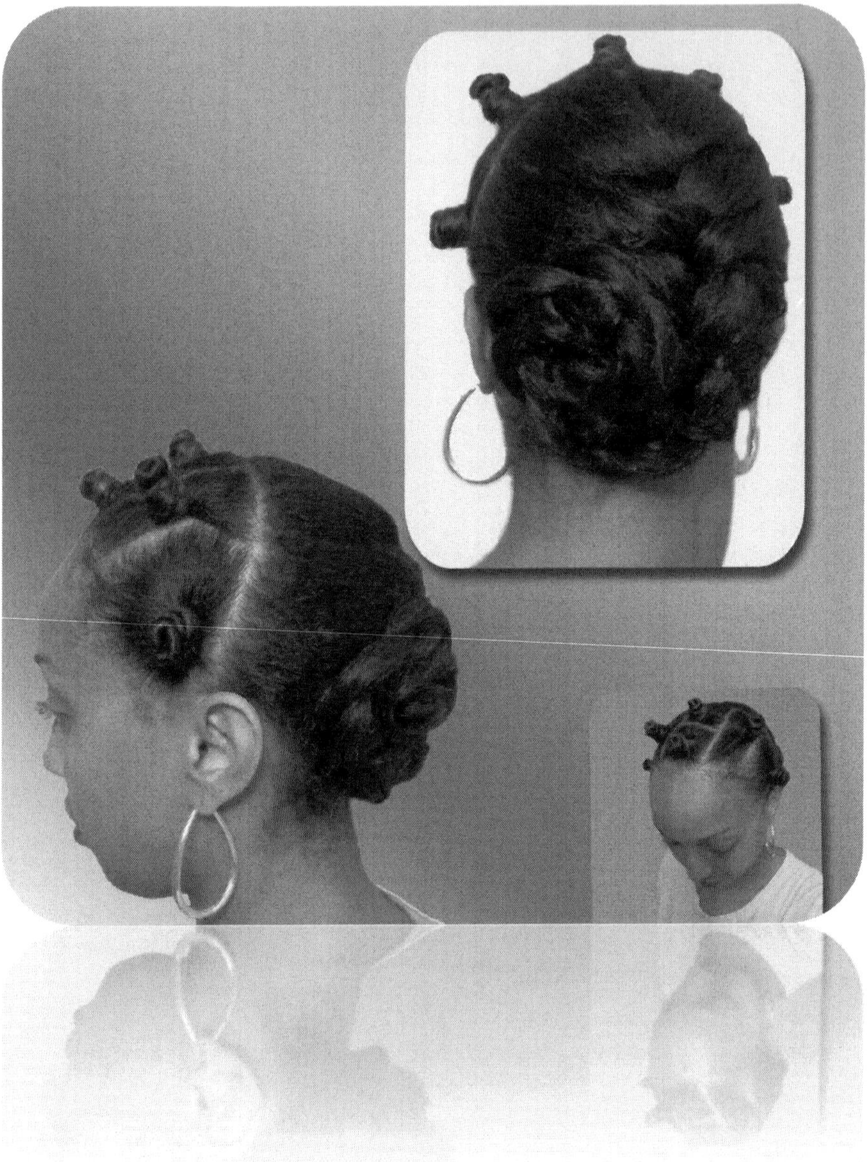

Flower Braid With Bantu Knots

Items you'll need:

- ✓ Comb
- ✓ Soft brush
- ✓ Butterfly clips
- ✓ Hair pins
- ✓ Braiding hair (*same color and texture as your hair*)

Here's how to create the hairstyle:

1. Comb through the hair to get rid of any tangles.
2. Make a part from ear to ear across the head horizontally (about 4 inches wide from front to back), then section off the back portion of the hair for now.
3. Start **making parts for the Bantu knots**. Do so by making two parallel parts going back at the front center of the head, section off the sections of hair at the sides of the head with butterfly clips for now. Divide the top section of hair into 2 more sections (front and back) and proceed to create Bantu knots with them.
4. Undo the butterfly clips from one side of the head and proceed to part the hair in half going back, and then create 2 separate Bantu knots with the 2 sections of hair. Repeat this same step for the opposite side. (*Please see "tips before styling" section to learn how to do Bantu knots.*)
5. **Cornrowing the back**. Remove the butterfly clip from the back and comb through the hair gently to get rid of any knots.
6. Take the braiding hair from the package and take off about ½ of it. Section the braiding hair into 3 sections and place the hair down on a flat surface for a moment. Pick up 3 small pieces of hair from the top section of the back portion of your own hair, now take the braiding hair you divided into 3 earlier and place it on top of the 3 small pieces of hair you picked up from your own hair, pair each of the 3 pieces of braiding hair with the 3 pieces from your own, merge them together and proceed to do an inverted cornrow.
7. Braid the hair all the way to the end and then loosen the loops of one side of the braid. Now take the braid and place it on one side of the head in a spiral pattern and use the hair pins to secure the hair in place. Use the soft brush to smooth the edges.

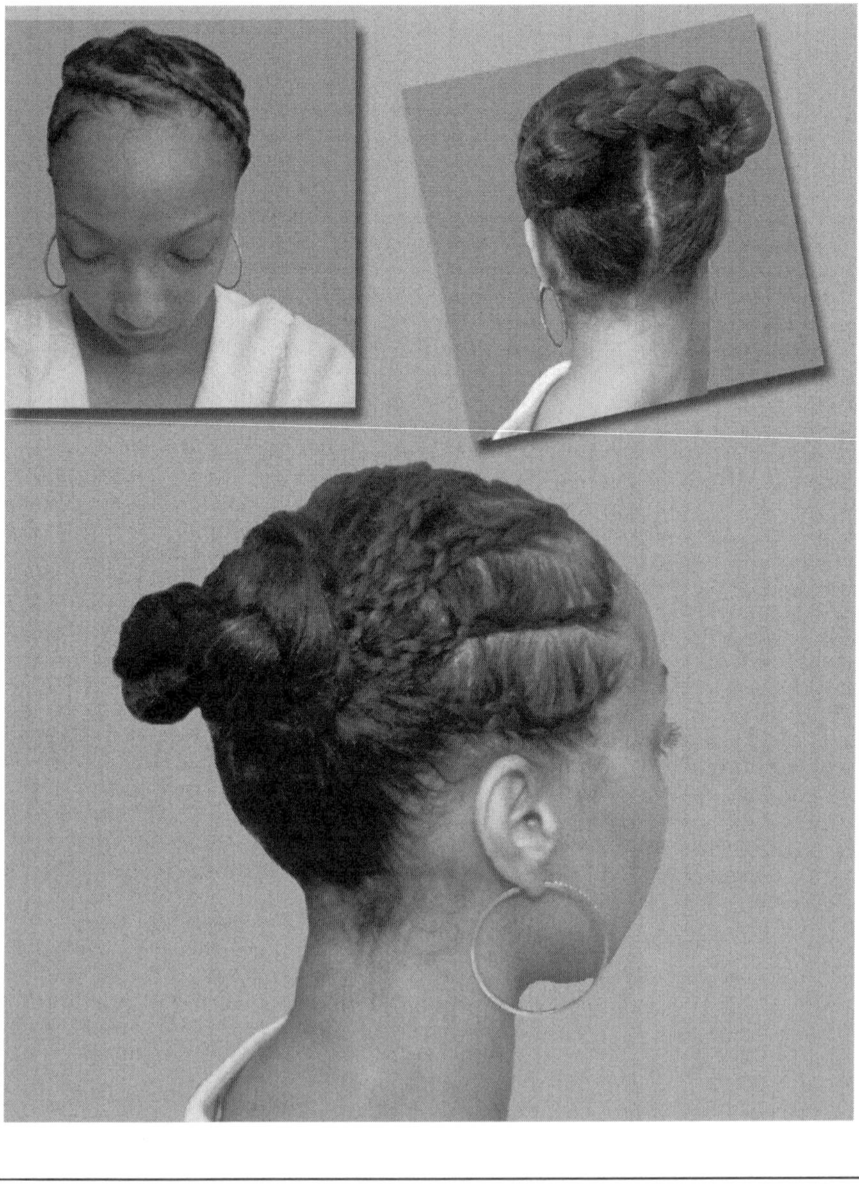

Braid Updo With Cornrows

Items you'll need:

- ✓ Comb
- ✓ Soft brush
- ✓ 2 hair bands
- ✓ Hair pins
- ✓ Gel or hair jam
- ✓ Braiding hair (*same color and texture as your hair*)
- ✓ Butterfly clips (*for sectioning off the hair*)

Here's how to create the hairstyle:

1. Comb through the hair gently to get rid of any tangles.
2. Begin to make a part from ear to ear horizontally going across the front of the head. (*This should be about 4 inches wide from front to back.*) Section off the back portion of hair with a butterfly clip.
3. **Cornrowing the front of the head**. Begin to make small parts going back, in the front of the head. First make two parallel parts going back in the middle of the section of hair (*the size of the parts depends on what size you prefer*), then section off the rest of the hair with butterfly clips. Proceed to start cornrowing the first section you part off.
4. Undo the butterfly clip from one side of the head and make another parallel part next to the section of hair you just cornrow (*this and all the following sections should be the same size*). Continue to part and cornrow this side and the opposite side of the head. When the front is completely cornrowed, proceed to the back.
5. **Styling the back**. Remove the butterfly clip from the back section of hair and begin to divide the back section into 2 equal parts. Do this by making a vertical part from top to bottom. Use the butterfly clip to section off one section for now. Take the braiding hair from the package and separate it into 2 equal parts.
6. Apply some gel or hair jam on the edges and then use the soft brush to brush and smooth the hair out. Gather all the hair into one high ponytail and place a hair band around the base to secure the hair in place. Pick up one of the bundle of braiding hair you split into ½ earlier and proceed to arrange the hair into 3 equal sections (*the hair from the ponytail should be separated into 3 equal parts as well*). Now place the braiding hair at the base of the ponytail, matching the 3 sections from the braiding hair to the 3 sections from your own hair. After you pair each section of hair up merge them together and proceed to braid the hair to the end.
7. Remove the butterfly clip from the next section of hair and REPEAT steps # 5 & 6.
8. **Wrapping the braid around**. Take one of the braided ponytail and bring it horizontally across the head and place it on top of the other braided ponytail right at the base. Continue to wrap the remaining hair from the

braided ponytail around the base until there's no more hair left. Then use the couple hair pins to secure the hair in place.

9. REPEAT step # 8 for the other braided ponytail.

Beautiful Braided Side Bun

Items you'll need:

- ✓ Comb
- ✓ Soft brush
- ✓ Gel or hair jam
- ✓ Hair pins
- ✓ 2 Hair bands
- ✓ Decorative hair clips
- ✓ Butterfly clip (*for sectioning off hair*)
- ✓ Braiding hair (*same color and texture as your own hair*)

Here's how to create the hairstyle:

1. First comb through the hair to get rid of any tangles.
2. Make a part at the side of the head parallel to the hair line. Stop parting when you get to the back of the head. (*This section of hair should be about 1 inch wide.*) Section off the rest of the hair with the butterfly clip and proceed to cornrow the hair.
3. Remove the butterfly clip from the rest of the hair. Make another 1 inch wide part from the front to the back parallel to the hair you just cornrowed. Section off the rest the hair again and proceed to cornrow the small section of hair. At this point you should have 2 small cornrows at the side of the head.
4. Remove the butterfly clip again from the rest of the hair. Proceed apply some gel or hair jam on the edges of the hair and use the soft brush to brush and smooth the hair.
5. As you brush the hair, swoop all the hair to the opposite side from where the cornrows are, and proceed to gather all the hair (*including the ends of the cornrows*) into a low ponytail. Place a hair band around the base of the ponytail to secure in place. Braid or twist the ponytail and wrap it around its base and use a couple of hair pins to secure the hair.
6. **Preparing the braiding hair**. Take the braiding hair from the package and proceed to braid it into one. Place a hair band at the end to secure the ends of the braid.
7. Place one end of the braiding hair onto the center of the braided ponytail bun on your head and secure with a hair pin. Begin to wrap the braiding hair around the braided ponytail bun into a spiral shape. As you wrap the hair, use hair pins to secure the hair in place.
8. Take the decorative hair clips and place them at the base of the bun on top.

Flower Braid With Tuck Front

Items you'll need:

- ✓ Comb
- ✓ Soft brush
- ✓ Hair pins
- ✓ Decorative clips
- ✓ Gel or hair jam
- ✓ Braiding hair (*same color and texture as your own hair*)

Here's how to create the hairstyle:

1. Comb through the hair to get rid of any tangles.
2. Make a part from ear to ear across the head horizontally (*about 4 inches wide from front to back*), then section off the back portion of the hair for now.
3. Apply some gel or hair jam on at the front edges and use the soft brush to brush and smooth out the hair. Now fold the hair underneath itself in the back and begin to secure the hair with hair pins.
4. **Cornrowing the back**. Remove the butterfly clip from the back and comb through the hair gently to get rid of any knots.
5. Take the braiding hair from the package and take off about ½ of it. Section the braiding hair into 3 sections and place the hair down on a flat surface for a moment. Pick up 3 small pieces of hair from the top section of the back portion of your own hair. Now take the braiding hair you divided into 3 earlier and place it on top of the 3 small pieces of hair you picked up from your own hair. Pair each of the 3 pieces of braiding hair with the 3 pieces from your own, merge them together and proceed to do an inverted cornrow.
6. Braid the hair all the way to the end and then loosen the loops of one side of the braid. Now take the braid and place it on one side of the head in a spiral pattern and use the hair pins to secure the hair in place. Use the soft brush to smooth the edges.

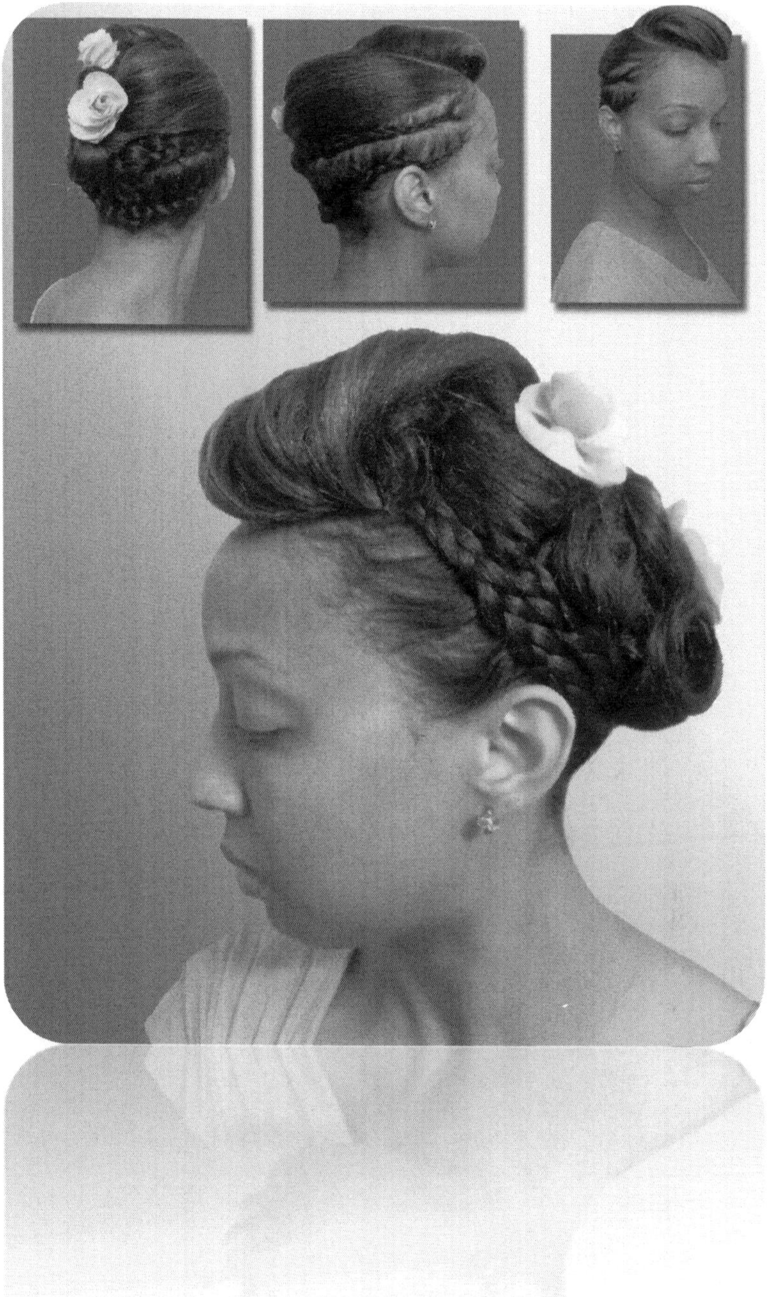

Side Pin Curls With Accent Cornrows

Items you'll need:

- ✓ Comb
- ✓ Soft brush
- ✓ Hair pins
- ✓ Hair jam or gel
- ✓ Braiding hair (color and texture as your own hair)
- ✓ Decorative clips
- ✓ Butterfly clips

Here's how to create the hairstyle:

1. First comb through the hair to get rid of any tangles.
2. Make a part at the side of the head parallel to the hair line. Stop parting when you get to the back of the head. (*The section of hair to be cornrowed should be about 1 inch wide*). Section off the rest of the hair with the butterfly clip. Pinch off a small piece of braiding hair and proceed to cornrow the hair with it.
3. Remove the butterfly clip from the rest of the hair and make another 1 inch wide part from the front to the back parallel to the hair you just cornrowed. Section off the rest the hair again and proceed to cornrow the small section of hair with another small piece of braiding hair.
4. Remove the butterfly clip from the rest of the hair and make a small "U" shape part at the front center of the head (*about 3 inches wide & 3 inches going back*) use the butterfly clip to section off this section for now.
5. **Pin curling the side of the head**. Take the middle section of hair and swoop it to the opposite side of the head away from the cornrows. Apply some gel or hair jam to the edges and use the soft brush to brush and smooth out the hair.
6. Begin to create about 5 flat pin curls on the side with small sections of hair and secure with hair pins. See photo.
7. Next, take the tail of the cornrows from the other side and bring them around the other side of the head where the pin curls are, and place them below the pin curls. Use the hair pins to secure the braids on the side of the head.
8. **Styling the "U" shape part in front**. Remove the butterfly clip from the "u" shape part and comb through it to smooth it out. Next, comb it over to the side of the pin curls and begin to create a raised pin curl by rolling the hair under itself (*make sure the raised pin curl is covering the ends of the braids*), then use the hair pins to secure the hair in place.
9. Finally, place the decorative clips on the side where the pin curls are.

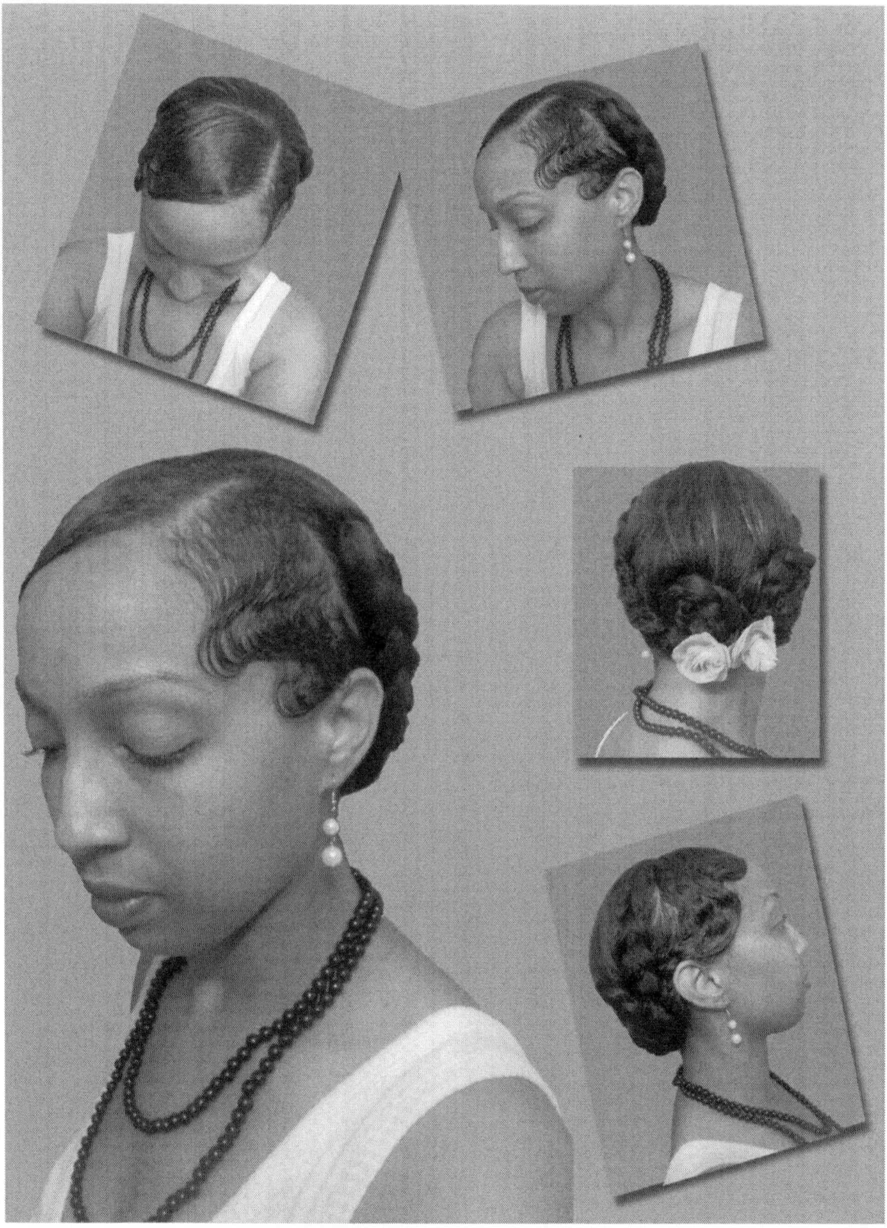

Finger Waves With Stylish Braids Pin Up

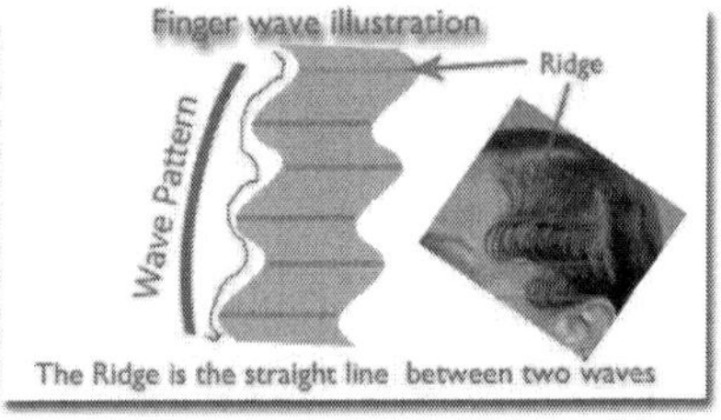

Items you'll need:

- ✓ Gel
- ✓ Spray bottle with water
- ✓ 2 Small teeth comb
- ✓ Butterfly clips
- ✓ Hair pins
- ✓ Decorative hair clips
- ✓ Braiding hair (*same color and texture as your own hair*)
- ✓ Duck bill clips or wave clips

Here's how to create the hairstyle:

1. Comb through the hair gently to get rid of any knots.
2. Make a part from ear to ear across the head horizontally (about 3 inches wide).
3. Take the butterfly clip and section off the back portion of hair for now.
4. **Creating finger waves in the front**. Make a side part going back. Section off the bigger section with the butterfly clip for now.
5. Take the water bottle and spray to saturate the smaller section of hair. Apply a good amount of gel to the wet hair and begin to comb through the hair (*getting the hair as straight as you can*), and comb the hair in a downward direction on the side of the head.
6. *For each **wave** that is on the top and bottom of the **ridge**, you will be combing the hair to the opposite direction.* So here goes…take the small teeth comb and place it horizontally about 1 inch from below the side part and hold it there for a moment (*this will form the ridge*).
7. Take another small teeth comb and place it in the same position as the first but **close under it**. Now, while holding the top comb against the head pull the bottom comb with the hair towards the face (*the hair between the 2 combs will result in the creation of a ridge*). Gently take both combs off the head and place one under and against the ridge. *(This will keep ridge in place while you are making the wave on the bottom.*)
8. Begin to comb the rest of the hair in a downward diagonal direction towards the face. When the hair is straight and smooth, take both combs off the head and place one back on the head about 1 inch below the first ridge. Take the other comb and place it below the first comb but close against it. Now use the comb on the bottom to pull the hair away from the face while holding the top comb in place.
9. Take both combs off the head and place one below but close to the second ridge and begin to comb the hair that's below away from the face in a diagonal downward direction. Remove the comb.
10. Again place both combs against the head about 1 inch below the last ridge (*the combs should be really close to each other, top and bottom*). Pull the bottom comb towards the face while holding the top comb. Take

both combs off the head and place one back under and against the last ridge...continue to repeat the process of pulling the hair back and forth by following steps 7-10. When you reach to the ear, simply swoop and tuck the rest of the hair behind the ear.

11. **Finger waving the next side of the head**. Remove the butterfly clip from the other side of the head and REPEAT steps 5-10 for this section. (*TIP: while finger waving the hair, each ridge that you complete, you can place a wave clip or a duck bill clip on the ridge to help hold the hair in place while you work. You can leave it there until the hair dries.)*
12. **Cornrowing the sides of the head.** Remove the butterfly clip from the back of the head and comb through the hair to smooth it out.
13. Take a small portion of braiding hair (*arrange it into 3 sections for braiding. See "tips before styling" section for demonstration*). Start to attach the braiding hair to your own hair at the side of the head (*about 4 to 5 inches above the ear*) cornrow the hair down and to the back of the head (*all the while following the contour of the side hair line. Also be sure to take some of the hair from the back while cornrowing the side of the head*).
14. When you reach the back of the head stop at the middle where the nape of the neck is. Then continue to braid the hair down to the end. **Loosening the braid**. When the hair is almost braided to the end, lightly hold the hair at the end and begin to loosen the loops on one side of the braid. Start to do this from the end and work your way up the beginning of the braid.
15. **Making the spiral pattern shape with the braid in the back of the head**. Take the braid and form it into a spiral shape on the back of the head on the bottom and then use the hair pins to secure the hair into place.
16. **Cornrowing the next side of the head**. Follow steps 13 & 14 for cornrowing this side.
17. Finally take the two decorative clips and place them at the back of the head at the bottom.

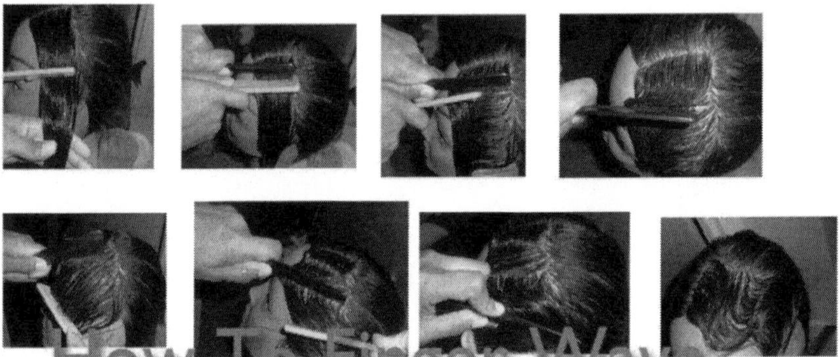

How To Finger Wave

Loosening The Braid

Suggestions for Styling Shorter Hair Types To Promote Length Retention.

If your hair is currently of a short length, for instance shoulder length or shorter, I would suggest you start out with hairstyles such as braid outs, twist outs, Bantu knot outs, flexi rod set, straw set, perm rod set, braids, twists, bantu knots, tuck under styles, clip on ponytail, and wigs. These hairstyles are excellent aids to take short hair lengths pass shoulder length area.

The reason why they are excellent aids in the length retention process is because they require absolutely no heat to style them and the styling process requires low manipulation. Also, since the hair is short even if you wear the hair out free flowing, especially if it is shorter than chin length, it doesn't have the opportunity to rub up against your shoulders. However, even though you can wear your hair out free flowing, please limit this practice. The ends need to be protected especially during the start of your healthy hair journey to ensure active progress of length retention.

Hairstyles I Plan To Incorporate In My Hair Regimen

Name of style:______________ Page #:__________

Name of style:______________ Page #:__________

Name of style:______________ Page #:__________

Name of style:______________ Page #:__________

Name of style:______________ Page #:__________

Name of style:______________ Page #:__________

Name of style:______________ Page #:__________

Name of style:______________ Page #:__________

Name of style:______________ Page #:__________

Name of style:______________ Page #:__________

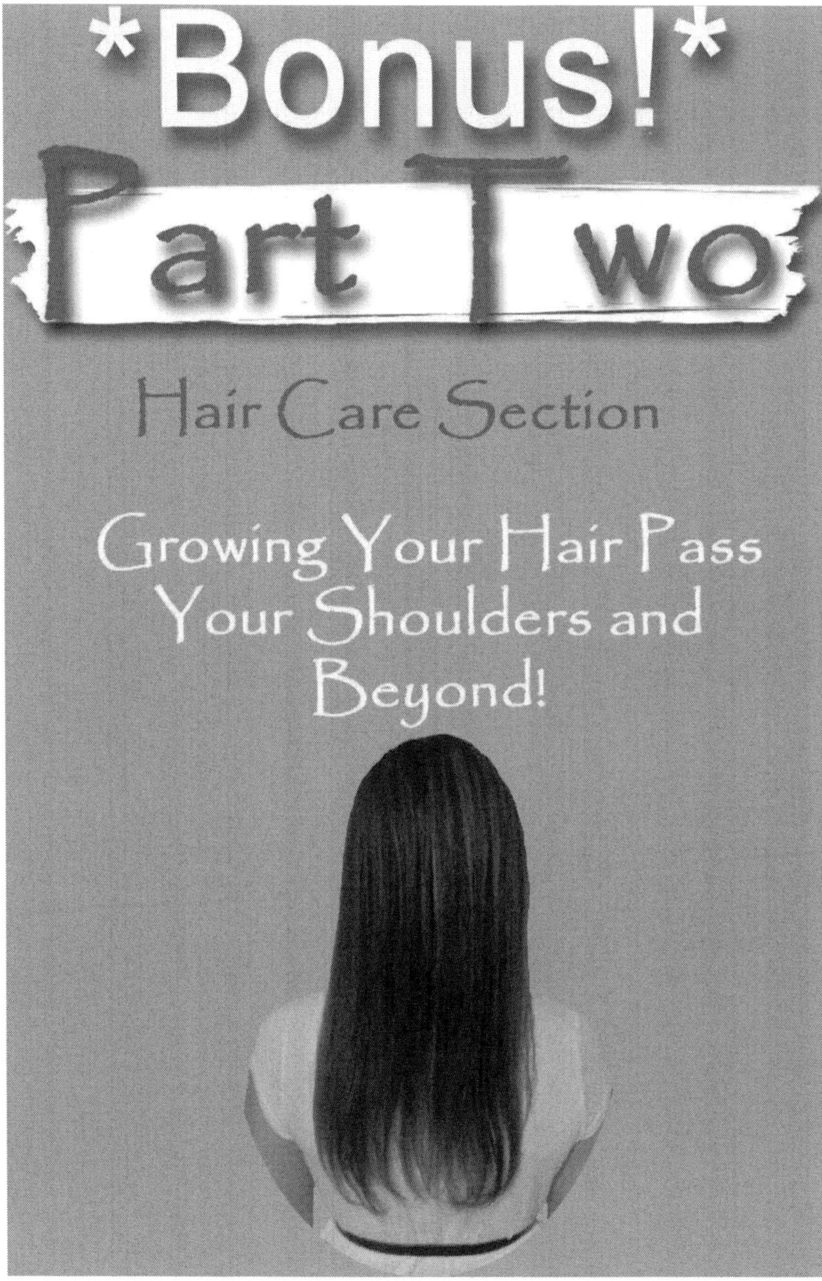
Bonus!
Part Two
Hair Care Section
Growing Your Hair Pass
Your Shoulders and
Beyond!

Hair Care Section.

This section is a **basic over view** of things I think you should know as a **beginner**. I included this section because just showing you how to create *protective and no heat hairstyles* alone **will not** take you to your goal of **longer hair**. Knowing how to properly take care of your black hair and knowing what works and what doesn't, is the first step in your long and healthy hair care endeavor. Protective & no heat hairstyles and proper hair care works hand in hand. Also, when you come to know something on a more personal level you will be able to deal with it in a less frustrating manner when things aren't going as planned during the course of your goal. Ok, so let's go…First my hair story.

~My Hair Story ~

Ever since I was a young girl, I always admired others with longer hair. Sometimes I would even put a T-shirt or something like that on my head and pretended that it was my own hair. My own natural hair was a decent length. It was about the arm pit length region or just about grazing it. I remember the little girls in my school use to play a lot in my hair after my mother spent time to style it. And needless to say, my mother got a little annoyed when that would happen.

Getting My Hair Washed

Oh girl, I use to hate getting my hair washed. I remember my mother had to chase both my sister and I down so that she could wash our hair. When she finally got a hold on me she would put me over her lap with my head facing up to the sky and hanging over a bucket of water. That wasn't the dreaded part though. It was what had to be done after getting my hair washed.

Combing Through My Hair After A Wash…ahhhhh!

Combing through my hair after washing it was a nightmare! There was no special consideration, technique or sympathy given to this process of grooming. It was a let's get these knots and tangles out of this head of hair by any means necessary type of thinking (LOL) and there was nothing I could have done about it. I just had to deal with it.

My First Relaxer

When I was about 14 years old my cousin relaxed my hair. I had a lot of hair and no one really wanted to be bothered with it. So it was decided that a relaxer was the best option to go with verses contending with my own natural hair. I was so happy, because that meant I didn't have to deal with painful styling sessions any more. Now, I could run the comb through my hair with ease, not to mention I thought I was all that with my relaxed hair. lol

Shortly after my first relaxer I began experimenting with my hair a lot. I had my first hair cut done by my cousin. I had it cut into a bob hairstyle with a long tail in the back. Shortly after that I decided that I didn't like the tail anymore and I decided to get it cut off. At some point I remember I went to the hair salon for the very first time to get my hair professionally cut and styled. I remember I wanted to look older so bad that I decided to go bold and have my hair cut way up to my chin area into a more sophisticated bob style with the back of my head shave ever so slightly. I LOVED IT! However, my dad wasn't so amused by what I've done to my hair. He believes that a woman should leave the hair that is on their head, because that is their beauty.

After that my hair started to grow out. And every time it would grow out a little I would take a pair of scissors and try to alter my hair a little bit. I remember one time I even put some type dye in my hair, it was blue but it came out purple instead or vice versa. Who knows? I guess was just bored or something.

In My 20's

In my 20's I continued to abuse my hair. I got bored with my hair very quickly and every second I would throw some type of permanent blond color in it. Every second, I would have a pair of scissors in my hands trying to alter my hair this way or that way. "Moisturize and seal", "washing in sections" and "gently detangling my hair" just wasn't in my hair care regimen vocabulary.

Late 20's early 30's....Turning Point

Around 2010, I had my hair cut to about shoulder length and it had blond highlights. I remember every time my hair started to grow out and reach a little pass my shoulders I would snip it back up to shoulder length.

After that my hair started growing out again and I really kind of left it alone as far as cutting is concern. I became pregnant in early 2011. During my pregnancy I didn't use any relaxer in my hair. I purposefully stayed away from it because I knew the repercussions of using chemicals while being pregnant. (*The chemicals from the relaxer can potentially get in your pores and enter your blood stream and go straight to the baby, which needless to say is not good for a developing fetus.*) So, for that reason, I stayed away from relaxing my hair for the duration of my pregnancy. Also for the most part I had my hair in a low ponytail and I hardly messed with my hair. Even when it was time to style it, I never really implemented any kind of care or consideration in the way I handled my hair. At the time I was not thinking of "healthy hair journey" or anything like that.

Ok, so after I gave birth I relaxed my hair shortly thereafter. And wow! I loved what I saw. I've gained a decent amount of length. So I thought, if during my pregnancy I did not really make any real effort to care for my hair, and I gained this amount of length, then I wondered what would really happen if I consciously implement good hair care practices in my daily and weekly routine? So, out of curiosity, I began to research ways to better take care of my hair. I can't remember the initial information I was looking for, but I do remember I stumbled upon a few ladies' videos that they had posted on a video sharing site. They were sharing information on how they grew their "black" hair long. I was truly amazed by this information because I didn't know such a thing could even happen to black hair.

I had the notion that black hair grew and then stopped at a screeching halt at about shoulder length and stayed at that point forever! And no matter what you do and how well you take care of it, it would never grow beyond your shoulders or arm pit. Well girl was I WRONG! In my quest to learn more about this phenomenon, of how black hair can grow at these amazing lengths, I became more and more intrigued and really excited about the possibilities of my own hair!

One of the tips that I learned was to *stretch my relaxers*. (*Meaning that instead of relaxing my hair every 8 weeks or so, I tried going for longer periods of time. This caused less trauma to the scalp from the chemicals used in the relaxer and also prevented double processing the previously relaxed hair, which would weaken and cause breakage of the hair.*) My initial plan was to stretch and not relaxed my hair for about 4 months or so. When I finally relaxed my hair, about 6 months had gone by. During the period of time of stretching my relaxer, I was being mindful and extra careful of how I handled my hair. *I must confess, it was hard and challenging to deal with my hair because I had so much new growth and I had to contend with the different textures of both the new growth and my already relaxed hair.*

In August 2012 I relaxed my hair again. From this point through July 2013 I stayed away from relaxing my hair. The reason why I went so long without any relaxer was really to see how long I could stretch. I surprisingly survived one whole year without relaxing! WOW!

That's pretty much it. These days I've been really aiming to preserve my hair the best I can by the way I style, wash, comb, detangle, and the products I use.

I included this section **"My Hair Story"** because I wanted to show you that if you have short hair, it can grow pass your shoulders or even further with proper knowledge and care. (*In my case, I had cut my hair very short and it still grew pass my shoulders.*)

The problem is not that black hair doesn't grow, it surely does or else you would not need to touch up the new growth. The problem is after it grows from your scalp what you do and don't do and also how you treat it is what determines length retention. Another important consideration that should be given when wanting to grow black hair to longer lengths is that the health of your scalp and body should be in good condition. If you have any ailments such as alopecia, or cancer the hair growing process would be impossible.

What is hair?

- **Basic Structure of Human Hair**
- **Bonds in the hair**
- **Hair Growth Cycle**
- **Hair Textures and types**
- **Why is black hair different?**
- **Relaxed hair**
- **Conditions that prevent hair growth**

First, before I start talking about how to grow black hair pass your shoulders, I would like to take it back to biology class for a moment. This is necessary because in order for you to get the hair that is on your head to do what you would like it to do, you must first come to know about it on a more personal level. You need to understand what it really is, how it behaves, its characteristics, its likes and dislikes, and how it response to different situations. Just like a real person, getting to know and forming a good relationship only enhances the interaction process.

Trust me, with this information in your hair care regimen, you'll be able to make wiser decisions concerning your hair. So let's jump right into it!

So what is hair?

Hair is mostly made up of protein. This particular protein is call keratin (*keratin is a fibrous protein. This protein is hardened or keratinized.*) Hair grows from the follicle from the skin in a long pipe like shape.

As hair emerges from the scalp and enters the outside world, it is immediately being bombarded by so many things. The hair that you see is considered biologically DEAD! Each combing, brushing, curling, styling etc. that you do to it presents wear and tear to the hair strand.

Think about it this way- just like the fibers and treads in your shirt are not living; same is true for the very hair that you see on your head. And just like that favorite shirt of yours that you wear on a regular basis it eventually has to get washed, bleached, dried, and ironed. Then you wear it again and again and then you have to repeat the process of cleaning it again each time. Now let's think for a moment – after all that washing, drying and ironing over a period of time that shirt that is being worn and washed on a regular basis WILL inevitably become worn out, old and shabby looking. Now, you would have to go back to the store to purchase another one to replace the old shirt.

Well the same is true with your hair. With each wash, color treatment, relaxer, and heat application, the hair shaft becomes worn, depleted, start breaking off and then just looks as if it is just not growing at all, especially if proper care is not being implemented when doing these things. Once you are living and really don't have any medical issues concerning hair growth or hair loss trust me your hair is growing just like the longest hair person you see. It's what you do and how you treat the hair that is on your head is the PROBLEM. If your hair wasn't growing, you wouldn't need a relaxer touch up to your NEW GROWTH every couple of months, as I stated earlier.

As I said earlier the hair that you see on your head is considered biologically DEAD. Meaning there's no longer any cell division taking place once it pushes forth from the scalp, the protein is harden and the hair bulb and root has done its job in making the hair. The responsibility is now placed on YOU to preserve and maintain it by keeping it moisturized, clean, protected and detangled in a gentle manner at all times.

YOU must understand that there is absolutely NO product on the market that is able to grow hair *(such as shampoos, conditioners, butters etc.)* They can only help to **preserve** the hair strands by keeping them moisturized, clean detangle and so forth.

Example: in an effort to help preserve your DEAD hair strands and ultimately help assist it to reaching longer lengths. Using a moisturizing product can help the hair to be more pliable thus – preventing it from drying out, become brittle, and breaking off pre-maturely – eventually retaining the length of the hair.

Hair that is damaged from heat, chemicals and other factors is unable to repair itself. It is not like when you get a cut on your skin and then the skin starts to heal on its own. That's not how hair works. Skin has cells that are alive. The hair that you see on your head does not. So if you have damaged hair and want healthy hair again, you would have to wait until the hair grows from the scalp and reach several inches before you can see healthy hair again.

Ok let's get into **the basic structure of the human hair**. Hair is composed of four basic parts, the *Cuticle*, *cortex*, *medulla*, and the *hair bulb.*

Basic Structure of Human Hair

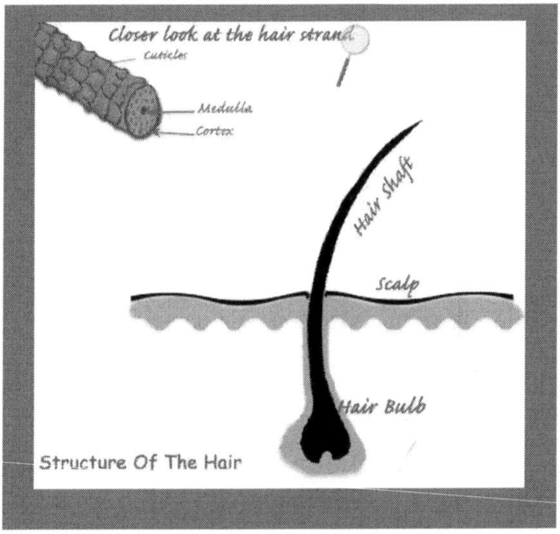

CUTICLE

Let's start with the **CUTICLE**. The cuticles serve as the first line of defense for the hair strand, protecting it from the outside elements. Its structure resembles that of shingles on a roof top or scales on a fish, overlapping over one another. The cuticles function is to help retain or keep moisture inside the hair strand. The cuticles inability to retain moisture effectively is considered to be *porous* hair. Hair that has moisture in it helps to keep it nice and supple and prevent the hair from prematurely breaking off.

Things like temperature, different pH levels, and chemicals can open and close the hair cuticle. The cuticles actually have no color which might be surprising to you since it is the outer most layer.

The cuticle does not last forever! So caution and care is advised whenever you style your hair. As I said earlier, with each time a brush (*especially hard ones*) or comb passes through your hair, it presents wear and tear to it. When the cuticles are damage that is it! Then hair strands cannot function effectively. It will start to lose moisture quickly which then leads to dry brittle hair that have to be replenish with moisture constantly. Hair strand will eventually degrade after cuticles are damage because now the cortex that was protected by it is now exposed.

CORTEX

Below the cuticles of the hair strand is the **CORTEX**. The cortex takes up most of the space within the hair strand and it is responsible for your individual hair color, because this is where the *melanin* is located. When moisture is applied to the hair strands, the cortex absorbs it like a sponge.

The hairs' strength and elasticity is located in this portion of the hair as well. The strength and elasticity comes from the long rope like structure that is in the cortex. These long rope like structures are the keratinized protein strands. They are coiled around each other and are held together by side bonds to maintain its shape. (*I'll discuss side bond in a moment.*)

MEDULLA

The **MEDULLA** is the inner most layer of the hair strand. Well, it depends on what hair type is being discussed any way. If you have thick course hair the medulla is most likely present. If you happen to have finer hair the medulla is not usually present. To my knowledge, the medulla serves no purpose in the hair shaft other than when it is present in the courser hair types it might give a little more thickness to the hair strand.

HAIR BULB

The hair bulb is the end of the hair root. It has a round shape and is located underneath the scalp of the head within the follicle. Within this region, the hair is being manufactured (*the cells are actively dividing*). As it pushes forth through the scalp, the hair comes out as harden protein called keratin and at this point cells that were once diving within the follicle bulb are no longer dividing and active. When the keratin is exposed through the scalp, the fiber that you see is what we call hair. The hair is basically comprised of dead cells. Hence whenever you try to manipulate the hair through styling and grooming such as cutting, you are not able to feel any pain because you are working with dead harden cells. At the end of 1 year you should have accumulated about an average of *6 inches* of hair give or take depending on a few factors (*Genetics, health condition, and personal care.*)

Bonds In The Hair

Inside the cortex of the hair locates bonds. These bonds serve the purpose of giving the hair its strength, elasticity, and shape. They are also each responsible for 1/3 of the hair strength. These side bonds are located at the side of the protein strands. *(Remember the protein strands are long cord like structures that are located in the cortex of the hair and they coil around each other to give the hair its natural shape).* To help keep the coils of the protein strands in its natural shape or positions, are the purpose of the side bonds. Each side bond is attached to one side of one protein strand to the side of another protein strand.

Each of these side bonds has a different degree of strength and purpose within the hair. To help you to visualize and understand the structures I've just explained, I like to think of a **ladder** and how it is constructed.

Imagine the two long parallel vertical posts that are on both sides of the ladder. Picture those as been the long protein strands in the cortex of the hair. Now the shorter horizontal more numerous posts that are between the 2 posts holding them up are maintaining the structure of the ladder. The side bonds between the protein strands would serve the same purpose as the post in between the ladder which is to maintain the shape of the protein strands, thus giving the hair its shape.

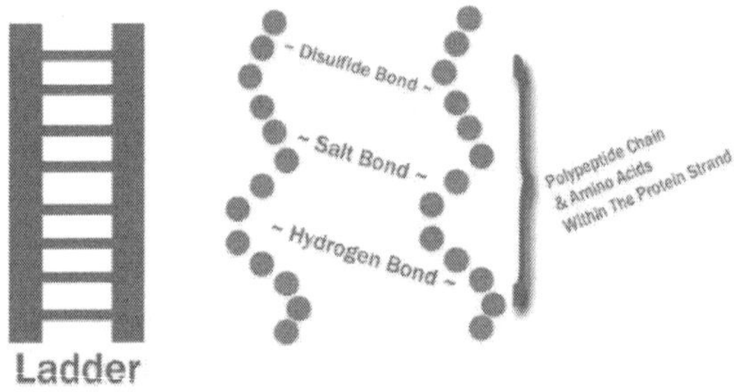

Ok lets' see the role that each of these bonds play within the hair strand.

Hydrogen Bonds
Hydrogen bonds are a weak form of bond in the hair strand. They can be disrupted by the presents of water or heat. For example when you wet your hair with water the water molecules move the positions of the hydrogen bonds that are already in the hair and reshape them in a different way. When the hair dries and the excess water is gone out the hair the hydrogen bonds resume their original positions. Whatever position the hair strands are in during this process that is exactly how the hair will remain (*A good example of this is wet roller sets*). The same concept is true when the hair is styled by heat. Heat temporarily breaks the hydrogen bonds in the hair and reform when it's cooled off.

Salt Bonds
Salt bonds can also be easily broken just like hydrogen bonds. They can be broken by pH levels either acidic or alkaline. To get the salt bonds back to their original positions, the pH levels in the hair would have to be normalized again at about 4.5 to 5.5 on the pH scale.

Disulfide Bonds
Unlike hydrogen bonds and salt bonds, disulfide bonds (2 *sulfur atoms*) are much stronger but fewer. These bonds can only be broken by chemicals such as relaxers. Disulfide bonds are responsible for the curls in the hair. The more disulfide bonds

present and the location of them, the curlier and kinkier the hair strands become. The less that are present, the looser and straighter the curl pattern will be.

Hair Growth Cycle
All the hair that is on your head right now are not all the same length and did not emerge from your scalp at the same time. They all started growing at different periods and continue to go through their *own* growth cycle.
The different cycles are as follows: ***anagen, catagen,*** and ***telogen***. Let's define each phase.

Anagen
This phase is the *growth* phase for the hair strand and the majority of the hair that's on your head are in this phase at any given time. During this phase the hair begins its journey of growth from the follicles* and continues to grow for about 2 to 8 years. The longest your hair can grow during the anagen phase is referred to as the *terminal length*. The length of your growth phase depends on **your own genetics.** Also experiencing terminal length might not be realized due to breakage beyond your control.

*(*Remember the follicles are where the cells are actively dividing to form the keratinized protein. Once the protein has been keratinized, new cells below it continues to divide and harden to form new keratin thus adding to the keratin that is being push through the scalp. This process continues to happen over and over to add* to the *previous keratin. The hair that you see is the result of this process and it lasts for the whole duration of the anagen phase)*

Catagen
At the end of the anagen growing phase, the hair comes to a rest. This phase is call the catagen phase. It can last for a couple of weeks to a couple of months.

Telogen
The last phase of the growing cycle is the shedding phase. This is when the hair follicle releases the hair from its cavity and prepares to make accommodations for another journey of growth for the hair.

Hair Texture
The *texture* of the hair is defined as the diameter across the cortex of the hair strand. Therefore the size of the hair strands has various sizes. When the hair strand is a little bigger it is considered **coarse**. When the diameter is smaller it is **medium**. And when the diameter of the hair measures smaller the hair is **fine**.
Try this: take a couple pieces of crochet thread, hair weaving thread and regular sewing thread. Separately roll a couple of pieces from each category between your fingers. Notice you feel the texture more of the crochet because it is bigger. When you roll the pieces from the regular sewing thread between your fingers it feels a lot smoother because the diameters of the sewing threads are smaller. So the same concept applies for the definition of hair texture.

Hair types/ wave patterns
Just like there are different hair textures there are also various hair types, meaning the curl patterns of the hair strands. The curl pattern or types can range from being bone straight (Asian hair) to coily and kinky such as our black hair.

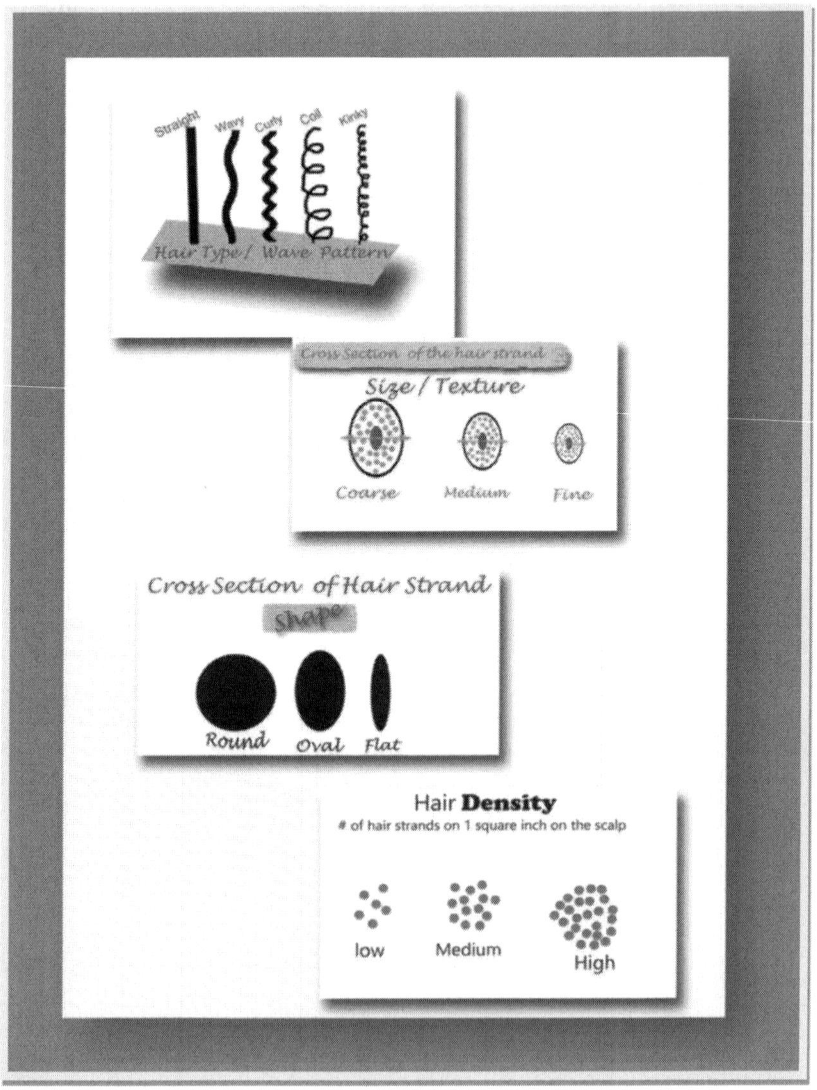

Why Is Black Hair Different?
Ok here is the BIG question. Why is black hair different? Black hair is different because of its shape and the chemical structure within the hair strand. Let's start with the shape of the hair. Each person is different and so are the follicles on our individual head. The follicles are not only responsible to guide the emerging hair through the scalp. They are also responsible for the molding and shape of the emerging hair. That's right. Follicles also have their own unique shape (*based on your own genetic make up).*

When you take a look at the cross section of the hair strand under a microscope, you'll notice a round shape, an oval/elliptical shape or a more flatten shape. The hair that comes out of the round shape follicle is said to be straight *(Caucasian and Asian hair)*. The more oval and flatten the shape tend to be, the hair comes out curlier and kinkier in the case of our black hair. It is also important to know that the kinkier or more coiled the hair is, it tends to have weak points where the hair kinks which tends to break easily. This pose a problem for our black hair because the natural oil *(sebum)* that the scalp produces cannot freely run down the kinks of the hair strands as it would a natural straighter strand of hair.

As far as the chemical structure of the hair goes, the bonds that are located within the hair plays a role in the difference of our hair, especially the disulfide bonds. In kinkier hair types, these bonds are more numerous than that of naturally straighter hair.

So, in a nut shell, the difference between our black hair and other hair types is the oval or more flatten shape of the hair shaft, the amount of disulfide bonds, and the inability for the sebum to freely run down the kinky hair strand to naturally keep it moisturized.

Shape- Flat
Chemical make up- # of disulfide bonds in hair
Dryness- lack of sebum on hair strand

Conditions that prevents hair growth

It is important to keep in mind that there are obstacles that might interfere with the hairs natural growing cycles. And as a result prevent you from reaching your personal hair goals. The list below is just a quick overview of *some* conditions that could be a factor.

- Alopecia (*Is when the immune system attacks the hair follicles, thus stopping the growth of the hair*)
- Certain medication
- Severe stress
- Thyroid and hormonal problems
- Pulling the hair from the scalp too tight *(weaves braids etc.)*
- Fungal infection on the scalp
- Age

~~~~~~
~~~~~~

Relaxed Hair

Relaxed hair and **perm** hair, are they the same thing? No they are not. Even though you might hear others (or yourself) use the two terms interchangeably describing the same procedure, they are actually two completely different things. Here are the definitions for both terms.

Relaxed- hair is chemically straightened from a state of curly, coily or kinky.
Perm- or permanent wave is the process of chemically adding curls to naturally straight hair.

Let me start out by saying using chemicals to straighten our tightly coiled hair shouldn't be taken lightly. I think that you should have some idea of what's really taking place to avoid irreversible damage and misusing this very strong chemical.

Let's take a look at the illustration below for a moment. This is call a pH scale and in essence it measures the presents of ions in any water base substance. pH, by the way, stands for *potential hydrogen.*

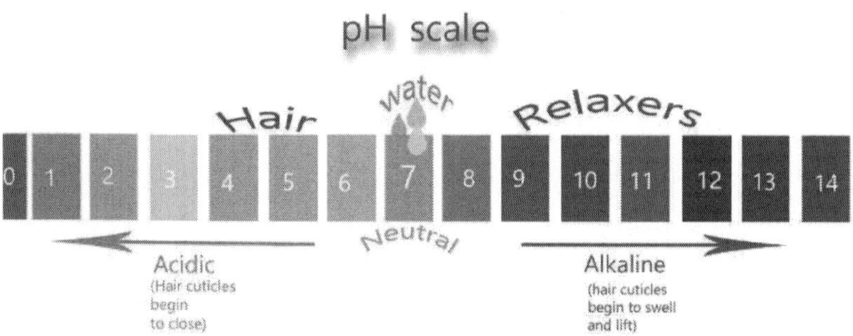

If there are higher amounts of hydrogen ions, the substance is considered to be acidic which closes or constrict the cuticles of the hair. If the water base substance contains higher amounts of hydroxide ions it is considered alkaline which opens and lift the hair cuticles. A normal pH for hair is about 4 to 5, which means that the hair is laying in a flat position. Water has a pH of 7, which is neutral. When you wash your hair with water it's slightly higher pH level of 7 lifts the hair cuticles. After every washing session it is important to use a conditioner to finish the washing process. Because of the conditioners lower pH level it will return the lifted cuticles down close to its normal pH level of 4 to 5. Chemicals such as relaxers are very alkaline, and open the hair cuticles dramatically. Any water base substance that falls below 7 on the scale is consider acidic (close cuticles) and any water base substance product that is higher than 7 is alkaline (opens the cuticles). You can purchase something call litmus strips to test water base substance for their pH levels in your hair products.

For a moment, let's discuss what happens during the relaxing process.
Earlier I talked about bonds in the hair (*disulfide bonds, hydrogen bonds, and salt bonds*). These bonds are important and are responsible for the strength and natural shape or curl of the hair. Chemical relaxers with hydroxide have a high pH level or alkalinity. Because of this the chemical begin to swell and open the hair cuticles dramatically to allow the chemicals to gain access into the cortex of the hair strand. At this point the chemicals begin to undo the natural setup of the disulfide bonds, breaking them apart and then reforming the disulfide bonds in a much weaker state. This process is call lanthionization. *The protein strand is joined by two sulfur atom naturally so during the relaxing process they are broken apart and reform as one weaker bond.* This process of course is permanent and can never be reverse.

When the relaxing process is complete it is time to close back the cuticles of the hair back into a flat like orientation. This is the purpose of the neutralizing shampoo.

Lye and no-lye relaxers

Have you ever been faced with the dilemma of trying to choose between lye or no lye relaxer brand? Which is better? And what is the difference between the two? Well, let me first start by saying that both kinds of relaxers contain very strong chemicals that help straighten your hair. They both contain very high pH levels that take hair from its normal pH level of 4-5 to about 9 to 12 which is a very large jump.
The main difference between lye and no-lye relaxers is the chemicals used to break the bonds in the hair. Let's start with lye relaxers

Lye

Lye relaxers use *sodium hydroxide* to break the bonds in the hair. It has a higher pH of about 10-12. Lye relaxers usually comes in a tub already mixed and are used mostly by professionals. This chemical is very strong and works very fast. However, because of the quick acting chemical it tends to cause tingling and burning to the scalp very quickly and as a result of this, less bonds get broken down in the process thus leaving the hair not so bone straight but with a little texture to it. Some of the hairs' natural strength and elasticity also remains as well. The hair also tends to feel soft after the relaxing process. Because the chemicals in the relaxer does not leave residues on the hair that will make it look dull and prevent moisture to enter into it the hair strand.

No-lye

No-lye relaxers have a lower pH level (9-10) than that of a lye relaxer. These relaxers usually come in a kit to be mixed and activated before use. Some of the active ingredients use to break down the disulfide bonds in the hair are guanidine hydroxide and calcium hydroxide. Unlike lye relaxers, the processing time for no-lye relaxers are longer, this allow more time for more bonds to broken within the hair and as a result produce a more straighter hair than of the a lye relaxer. Because of the calcium that is present in the No- lye mixture, it tends to leave residues behind on the hair strand after the relaxing and washing process is complete. This can cause dryness. The residues that are left behind can prevent moisture to enter into the hair and effectively keep the hair moisturized.

New growth

- New growth
- Demarcation point
- Touch up

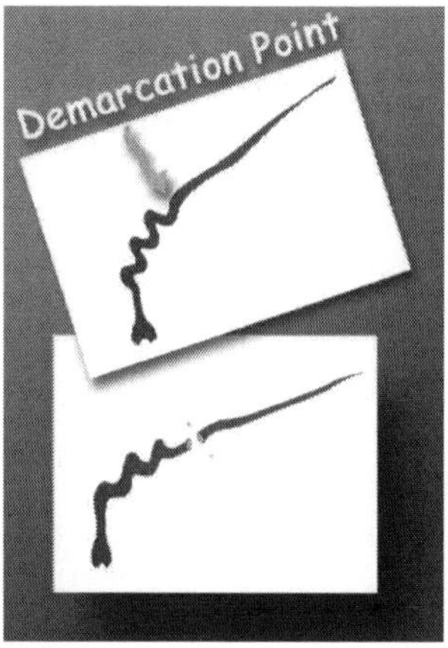

After a fresh relaxer, time will go by and your hair will naturally begin to grow out. The hair that is between the scalp and the previously relaxed hair is called "*new growth*" the point where the new growth and the relaxed hair meet is the *demarcation point*. This point is very fragile and you should take great care when handling both textures. Since your natural hair is much stronger than the relaxed portion, you should take heed in how you comb the hair. Sometimes what happens if you are not paying attention is you will comb the entire length of the hair from root to end with the same force you use when you comb through the natural hair/ new growth. This will definitely cause snapping, which you're trying to avoid.

I remember years ago before I became proactive in taking better care of my hair, every 6 weeks or so when I would see a sprout of new growth I would immediately throw some relaxer in my hair to keep my hair looking silky straight. Little did I know I was causing damage to my scalp and possible hair! Think about it, in a time span of 6 weeks I would have attain about ½ inch of new growth, imagine applying a chemical relaxer to that small section of hair as often as every month and a half to two months. First of all, such frequent chemical application to the scalp is damaging to the hair follicles which are responsible for the birth of the hair strands. When the follicles are destroyed, no more hair production is possible from that follicle.

To prevent frequent and over exposure of chemicals to the scalp I started to stretch my relaxers. What I mean by that is I began to wait for longer periods of time between a fresh relaxer and a touch up. This could be anywhere from 3 months to even a year! Yes I know. Everyone's tolerance is different and this kind of stretching will totally depend on your hair texture, schedule, and of course patience. It is worth it though because not only are you giving your scalp breathing room between relaxers you're also decreasing the risk of over processing, *which means relaxing hair that has already been relaxed*.

Caring for new growth. Passing the time you are accustomed to getting your touch ups can be a challenge. Now you have the natural texture of your hair as well as the chemically straighten portion. To get the new growth hair to look and feel similar to the relaxed hair, it should be kept in a moisturized state. Moisturizing and hot oil treatments will keep it soft and manageable. Now the type of product you use to moisturize the new growth may be different from the type you use to moisturize the relaxed hair. Generally, you would want to use a thicker conditioner to tame down the new growth hair; if you use the same heavy product on the relaxed hair it may weight it down causing it to look too limp. But all this depends on the texture of your hair. If your new growth hair is thick and unmanageable, then yes go with a thicker conditioner. If you have new growth that's not so thick then you can get away with using the same conditioner for both your new growth and relaxed hair.

Washing and conditioning hair during a *long* stretch/post relaxed

Things you'll need:

- ✓ Large tooth comb
- ✓ Butterfly clips
- ✓ Moisturizing shampoo
- ✓ Coconut oil *(soften and condition new growth before washing)*
- ✓ Thick conditioner *(or one for natural hair)*
- ✓ Regular conditioner *(for relaxed hair)*
- ✓ Leave-in conditioner
- ✓ Rollers and hair pins
- ✓ Water spray bottle w/ water
- ✓ Triangular mesh net *(optional)*
- ✓ Hooded dryer *(optional)*
- ✓ Applicator bottle *(for coconut oil)*
- ✓ Plastic shower cap
- ✓ Serum
- ✓ Flat iron
- ✓ Silk or satin scarf

Instructions:

1. First begin to **detangle** the hair gently. Use your **fingers first** to begin the detangling process.
2. Take the large tooth comb and begin to part and **divide the hair into about 4 to 5 sections**, separate each one with a butterfly clip.
3. Gently detangle each section with the large tooth comb starting from the ends of the hair and **work your way up slowly to the roots**. Create a 2 strand twist and temporarily secure the twist with the butterfly clip.
4. Put some coconut oil in an applicator bottle and begin to apply the oil in the roots and new growth and also to the relaxed hair. If possible leave the oil in the hair over night with a plastic shower cap on. Or go under a hooded dryer for about 15 to 20 min. to allow the oil to penetrate the hair shaft.
5. Go in the shower and saturate the hair with warm water. Take one section at a time and apply some **shampoo to the section in a downward position**, do so a few times (*never pile the hair on top of the head*). Next, hold the section as one with one hand, and with the other hand use the pads of your fingers to massage the scalp. Do so for each section.
6. Next squeeze out excess water from all sections of the hair and proceed to apply the thicker conditioner to the new growth and then the regular condition to the relaxed portion of hair. *(be sure to have all sections of hair back into their positions untangled)* *you can opt to apply some oil such as coconut oil, olive oil etc. to the hair for added conditioning
7. Place a plastic cap on the head and sit under a hooded dyer for about 30 min.
8. Wash out the conditioner in the same manner in which you applied it. In sections.
9. Squeeze the excess water from the hair and apply some leave in conditioner.
10. Roller set the hair. This will help to stretch out the new growth a little while it dries.
11. Remove the rollers and apply some serum to the new growth and **flat iron the new growth in small sections** at a time. **try to limit using direct heat to the hair more than 4 times a month.*
12. Moisturize and seal the ends and the length of your hair then proceed to place the hair into a criss cross wrap. Place a silk or satin scarf on the head overnight.

**when I'm going through a long stretch I usually refrain from wrapping my hair the traditional way and opt for a criss cross wrap instead. Reason being is that having so much new growth wrapping becomes more difficult and involves more combing and brushing to the hair. This is way too much manipulation to the hair and can result in unnecessary breakage. Also by doing a traditional wrap to the hair, it tends to make the hair poofy.*

**This washing process only applies if you have a lot of new growth. If you have about an inch or less exclude the two different types of conditioners.*

Touch up

It is finally the end of your stretch and time for a touch- up baby, yes! If you've successfully made it through a long stretch it is now time to reward yourself with a much need touch up. Slow down a bit though. Don't just jump right into it. There are a few things you must do to prepare your hair before a relaxer touch up.

Things to avoid during the days leading up to a touch-up.

- Avoid scratching your scalp with your nails or using a comb to scratch.
- Don't color your hair a month prior to relaxer touch up.
- Avoid using gels or any products that hardens the hair a week before.
- Don't wear braids or extension hair, weaves, curly hairstyles a week before touch up. Hair should be free and straight.
- Avoid using hot appliances such as blow driers, and flat irons, especially on new growth a couple days prior.

Things you should do days leading up to a touch up.

- * Be sure that your hair is free from breakage and is in good health, otherwise please postpone the relaxer.
- Leave hair in a straight style a week before relaxer. Or wear a wig over a criss cross wrap.
- Criss cross wrap hair at night before bed. *(No traditional wrap. Hair wrapped around the head, too much manipulation.)*
- Wash and cleanse your hair a week prior to a relaxer touch up. Use a light protein treatment to help build up the hair.
- Roller set hair to help stretch out the new growth a week prior.
- Measure the *new growth hair* with a measuring tape when it's wet at your last wash before the relaxer touch up. Stretch the hair out and take note of how many inches long it is and mark it on the comb or whatever tool you'll be using to apply the relaxer to the hair, place a piece of tape at the point where you measured so that you can feel it. Purpose? Since your hair will be in a straight state when relaxing, it will be kind of hard to distinguish where the new growth hair ends. This helps to prevent you from overlapping and over processing the already relaxed hair. **While relaxing the hair take the piece of hair you are going to place the relaxer on, stretch it out and quickly place the* ***tool*** *you marked with the tape on the* ***scalp and next to the hair*** *to help determine where the new growth stops. Hold the hair at that point stretched out and apply the relaxer. REMEMBER don't stop or linger around when you are dealing with*

chemicals that you need to apply it in a set amount of time. Just practice this technique to get the hang of it before you enter into the relaxing session.

Supplies you'll need for a touch up.

- ✓ Cape *(to protect your back from the relaxer while in the shower)*
- ✓ Vaseline *(to protect your skin from the relaxer during application)*
- ✓ Coconut oil *(to protect the already relaxed hair when washing out relaxer)*
- ✓ Timer *(to keep you on track and prevent over processing)*
- ✓ Relaxer kit & the contents that comes with it
- ✓ Gloves *(to protect your hands)*
- ✓ Towel
- ✓ Mirror
- ✓ Large tooth comb *(for parting hair in sections)*
- ✓ Brush applicator *(to apply relaxer to hair)*
- ✓ 4 butterfly clips

Instructions for a relaxer touch up.

Before I begin I would like to mention that whenever I would wash my relaxer out I would go under the shower not the sink. My hair is laying straight down, I do not pile my hair on top of my head. I also make sure that the shower is ready and available when it's time to wash the relaxer out.

1. Get all your supplies ready on a table. Mix the relaxer cream well.
2. Gently part your hair into 4 equal sections, and gently detangle each section from ends to roots. Next use the butterfly clips to hold the detangled sectioned hair temporarily in place.
3. Apply some Vaseline around the perimeter of the hair line and on the ears for protection.
4. Apply some coconut oil on the length and ends of your hair.
5. Put on your gloves.
6. Wear a robe or loose clothes to easily take off when ready to enter the shower.
7. Place and secure the cape around your shoulders.
8. Start the timer to the appropriate time according to the manufactures time in the relaxer kit.
9. Begin to apply the relaxer to the **new growth only** from each section of the *hair (remember to remove the butterfly clips from each section before applying the relaxer).* Start from the 2 back sections and work your way to the front sections. REMEMBER new growth only no over lapping.
10. When relaxer application is complete, begin to smooth the relaxer cream into the hair to help with the straightening process. Work quickly but neatly. Use the wooden stick that comes with the kit or the back of a

comb to smooth. Never comb through and stretch hair with chemicals on it, hair will break.

11. Turn on the water in the shower and set it to warm, be sure to have the cape on while in the shower.
12. To RINSE out the relaxer gather the hair into a ponytail or a smaller section and lift the hair so that is about 90 degrees off the scalp. Go under the shower and let the water run and focus where the relaxer cream is. Use your other hand to help rub, loosen and wash out the relaxer. *This method will help the relaxer to run off the scalp and down verses running down the length of your hair.*
13. When all the cream is out, apply some of the neutralizing shampoo mainly to where you had applied the relaxer, but also to the rest of the hair too. *(The neutralizing shampoo stops the relaxing process so* ***this step is very important.****)* Apply and lather the shampoo in a downward direction from roots to ends. Never pile hair on top of head. Apply some more of the neutralizing shampoo to the hair and leave it there for about 10 minutes then rinse in a downward direction. Continue to apply the neutralizing shampoo to the hair until the color signal is no longer there.
14. Follow the rest of the directions in the relaxer kit and apply conditioner, leave- ins, and moisturizers as directed. Also don't forget to do a deep condition.
15. Next, roller set the hair and go under a hood dryer or allow to air dry.

After a relaxer the hair might seem dry. This is because some of the calcium residues from the no lye relaxer are still sitting on the hair. Simply use a chelating shampoo at your next wash about a week later to help lift the residues off the hair strands. It is important to immediately add moisture back to the hair since this shampoo will strip your hair of moisture.

****

Since our black hair is naturally weak and dry from the start, applying a relaxer to the hair causes more dryness and weakens the hair structure. That is why it is imperative that action is taken on your part to **maintain, protect** and **preserve** the hair the best you can especially when your goal is to a achieve longer healthier hair.

****

Hair assessment and goals

Ok so now you've gained a better understanding of what your hair really is. Now it is time to make some assessments and some goals regarding your hair.

It is important that you stop for a moment and examine the current condition of your hair before going out on your hair journey. In doing this you can address potential problems such as split ends that could cause draw backs and discouragement during your hair journey experience.

Splitting of your hair ends as I just mentioned could be a result of heavy and hard brushing, over usage of hot hair appliances, or even unprotected hair ends. Leaving the ends of your hair exposed to the elements for long periods of time or not tying up your hair at night before you go to sleep can have negative consequences. Another potential problem you need to look out for is dryness. This could be a result of lack of daily moisture or color treated hair.

My suggestions: Correct any issues you might have before you proceed to start on your journey. Please take the time to **trim or cut off those splitting ends**, even if your hair might not seem to have any do it anyway. Think about it. Your hair is getting ready to go through a long journey of hair growth. *The ends are the oldest and weakest part of your hair,* along the way it will experience natural weathering. By you trimming the ends you are in essence helping it to stay in tip top shape so to speak and endure the whole hair journey process more successfully.
Secondly, give your hair a really nice **deep condition treatment** and **hot oil treatment**. This will give your hair a boost by adding much needed moisture.
****

After hair assessments are made it is time to make some hair goals. These goals should be realistic and specific. *(WARNING: don't expect your hair to grow to mid back length over night because in reality hair grows and average of ½ inch per month).*
Setting goals for your hair keeps you focus, in line, and on track. It keeps you accountable for the things you have to do each day and week to draw you closer to the ultimate goal. There are two steps in the goal setting process. **1).** the specific thing you want to accomplish and **2).** And the bite size action steps in which you will be doing to make it realized.

STEP # 1.

Here are some examples of specific hair goals.

- Date: 4/5/2015 my hair is currently at chin length. My ultimate goal length is bra strap length in about 28 months.
- I want my hair to be all one length in the back with no split ends.
- I want my hair to be fuller and healthier.

STEP # 2.

Breaking down the ultimate or end goals into more doable sizes.
I recommend for at least the first year of the beginning of your hair journey to have a weekly check list of things you are doing to your hair. This will get you into a routine and form a habit of doing the things you need to do to bring you closer to your hair goal. Below are pictures of pages from my hair journal I created. I created this to help you as a beginner to get you started and keep you on track.

Beginners' Healthy Hair Journey Kit

Below is a **basic checklist of products and tools** to **get you started** on your healthy hair journey. The specific brand of hair product would have to be decided by you. You may find that one brand type works best verses the other.

Products:

- ✓ 1 moisturizing shampoo *(sulfate free)* & 1 clarifying shampoo
- ✓ 1 moisturizing conditioner & protein conditioner
- ✓ 1 Leave-in conditioner
- ✓ 1 water based moisturizer *(daily for ENDS and hair length)*
- ✓ Natural oil(s) *(for sealing moisture in in hair) (coconut oil, grape seed oil, olive oil etc.)*

How to use the products: Example of hair regimen at a glance

****

MONTHLY: *At the end of the month use the clarifying shampoo to rid the hair of all dirt and product build up; this will give you a fresh start for the following month.*

WEEKLY: *Use the moisturizing shampoo once a week to wash and cleanse your hair. After shampooing do a deep condition or a protein treatment to the hair, depending on what the hair needs at the time (moisture or protein). Apply leave-in conditioner to the hair and roller set hair and leave to air dry or go under a hooded dryer.*

MID WEEK: *co wash in between regular washes to add moisture in hair and opt for a no heat hairstyle.*

DAILY: *Moisturize and seal the hair twice a day with the water based moisturizer and seal in the moisture with a natural oil of your choice. Wear protective styles about 4 to 5 days out of the week.*

AT NIGHT: *Neatly tie hair up with a silk or satin scarf.*

****

Tools:

- ✓ Large tooth comb
- ✓ Soft bristle brush
- ✓ Rollers *(or other no heat curling devices)*
- ✓ Hair pins *(no snag)*
- ✓ Plastic shower caps *(for deep conditioning)*
- ✓ Hooded dryer *(for roller sets)*. No blow dryers
- ✓ Silk or satin scarf
- ✓ Measuring tape *(for measuring hair length progress)*
- ✓ Camera *(for hair growth documentation)*
- ✓ Hair journal *(to jot thoughts down)*

Optional products: for styling

- Oil moisture
- Serum
- Setting lotion or mousse
- Gel or edge control
- Hair spray
- Cleansing conditioner (for co washes)

Optional Tools:

- Applicator brush for relaxing hair

OILS

Some types of natural oils

- ❖ Coconut
- ❖ Grape seed
- ❖ Olive
- ❖ Castor
- ❖ Jojoba
- ❖ Argon

Let's get started…hair we grow! (MDCM-PTHM) = Longer Hair

In addition to using *protective styles* to help promote longer hair, there are other important factors that play a role as well. Lets' explore the list below to see how to execute each factor effectively.

Mindset, Detangling, Cleansing, Moisturizing, Protecting, Trimming, Health and Massaging

Mindset

Purpose: *(To keep you on track despite any obstacles you might come across)*

Before YOU set out to do anything especially to achieve a goal, your thinking and frame of mind have to be right. As it goes for growing out your hair, sometimes your expectations for the process might be a little unrealistic as a beginner. We all want long flowing hair tomorrow, however from the information I provide earlier you know that expectation is not real. The natural hair growing cycle is a slow process. So growing out your hair is going to involve having a positive attitude, realistic expectations, along with a bag load of patience. As you'll soon come to realize, during your hair journey you are going to have some setbacks that will delay goals concerning your hair, this can be discouraging. But armed with a positive attitude and patience any obstacles that may come your way will be more easily overcome and get pass.

Detangling

Purpose: *(To keep hair loose and free thus prevent unnecessary breakage)*

When detangling your hair, just be sure to give this activity your undivided attention. Any rushed movement while the comb passes between the hair strands while navigating your way around any knots can cause premature breakage which will over a period of time shorten your length. Since black relaxed hair is extra fragile, we should always take care whenever we handled those precious strands. It is important to keep your hair in a detangled state 100% of the time. Also before you enter into washing session, I would advise you to detangle as well, as this will prevent you from having more tangles after a wash.

Things you'll need to detangle:

- ✓ Large tooth comb
- ✓ Butterfly clips
- ✓ Patience and time

Proper way to detangle hair (wet or dry)

1. First section your hair into 4 sections with your hands, not comb.
2. Place a butterfly clip on each individual section to temporally secure each one.
3. Use your fingers to go through each section at time and gently detangle working your up from the ends to roots.
4. Use the large tooth comb to further detangle the hair slowly and gently from ends to roots.

Cleansing
Purpose: *(To keep hair free from buildup of dirt and hair products)*
Despite the fact that our black hair is naturally dry, it is still very important to cleanse it on a regular basis. It has been said that if you leave black hair dirty and do not wash it for a while this will make it grow. First of all, buildup of dirt will break your hair off. And secondly hair needs moisture. Water is by far the best moisture you can find.

How often should you be washing your hair? I would say once a week is ideal. This keeps unnecessary buildup of **dirt off your hair** that may prevent moisture to effectively enter the hair strand and cause breakage.
There a few things to consider when cleansing your hair.

- How often?
- How?
- With what?
- Type of water you're using

How often should you be washing your hair?
Once a week is sufficient when it comes to washing and keeping your hair clean. You don't want to go for longer periods of time with dirt and product build up sitting on your hair. For hair to thrive and grow to newer lengths, keeping your scalp and hair clean is very important. If you happen to go to the gym and work out, perspiration may cause a problem. This may cause an unpleasant odor. If that is the case try doing a co wash in-between your regular shampoo washes. (***Conditioner wash**/co-washing use conditioners only. No shampoo. There are even co wash conditioners or cleansing conditioners on the market that are design specifically for the purpose of doing co washes)*. This will help the hair smell good and also add moisture to the hair. If you are co washing your hair please opt for hairstyles that do not require heat to achieve a style. No heat hairstyling methods would include but not limited to braid outs and Bantu knot outs.

How should you be washing your hair?
Before my healthy hair journey, I used to take all my hair and create a pile on top of my head and begin to lather and wash my hair. I'm pretty sure you are guilty of this as well. Little did I know I was washing my hair all wrong! Because our black hair is so fragile, great care should be taken when handling it. When it comes to washing, all the hair should be facing in a down position. If your hair is shoulder length or shorter, having it hanging loose in a downward position is fine. However when your hair starts to grow and becomes longer detangling and dividing the hair into sections becomes a must. Simply divide the hair into 4

sections and detangle each section gently from ends to root. Next twist or loosely braid each one. Go in the shower and soak the hair with water.

Take each section at a time and undo the twist or braid and start to apply the shampoo in a downward position along the hair length. Stroke the hair a few times with shampoo to help lift the dirt off the hair. Use the pads of your fingers to massage the scalp to loosen any dirt as well. Rinse that section, squeeze the excess water out of the hair, apply the conditioner to the hair in the same downward direction you applied the shampoo. Re-twist the hair and clip it away with a butterfly clip for now. Repeat this same process for the rest of the sections.

After applying the conditioner to the hair, leave it there for about 30 minutes with a plastic cap on your head. You can either go under a hooded dryer or as is. When the time is up go back in the shower and rinse out the conditioner section by section. Squeeze out the excess water and apply your leave-in conditioner.

Wash day run down:

- Pre poo treatment *(w/ oils, conditioner, or a mixture of both)*
- Shampoo *(w/ sulfate or sulfate free , or clarifying shampoo. depends on product build up)*
- Deep condition or protein treatment *(depends on what your hair needs)*
- Leave-in conditioner
- Roller set & dry *(under a hooded dryer or air dry)*
- Moisturize and seal *(w/ water based moisturizer & natural oil)*

With what should you be washing your hair with?

Just as how the manner in which you wash your hair is important. What you use to wash your hair with is just as important. Shampoos are made to remove dirt and product buildup off the hair. The ingredients that are in the shampoo that's responsible for removing product build up and dirt can be quit harsh on our black hair. Remember, our hair is naturally dry already so choosing a shampoo to cleanse your hair that does not completely strip and leave it even drier is going to be very important.

So what exactly are in shampoos, and what kind should you be using? Shampoos contain cleaning agents call ***surfactants***, basically cleaning agents that remove the dirt and product build up off the hair strand. ***Sulfates*** are a type of surfactant that are in shampoos and can be very harsh. If you take a look at the back of your shampoo bottle, you would see that it contains one of these common types of sulfates: *(Ammonium lauryl sulfate, Ammonium laureth sulfate, Sodium lauryl sulfate, Sodium laureth sulfate)* each one is different in their level of cleaning. Because these sulfate cleaners really get the job done during shampooing, they tend to also strip the hair of its natural oils and moisture as well. That is why you add **moisture** back into the hair via conditioning.

So what should you be using? An alternative to shampoos that contain sulfates are **sulfate free shampoos**, these shampoos are gentler and won't strip your hair. Sometimes what I like to do as well is dilute my **regular sulfate shampoos** *(not the whole bottle at once but rather just the amount that I'll be using during a cleansing session. Just take a small bottle and pour some of the shampoo in it and then dilute it with some water)*

Since sulfate free shampoos are gentler on the hair, you can start using that for your weekly shampooing. For a once a month product build removal, use a **clarifying shampoo** *(much stronger than regular shampoo and design to remove stubborn dirt and oils)*

*If you happen to use a lot of products during the week, a sulfate free shampoo might not be suitable as it may not remove sufficient amounts of dirt off your hair. Try using a regular **moisturizing shampoo** instead. Moisturizing shampoos do contain sulfates to help remove the dirt off the hair and also moisturizing ingredients to add moisture back into the hair. That is what I use sometimes, followed up by a conditioner as well.

Pre poo before shampooing can be very helpful to fight against moisture loss especially when using sulfate shampoos. **Pre poo (pre shampoo treatments)** is a treatment done to the hair by adding moisture and conditioning to the hair before cleansing with a shampoo. This can be done by using natural oils, conditioners, or a combination of both. If you are using **oil(s)** to pre poo, place a towel around your shoulders to prevent oils from dripping down on your clothes. Place the oil(s) in an applicator bottle for easier application. Be sure that the hair is fully detangled and are in sections. Begin to apply the oil(s) to dry hair at the ends of your hair *(driest, oldest, and most fragile).* And work your way up the hair strand until you reach the root. Do this until the entire head is completed. Secure the hair on the head with a butterfly clip and place a plastic shower cap over your head. Leave oil(s) in the

hair for about 30 min. to 1 hour. If you can, go under a hooded dryer for about 20 minutes, this will help the oils to penetrate in the hair strand.
You can also use **conditioners or a mixture of conditioners and oils to pre poo hair**. Do this by selecting the conditioner and oil(s) you would like to use and pour the amount you'll be using for this pre-pooing session. Mix it well and begin to apply it to the hair in the same manner you would the oils. Also, leave it in the hair for about 30 min to 1 hr. or go under a hooded dryer for about 20 min to help the product to penetrate the hair strand.

After the pre shampoo session, proceed with regular shampooing.

Some types of shampoos:

Sulfate free shampoo: Gentle form of shampoo that contains no harsh sulfate.
Regular sulfate shampoo: Shampoo that contains harsh cleaning agents such as sulfates can be used for once a week washes.
Moisturizing shampoo: These shampoos contain sulfates to lift dirt, and also moisturizing qualities to add moisture back in the hair. Can be used for weekly washes.
Clarifying shampoo: This shampoo is great for removal of a lot of product buildup that you've accumulated within the month. Because the ingredients are much stronger, limit the use to only once a month as this will strip your hair.
Chelating shampoo: Are made to remove mineral build up off the hair resulting from hard water.
Neutralizing shampoo: Are made with a low pH to bring the cuticle back to their normal position after a relaxer.

What type of water are you using?

The type of water that comes out of your pipe can potentially be damaging to your hair. Sometimes minerals such as calcium and magnesium are present in water. High concentration of minerals can pose a problem to our hair. After washing your hair with hard water, minerals such as calcium residues are left behind on the hair. These minerals sit on the hair and block moisture from entering into the hair strand. As a result of this, hair becomes dull hard to manage, and breakage certainly will become an issue. If you have hard water you might notice that your shampoo does not lather the way it supposed to. This is because the minerals in the water block the ability of the ingredients in the shampoo to effectively do its job.

How to treat hard water?
There are a few things available on the market to help eliminate some of the minerals present in the water. They range from shower head filters to treatment in your water supply.

Moisturizing

Purpose: *(To keep hair pliable and prevent premature breakage)*

Keeping black hair in a moisturized state is an absolute must if you want longer hair.

I remember as a little girl whenever I would get my hair combed, my mother or whoever did my hair use to put grease in my hair as a moisturizer because my hair was too dry. As I now know, putting grease in hair as a moisturizer actually does the opposite of what is intended. Grease BLOCKS out moisture. Yes hair will look shiny and appear to be healthy but that is just an illusion of hair being moisturized. True moisture comes from water or water based products, such as conditioners and water based moisturizers. Water molecules are smaller and penetrate into the hair more easily verses the bigger molecules from oils and grease which tends to sit on the hair strand.

The protein structure in hair also craves water so it makes sense to feed it and give it what it wants so that it stays pliable and thrive.

You can keep the hair in a moisturized state through your regular weekly washes and deep condition treatments, co washes in between your regular washes and daily moisturizing and sealing.

Here's how to incorporate moisture in your hair daily:

This process is call "moisturizing & sealing". First you will be adding moisture to the hair and then sealing in that moisture with an oil so that the moisture stays in a little longer.

You'll need:

- ✓ Water based moisturizer *(water as the first ingredient)*
- ✓ Natural oil *(example: coconut oil, olive oil etc.)*
- ✓ Butterfly clip *(to section off the hair while working)*
- ✓ Large tooth comb *(to detangle hair)*

How to moisturize:

1. First gently detangle hair from ends to roots.
2. Take a small section of your hair and apply about a pea size amount of moisturizer to the ends first *(since this is the oldest, weakest, and fragile part of the hair you want to baby and take care of it first)* and then work your way up the length of the hair to the roots, all the while applying the moisturizer to the hair in a downward direction.
3. Take a drop of the oil and apply it in the same manner you applied the moisturizer. *Be careful not to apply too much moisturizer and oil to the hair as this will make the hair look too limp.
4. Section that part of the hair off with a butterfly clip and repeat the process for the rest of the hair.

Protecting
Purpose: *(to keep the hair strand intact for as long as possible)*
Since the hair that you see on your head is considered dead, your goal then is to preserve what you got the best you can an as long as you can. If every day you get up and ignore the needs of your hair and sort of did whatever you like without any regards to the health of your hair, you would never see any length retention. Sometimes it may seem as if black hair does not grow pass a certain length because the ends of the hair is breaking off at the same rate that your hair is growing from the roots.

Below I've created an illustration showing what happens during each month that goes by when hair is protected and cared for in a gentle way verse showing no regard to the health of your hair.

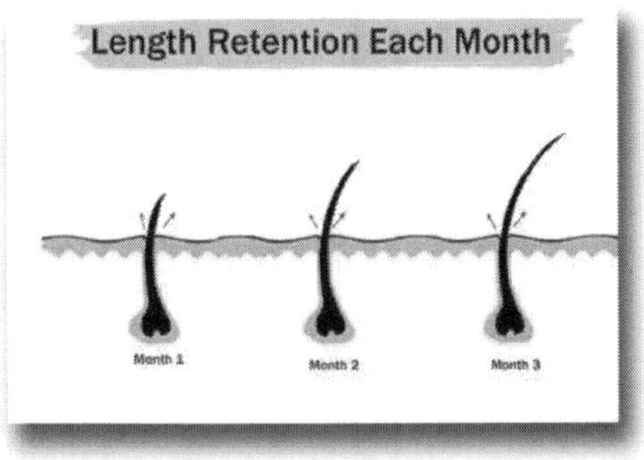

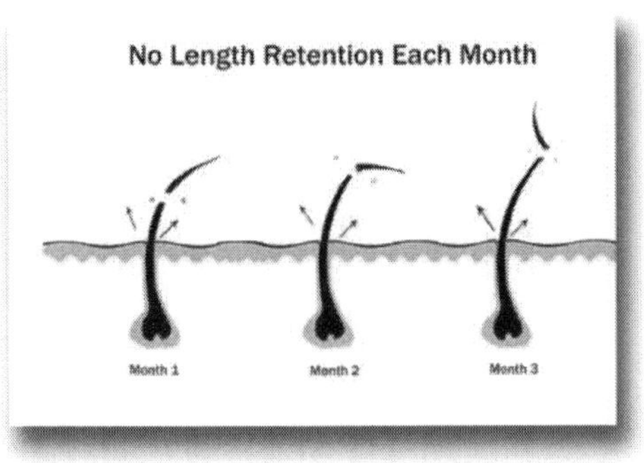

As you can see during the length retention process hair is kept intact at the ends to show progress. In the no length retention illustration, hair keeps snapping off at the ends each month giving the illusion of no growth. So what causes this? Lack of moisture, rough combing, blow drying hair in a rough manner, not wrapping hair at night, hair that's left unprotected and loose majority of the time, rubbing up against clothes and snapping off in pocket book handles, and improper use of chemicals. All this might seems like nothing by themselves but combining all of those actions and perpetuate them over a long period of time only results in unhealthy hair.

This book provides you with a banquet of protective and no heat hairstyles to choose from to incorporate in your hair care regimen. I've also provided you with basic information of how to care for your hair to attain a healthier head of hair.

Trimming

Purpose: *(to keep ends in tip top shape and prevent slit ends from forming and traveling up the hair strand)*

Even though your goal is to grow out your hair long, trimming your hair might be a hard concept, at first. I know it was for me. After all that hard work I put in to growing out my hair I couldn't imagine letting go of even 1/4 inch! I know it's crazy. After realizing that this is a necessary part of the healthy hair journey process I slowly gave in and embraced the idea.

The ends are the oldest part of your hair. Despite your earnest efforts of taking the best care of your hair, split ends can creep up on you due to natural weathering. If left alone over time, they'll just get worse. To keep split ends under control, do a light trim after a relaxer touch up. In-between your relaxer touchups you can also do a light **dusting**. This method of trimming your ends only require for a very small amount of hair to be removed from the ends. When the hair is removed it should literally look like "dust". **Search and destroy** is another method of snipping off those unwanted split ends. This method is a little tedious as it requires you to search out for individual strands of hair that are split and damaged.

Here's how to dust~~~~~~~~~~Things you'll need:

- ✓ A pair of scissors made for cutting hair.(sheers)
- ✓ Good lighting
- ✓ Comb
- ✓ Clips for sectioning hair

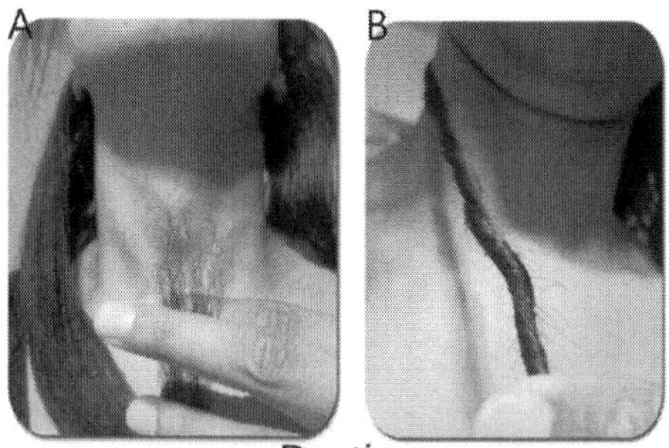

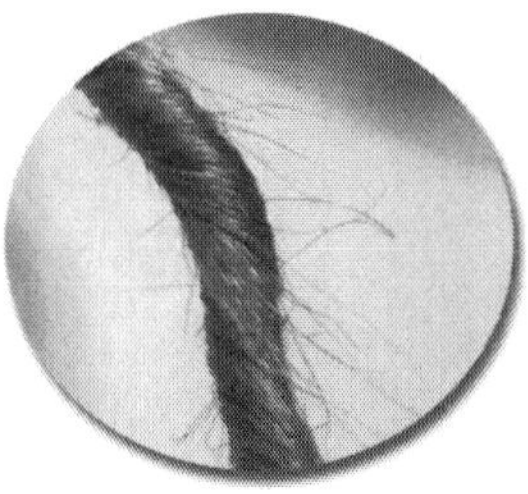

Dusting

To dust your hair, first divide your hair into 4 sections and separate each one with a clip. Start with one of the 4 sections and take a smaller piece of hair, comb through it to smooth it out. Hold the hair with a little tension in a downward direction away from the scalp so the hair is straight and smooth, slide your fingers with the hair between them all the way to the ends and begin to "dust" or cut tiny pieces off the ends.

Next, begin to roll and twist the hair between your fingers starting from the roots all the way down to the ends. Any piece of hair that you see sticking out of the piece of hair that you twisted, snip them off. These pieces of hair are shorter hairs that are not as long as the rest of your hair and were missed when you dust the ends. Do this until you've completed the whole head.

With the **Search and destroy method,** your hair have to be long enough so you can actually see potential split ends to be removed. Basically you are going to take small sections of hair and examine and search out for potential damaged or slit ends. Then cut off any damage portion of hair off that individual strand just above the point of damage.

Health

Purpose: *(to promote healthier hair growth and body too)*

Your health is the basis and foundation for good strong hair. The things that you put in your body reflect in the quality of your hair! Try to incorporate vegetables, fruit, nuts, vitamins, and lots of water to nourish and hydrate your body and hair. Foods like meat, fish, chicken, and eggs contain amino acids that are important to the proper function of your body as well as the health of your hair.

Massaging

Purpose: *(to nourish hair follicles)*

It is said that a good scalp massage improves blood circulation to the follicles on the scalp and encourages hair growth, not to mention how rejuvenated and relaxed you feel after a good scalp massage.

How to do a scalp massage

Things you'll need:

- Oil in a applicator bottle *(warm a little)*
- Finger tips
- Couple of clips for sectioning off hair
- 10 minutes

Divide your hair into 4 sections as you would for a relaxer. Clip away the 2 front sections and focus on the 2 back sections for now. Take the applicator bottle with the oil in it and squeeze a few drops of oil on the scalp of the two back sections. Spread out your fingers a little and insert them in the root of the hair, place the pads of your fingers *(not the nails)* on the scalp with a little pressure and begin to move your fingers into small circular motions. Do this for the whole back section of hair for about 5 minutes. Repeat this same process for the front section.

Summary

Hair is a dead keratinized fiber that has to be preserved by keeping it clean, moisturized, protected, and handled delicately. When these steps are seriously put into action, length retention will become evident.

Be gentle with your **ends**, moisturize your ends on a daily basis, deep condition, do hot oil treatments once a week, trim your ends, do protective styling, stretch your relaxers, eat healthy, incorporate scalp massages, try not to use color in your hair or if so try a temporary highlight. And keep a journal to document your journey *(bad and the good).*

As a beginner, try to keep away from heat or limit the use to a maximum of 4 times a month. This could be from drying your hair under a hooded dryer or using a flat iron to straighten your hair. The purpose is that you want to give your hair some breathing room and a chance to show you that it can grow. When you start to see actual length retention each month, this will only boost your confidence and assure you that this can be done. As a result of this, you'll begin to create a routine and hair care regimen that yields positive results.

As your hair begins to grow to longer and newer lengths the regimens you used in the beginning or at a certain hair length might have to be tweaked to accommodate the new hair length.

Glossary
Hair terms

Anagen: One of the three phases the hair goes through. This phase is the growth phase which last for about 2 to 8 years.
Afro textured hair: Black hair that has not been chemically altered.
Amino Acid: Are the building blocks of protein.
Ammonium laureth sulfate and Ammonium lauryl sulfate (ALS): Are harsh detergents in shampoos that strip the hair.
Apple cider vinegar (ACV): Can be used as a rinse after conditioning. Because of its acidity, it helps to close the cuticles of the hair and make the hair less frizzy. When using ACV as a rinse, be sure to dilute it with water before applying it to your hair.
Banding method: Stretching the hair with the aid of hair bands on the length of small sections of hair. (Drying the hair without heat)
Breakage: Fracture of hair strand along any given point of the hair. This is due to over manipulation or rough styling. This is different from shedding. *See shedding.*
Catagen: This is the transitional and second phase of the hair cycle and it indicates the end of the growth cycle.
Chelating shampoo: Are made to remove the metal deposits off hair.
Clarifying shampoo: Removes dirt and product build up off the hair.
Co washing: Washing the hair using only conditioner (conditioner wash) can be done to add moisture in between regular washes.
Cortex: The middle layer of the hair strand. It accounts for most of the hair size. This is where the melanin (color) and the bonds of the hair are located. The disulfide bonds are responsible for the curl pattern of the hair.
Cuticle: The shingle like structure and outer most part of the hair. This protects the inside of the hair and also keeps the moisture in.
Dead ends: This refers to the damaged or split ends.
Demarcation point: The point on the hair strand where the natural hair and the relaxed hair meet.
Density: Is measured by the number of hair that is on a square inch on the scalp. Density can be low, medium, or high.
Detangling: untangling and freeing the hair from knots.
Disulfide bonds: Bond between sulfur atoms. The sulfur atoms attach two protein strands together thus giving the hair its unique curliness. The more present in the hair the curlier the hair. The less present, the less curly the hair will be. These are chemical side bonds and are only broken by chemicals.
Dusting: Cutting of small amounts of hair off the ends. The hair that is removed should look like dust.
Elasticity: The ability of the hair strand to stretch and return back without snapping off.
Hair: A fiber made of mostly protein that is hardened and is no longer living. (Keratinized)

Hair bulb: The end of the hair root that is located under the scalp inside the follicle. It has a round shape.
Hair Journal: A book kept for the purpose of recording and documenting things about your hair.
Hair Journey: Refers to the period of time spent caring for the hair for the purpose of hair growth and health. This can last months or years.
Hair shaft: The keratinized part of the hair that you see emerging from the scalp.
Hair Typed or curl pattern: The degree of curliness the hair has. (Wavy, curly, coil, kinky)
Hard water: Water that contains excessive amounts of mineral such as calcium and magnesium. This can sit on the hair and prevent moisture to enter in the hair, as a result cause breakage. Also hard water can cause shampoos to not lather as normal.
Humectant: Is a substance that helps to keep moisture in the hair. Example: glycerin
Hydrogen bonds: Are what gives the hair its elasticity. These bonds are physical. Bonds can easily be broken when moisture or heat are introduced into the hair. They return back to their original position when the hair is dried or cooled off again.
Hydrophilic: A strong attraction to water.
Hydroxide relaxers: Are lye and no lye relaxers. Lye is stronger and uses sodium hydroxide to break the bonds. No lye is milder than lye and uses guanidine… *see sodium hydroxide*
Ion: A molecule that carries an electrical charge. Can be positive or negative. *See pH*
Length Check: A measurement taken of the length of the hair periodically for length retention.
Length Retention: The ability to keep the hair strands intact especially the ends over a period of time, to show growth progression.
Lipophilic: Able to attract oil.
Low manipulation styles: Styles that are done with minimal movement of the hair when styling it, also hairstyles that does not require too much combing, brushing, and heat.
Lye relaxer: Relaxers that have a high pH and are able penetrate the hair quickly and break the bonds of the hair. The chemical component sodium hydroxide is responsible for breaking the disulfide bonds.
Medulla: The inner most part of the hair strand.
Moisturizing and sealing: Adding moisture to the hair then trapping or sealing in that moisture with a natural oil.
Neutralizing shampoo: A shampoo with a lower pH than that of a relaxer, it is used to close back the cuticles and bring the pH back close to the hairs' natural pH.
New growth: Virgin hair that is between the scalp and the relaxed hair.
No heat hairstyles: Creating hairstyles without the aid of heat.

No lye relaxer: Lower pH than that of lye relaxers. Gentler on the scalp but can be drying to the hair because of calcium deposits on the hair stands. The chemical that is use to break the bonds in the hair are guanidine hydroxide.
Permed hair: Chemically altering naturally straight hair to make it curly.
pH: Stands for potential hydrogen. pH measures the amount of ions present in a water base substance. The more hydrogen ions detected it is acidic, the more hydroxide ions detected it is alkaline. *See ion.*
Polypeptide chain: A chain of amino acids, these are the building blocks of protein strands.
Porous hair: The hair inability to keep in moisture.
Post relaxer: The time between two relaxer applications, or a period of time after a relaxer application.
Pre-Poo: Pre shampoo treatment
Protective Styles: Protective hairstyles are styles that are done with the goal of hiding the ends of the hair from the outside elements. The idea is to protect the ends from anything that might come in contact with the hair and snag or rub against it, and as a result breaking it off prematurely.
Protein: Strands that are located in the cortex of the hair and are made up of a chain of amino acids.
Regimen: A way of doing something.
Relaxed Hair: Chemically altering naturally curly, coil, or kinky hair to make straight.
Salt bonds: Are one of the three side bonds in the hair. These are physical bonds and can temporarily be broken by shifts of pH in the hair. Regulating the pH helps to reset the salt bonds.
Scalp: The skin that is located on top of the head.
Sebum: The hair's natural oil.
Shedding: Is a natural process and it is caused when the follicle is at the last stage of the growing cycle and is preparing to release the hair, then a new growing cycle will begin. Shed hair has a white bulb at the end of the strand. Shedding is different from breakage. *See breakage.*
Sodium hydroxide: Is a strong chemical compound also referred to as (lye), it is alkaline and can be irritating to the skin. It is also used in a variety of ways in different quantities. It can be found in things such as soaps, shampoos, and relaxers.
Sodium laureth sulfate and Sodium lauryl sulfate (SLS): Are types of detergent that strip the hair. SLS detergents are gentler that ALS detergents.
Split ends or Trichoptilosis: Hair ends that are damaged due to wear and tear or inadequate care.
Sulfates: Are a type of detergent found in shampoo.
Sulfur atoms: Are two atoms joined together by a bond call disulfide bond, they are located between 2 peptide chains that make up the protein strand.
Surfactants: Are cleaning agents in shampoos.

Telogen: Last phase of the hair cycle and it is the resting phase. Hair stops growing and sits in the follicle until it naturally falls out or the new hair that's coming in pushes it out. This phase can also be referred to as shedding. You can shed an average of 40 to100 hairs a day which is normal.
Telax: Hair that is purposely under process with a relaxer to achieve some texture oppose to bone straight hair.
Terminal length: The longest the hair can grow during the anagen or growing phase.
Texture: Is defined as the diameter across the cross section of a hair strand. Hair textures can be fine, medium, or course.
Thio relaxers: (Thioglycolate) are relaxers that have a milder pH than that of hydroxide (lye and no lye) relaxers. Thio relaxer loosens the curls but does not get it as straight as hydroxide relaxers. Thio relaxers can be harsh on black hair.
Trimming: Cutting off the ends of the hair in an attempt to keep hair healthy and free of slit ends.

Index For Hairstyles

Hairstyles At A Glance

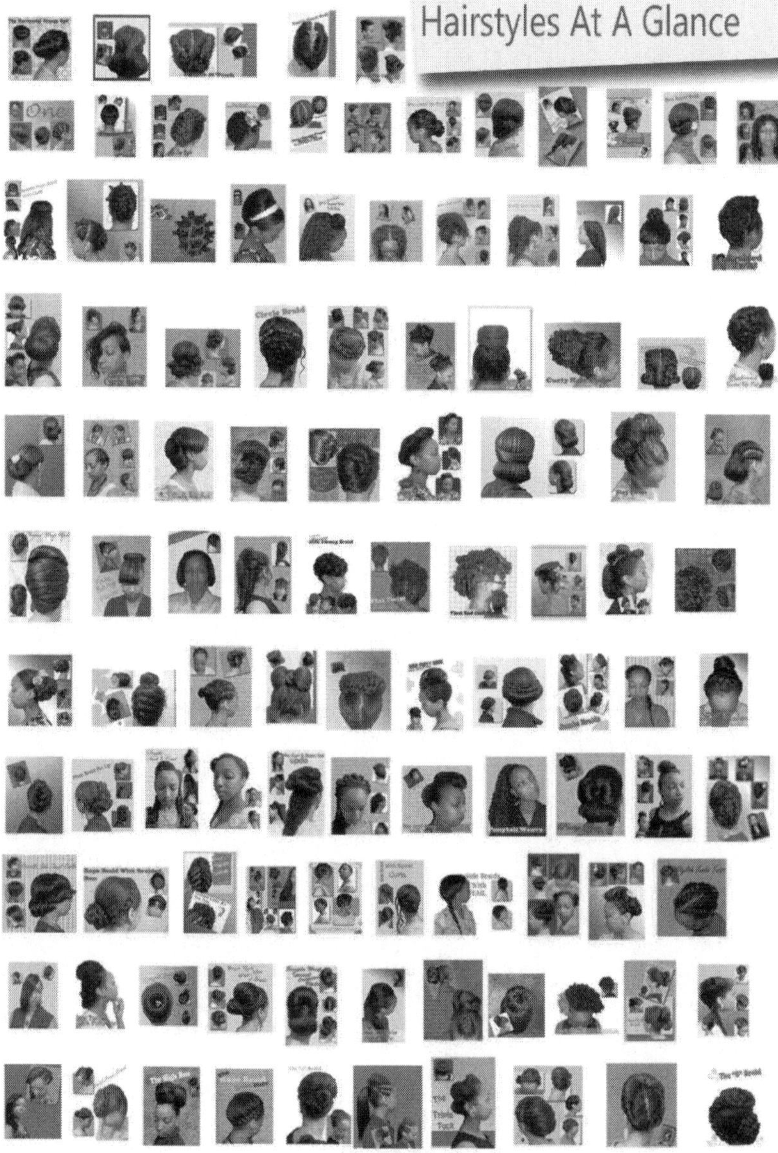

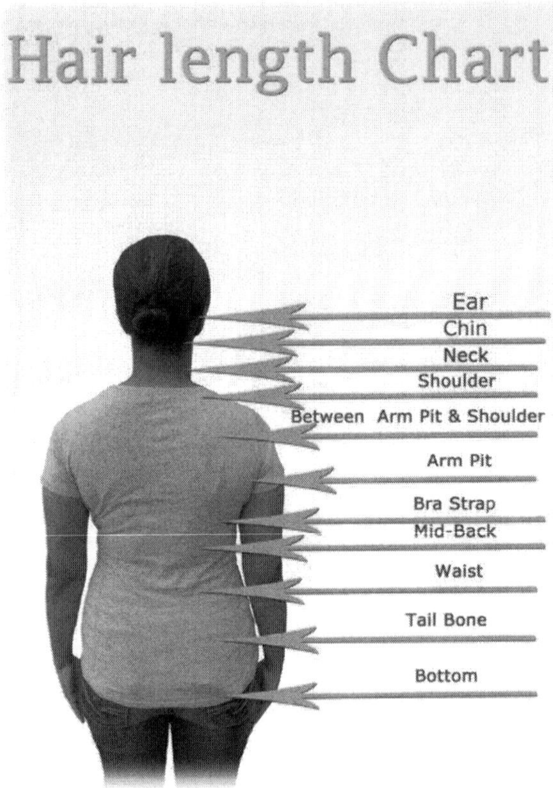

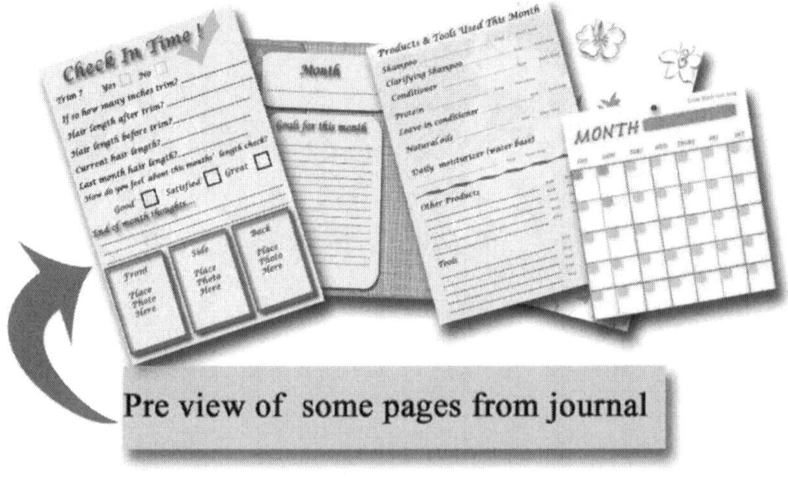

Pre view of some pages from journal

My Online "How To" Videos
hairstylings101

Notes:

Psst!

Please Visit: www.LearnHairAndDo.com

"Growth Through Easy Fun Fabulous Hairstyles!"

"My **Get It Done** Healthy Hair Journal"

"Over 100 Fabulous No Heat Hairstyling Ideas!" LOOKBOOK

"My Fab-hair-Lous Note Book"

16309481R00194

Printed in Great Britain
by Amazon